COMPARATIVE INQUIRY IN POLITICS AND POLITICAL ECONOMY

COMPARATIVE INQUIRY IN POLITICS AND POLITICAL ECONOMY

Theories and Issues

Ronald H. Chilcote
University of California at Riverside

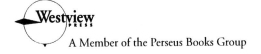

A Member of the Perseus Books Group

Copyright © 2000 by Westview Press, A Member of the Perseus Books Group

Published in 2000 in the United States of America by Westview Press, 5500 Central Avenue, Boulder, Colorado 80301-2877, and in the United Kingdom by Westview Press, 12 Hid's Copse Road, Cumnor Hill, Oxford OX2 9JJ

Find us on the World Wide Web at www.westviewpress.com

Library of Congress Cataloging-in-Publication Data
Chilcote, Ronald H.
    Comparative inquiry in politics and political economy : theories and issues / Ronald H. Chilcote.
        p. cm.
    Includes bibliographical references and index.
    ISBN 0-8133-8151-7 (hc.) —ISBN 0-8133-8152-5 (pbk.)
    1. Comparative government.   2. Comparative economics.   I. Title.
JF51.C453   1999
320.3—dc21
                                                                99-34286
                                                                        CIP

The paper used in this publication meets the requirements of the American National Standard for Permanence of Paper for Printed Library Materials Z39.48-1984.

CONTENTS

PREFACE

This book is intended as an introductory text for students involved in comparative inquiry in politics and political economy. My assumption is that inquiry becomes or should become comparative and that although study of a single theory, issue, country, or institution may be appropriate or necessary at any particular time, ultimately reference must be made to parallel or alternative phenomena. The willingness to examine a variety of perspectives and to explore alternative possibilities arouses curiosity, stimulates creativity, builds interest and self-motivation, and enhances comprehension of complex matters.

Two decades ago I began to synthesize and find order to the wide-ranging themes in and multitude of approaches to the comparative study of politics. The result was a book, *Theories of Comparative Politics* (1982), which presented a framework of the major trends and theoretical directions in contemporary politics. It focused on a juxtaposition of theories of political system and the state; particular and total political conceptions of culture; development and underdevelopment; and the distinctions between elites and masses through various approaches to a theory of class. The book was intended to guide advanced undergraduate and graduate students in a comprehensive and critical overview of comparative politics and to serve as a resource for teachers and as a reference work for scholars already familiar with the field. In fact, it proved especially popular among graduate students, especially at the doctoral level, although it was used at the undergraduate level and occasionally served as an introductory text. This book has been refined, rewritten, and substantially updated in a second edition (1994). A sequel also has been written, entitled *Theories of Comparative Political Economy* (forthcoming), which emanates from the plea in the conclusion of the first book for the study of politics and economics; the sequel emphasizes comparative historical themes and theories of transition, class, imperialism, state, and democracy.

The present text draws from both these books, digesting their content in a way that facilitates and provides the introductory student of social science with a theoretical basis and the foundations for comparative inquiry in politics and political economy. Its purpose is threefold: to provide an overview of the major theories and concepts; to expose issues and summarize arguments and counterarguments; and to encourage the beginning student to pursue critical thinking in the recognition that mainstream ideas deserve scrutiny, that many essential questions remain unsettled, and that the outcome may result in the formulation and reinforcement of a personal perspective premised on one's individual learning. Those desiring to delve into a more extensive array of theories and ideas, trends, information, and sources should consult the above works.

I wish to thank Sheryl Lutjens for suggestions, insights, and criticisms in her careful reading of the manuscript. I am grateful for three anonymous reviewers, two of whom were enthusiastic about this book because it is strong in its historical grounding and comprehensive in its incorporation of classical and current social theory; the third reviewer was helpful in filling gaps in current debates and updating a draft that had become somewhat uneven as I elaborated it over many years of writing. This reviewer complained, however, that introductory undergraduate students do not have enough background to engage in theoretical debates around the issues herein. I have tried to draw out some of these debates in the present version, but I have not introduced many examples of particular countries, simply because contemporary events become rapidly dated and do not necessarily conform to individual preferences. I shall leave it to readers to search for examples, which are abundant in the comparative literature. A further complaint was that most instructors do not approach the subject from a Marxist viewpoint. I caution, however, that my work was not intended to do so. I juxtapose mainstream and alternative perspectives to awaken students to the possibility of employing various theories and methodologies, including Marxist, in their study and thinking. The desire here is to open minds to critical thinking, not to close theory to ideas that may be popular today but become obscure in the future.

Ronald H. Chilcote

PART ONE

Introduction
FOUNDATIONS FOR INQUIRY

This introduction identifies and explains key issues, defines essential concepts, delineates theoretical directions, and notes the limitations and parameters of inquiry in (comparative) politics and political economy. My purpose is to show the importance of theory in coming to grips with the disparate material, to lay the foundations for further study, and to encourage the reader to assume a questioning stance in the recognition that all questions remain open and unsettled.[1]

ISSUES

The specialist tends to view comparative politics as the study of everything political. Any lesser conception obscures the criteria for selection and exclusion of what the field might study. There is no consensus on this view, however, and defining comparative politics evokes much confusion for student and scholar alike. More concretely, comparative politics studies a broad range of political activity, including governments and their institutions as well as other forms of organizations not directly related to national government, for example, tribes, communities, associations, and unions. The term **comparative politics** sometimes is used loosely and

---

[1]Bibliographic information for works cited in the text can be found in the References section at the end of this book. The reader will also find a glossary of terms that appear throughout the book. These terms are printed in bold in the text where an explanation occurs. Those readers desiring considerably more detail and explanation, including criticisms and annotations to an extensive survey of relevant literature, should consult my *Theories of Comparative Politics: The Search for a Paradigm Revisited* (Westview Press, 1994) and *Theories of Comparative Political Economy* (Westview Press, forthcoming).

interchangeably with **comparative government**, which usually refers to the study of countries or nation-states in Europe; the focus of that field of study is on the political institutions or structures and the activities or functions of those countries, with attention to their executives, legislatures, and judiciaries as well as such supplementary organizations as political parties and pressure groups. Stated more simply, the comparative study of government often refers to the study of foreign governments and regimes, and the term comparative politics is used for comparisons in the study of all forms of political activity—governmental and nongovernmental.

Comparative inquiry necessarily relates to economic as well as political phenomena. Increasingly, political scientists look to economic causes for political understanding, whereas economists look to political explanations. **Political economy** thus overlaps these disciplinary preferences. *Webster's New International Dictionary* (3d ed.) identifies political economy in the eighteenth century as a field of government concerned with directing policies toward the enhancement of government and community wealth. The dictionary adds that in the nineteenth century political economy was a social science related to economics but primarily concerned with government rather than commercial or personal economics. Not until recently has a tradition of political economy established itself in political science, but during the 1980s and 1990s it was clearly in vogue. Political economy has always been of interest in economics, dating back especially to nineteenth-century studies and polemics associated with the rise of **capitalism** and the implantation of bourgeois society and, since the Second World War, to the resurgence of attention by radical and Marxist political economists.

Political science, comparative politics, and political economy relate to both theory and method. **Theory** refers to sets of systematically related generalizations premised on what is happening or might happen in the real world; theory can lead to changes in the world, and the experiences of the world can shape, revise, and refine theory. **Method** is a procedure or process that involves the techniques and tools used in inquiry and for the examination, testing, and evaluation of theory; methods may be experimental, statistical, or linguistic, but the case study method, with its possibilities for theory building and gathering information, has been especially fruitful for comparative inquiry. **Dialectics** may be employed as a method in the weighing of tensions or oppositions between interacting forces, such as the search for relevant theory, and allows for the building of theory on new facts as well as for the interpreting of facts in relation to new theory. **Methodology** consists of methods, procedures, working concepts, rules, and the like used for testing theory, guiding inquiry, and searching for solutions to problems of the real world. Methodology is a particular way of viewing, organizing, and giving shape to inquiry. Both theory and method owe a great deal to the classical political philosophers Aristotle and Plato, Machiavelli and Montesquieu, and Hegel, Marx, and Mill. Comparative politics also is indebted to the early-twentieth-century contributions of Woodrow Wilson, James Bryce, and Carl Friedrich, whose attention was directed toward the formal study of government and state. Comparative political economy finds its roots in the thought of Adam Smith, David Ricardo, and Karl Marx, among other classical thinkers.

The present text draws on the ideas of these early thinkers but emphasizes the contributions of more contemporary comparative political scientists. The Second World War heightened interest among scholars in the study of foreign systems, especially systems in Europe, Asia, and Latin America. The decline of empires after the war and the turmoil of independence in Asia, Africa, and the Middle East influenced scholars to turn their attention from the established to the new nations. The primacy of comparative politics was conspicuous in the ensuing period as this interest in research was facilitated by new technology and funded by private foundations and governments. At the same time, however, a fragmentation of case materials ensued due to differences over methods in the gathering of data, imprecision in the use of terminology, and uncertain conditions, which resulted in an unevenness in the accumulation of knowledge. Additionally, there were problems with grand theorizing politics as total systems on one level and with micro theorizing politics as analysis of human behavior on another level. There was also a tendency toward model building and the use of unrealistic classificatory schemes based on the Anglo-American experience; ethnocentrism combined with unreliable and tentative data often resulted in distorted analyses and misunderstandings of actual experiences.

Students of comparative politics face yet another problem, that of value-free investigation. Many political scientists emphasize attention to explicit assumptions and to systematic and quantitative investigations. Such investigators assume the role of objective social scientists, separating themselves from the role of active citizens, but there is now a widespread understanding that values enter into all investigations of politics and that we must be aware of the consequences of bias in problem selection, concept formation, gathering of data, interpretation, and theory construction and verification.

The above discussion implies a systematic procedure for social science investigation, similar to the work of natural scientists, who look for regularities in the abstractions that they identify in the nonhuman world. Social science often borrows the theories and rules of natural science to study the human world, but human behavior tends to be ubiquitous and consequently unpredictable; the emphasis on regularity may obscure any recognition of irregularity; and values, beliefs, and personal preferences might intrude on the scientific enterprise so that in the end little understanding will be gained. Such has been a concern of many people interested in comparative politics.

Comparative political science may insist on the primacy of politics, but the student should explore the relationship of politics to other disciplines to learn their relationship to comparative political inquiry. We could discover, for example, the contributions of A. R. Radcliffe-Brown and Bronislaw Malinowski in anthropology; Gaetano Mosca, Vilfredo Pareto, Max Weber, and Émile Durkheim in sociology and political sociology; and John Maynard Keynes, Karl Marx, and Adam Smith in economics and political economy. The emphasis on the meaning of value judgment and neutrality and the implications of objectivity in the study of politics, for example, may be attributable to Weber, who wrote about such problems in his *The Methodology of the Social Sciences* (1949). Durkheim in his *The Rules of Sociological Method* (1938) suggested rules for the observation of social facts, classification of social types, and explanation of social facts; such rules are widely applied in contemporary comparative politics. Unlike Weber and Durkheim, Marx did not prepare a manual on theory and method, but those concerns are evident throughout his writings. He was a comparativist who focused on the monarchies of Europe but also extended his analysis elsewhere, most notably to Asia. Marx would explain the societal equilibrium emphasized by Durkheim and Weber as a consequence of actions of a **ruling class**. The ruling class enforces rules and norms that legitimize the relations of production, which arise from particular means and forces of production and may become outmoded as change and equilibrium become dialectical parts of a single process. Later I elaborate on the contributions of Marx and demonstrate that his theory and methodology tend to run counter to the dominant tendencies of the contemporary literature of comparative politics.

TERMINOLOGY

Theory involves viewing and thinking. The student of comparative politics must relate theory to description, analysis, and synthesis. **Description** is a statement about the parts or relations of something; it may involve classification, identification, and specification. **Analysis** is the separation or breaking up of the whole into its fundamental parts and subjecting them to detailed qualitative or quantitative examination; analysis may involve clarification and explication. **Synthesis** is the combining of the parts into the whole, of diverse ideas and forces into a coherent or cohesive complex.

The literature tends to discuss theory in general terms, and definitions are likely to reflect the preferences of individual authors, so for the reader to gain a deeper understanding of theory and its usefulness in inquiry, I now turn to a discussion of some terms that appear throughout the text: concepts; generalizations, propositions, and hypotheses; types and levels; approaches; and models and paradigms.

Comparative politics and political economy suffer from ambiguity and imprecision of concepts. A **concept** is a theoretical construct or universal term. Conceptualization should be clear and well formulated, devoid of ambiguity and any multiplicity of meanings that may obfuscate connotation. Conceptualization must be realized prior to description and classification, prior to quantification and measurement, prior to the testing of theory. Comparative politics makes use of concepts in theory building. Concepts may be worked into definitional schema, classificatory arrangements, or systematic orderings that accompany a particular theoretical approach. Measurement and evaluation procedures may come into play. The resulting data and information are then subject to either qualitative or quantitative analysis. (**Qualitative analysis** relates to generality and sometimes imprecision, whereas **quantitative analysis** relates to specificity and exactness, criteria often exaggerated in an age of technological advances.) The more essential economic concepts used in political economy include, for example, **necessary production** in the satisfaction of basic human needs for food, drink, and so on and **surplus production,** which evolves with inventions and new knowledge that make possible increases in labor productivity. These types of production, of course, relate to the **economic base,** or **infrastructure,** and to concepts such as **mode of production, forces of production, relations of production,** and **means of production**. On the political side, attention to the political **superstructure** may focus on the **state, class,** and **ideology.**

Comparative politics and political economy tend to combine qualitative and quantitative techniques of research. In research, concepts sometimes are called variables. **Variables** are concepts that have quantitative or qualitative attributes. Numerical values, such as age or size, can be utilized with **quantitative variables,** whereas nonnumerical values are employed with **qualitative variables.** Variables also may be dependent or independent. **Dependent variables** depend on at least one other variable; **independent variables** are completely autonomous from other variables. Although these definitions may assist the reader in understanding the terminology, a word of caution is in order. Sophisticated techniques are not an escape from questions of substantive theory nor do they necessarily help us to understand causality, that is, why and how dynamic changes occur and impact on the course of history. However precisely terms are defined, conceptualization undoubtedly will suffer in comparative investigation. Differing language connotations from culture to culture also may pose a problem.

The terms **generalization, proposition,** and **hypothesis** are often used interchangeably, although different connotations and nuances of language may be associated with each term. Certainly there is no widespread consensus as to the meaning of many terms, but the discussion that follows attempts clarification. Qualitative analysts usually stress the term "generalization", and quantitative analysts may employ the term "hypothesis"; "propositions" may be the concern of either type of analysis. A generalization is a general statement of uniformities and regularities. It is the simplest form of explanation. Knowledge of subject matter is essential to the capacity to generalize. Eugene Meehan (1965) identified three forms of generalization: a universal generalization that in some cases may be a law because it has withstood intensive testing; a probabilistic generalization that based on experience likely is valid (frequently referred to as a proposition); and a tendency generalization, expressed in tentative and conjectural terms (thus being a hypothesis, which may be true but is not yet tested). Thus laws are universal, propositions are probabilistic, and hypotheses are tentative.

Generalizations, propositions, and hypotheses are especially useful in sciences such as chemistry and physics, which rely on precise measurement and complex and detailed classifications. Classifications depend on uniformities and similarities. Political science and political economy find explanations of human behavior limited if only uniformities and similarities are noted, however. Since human behavior is usually unpredictable, diversity and dissimilar patterns of behavior become important in the study of politics. The demand for the study of patterns of dissimilarity, as well as irregularity, echoed by Roy Macridis (1955) and other specialists in comparative politics over the past decades, has caused skepticism about the application of science to politics.

Two types of explanatory reasoning are prominent in theory. **Induction** is the process of inferring a generalization from a pattern of specific observations, whereas **deduction** is the application of the rule that if a universal generalization is true then a lesser generalization can be true. In comparative politics, induced generalizations and propositions are suspect because they may be viewed as deterministic or deemed to be correct and true when in fact conclusive evidence may be lacking or deviant cases to disprove them may exist. Since political science has few if any universal generalizations or laws, deductive explanation is unlikely to have much impact on the discipline (this reservation is not held by the social scientists who emphasize such terms as "scientific method" and "rules of science" in the theoretical literature).

Three levels of theory are identifiable: global, middle range, and narrow gauge. **Global,** or **grand, theory** seeks universal conceptualizations; the efforts to establish such theories for comparative politics have been largely discredited because of their generality, vagueness, and abstraction. **Narrow-gauge theory** has suffered from a preoccupation with technique rather than substance; often sensitive issues of politics are obscured by limiting the scope of inquiry to small problems and to easily manageable data. Among the social sciences global theory is also known as **macro theory** and narrow-gauge theory may be called **micro theory.** Between these extremes is the **middle-range theory** preferred by most practitioners of comparative politics; this level emphasizes the study of institutions (structures) and their activities (functions).

Among the approaches to the study of politics are the normative, structural, and behavioral approaches. The **normative approach** represents a traditional tendency, dating to times before philosophy was divorced from politics; it looks to desirable cultural values in society and emphasizes norms in the form of rules or rights and obligations that are considered desirable. For example, it is often an assumption of U.S. political scientists that democracy is premised on shared rather than divisive values, and these investigators look for compromise, bargaining, and consensus as the components of a democratic society. Proponents of the **structural approach** tend to examine issues of system maintenance and stability; whole societies or nations are studied with an emphasis on separation of powers among the legal governmental institutions. Structures in the form of the **state** and its matrix of agencies and agents may evolve through law and enforcement and basic rules spelling out the limits of negotiation. Sometimes referred to as a sort of superstructure, the state and its apparatuses may delegate power to agents who follow the objectives of a ruler, as, say, in the redistributive societies of the ancient Egyptians or the slavery system of the Greek and Roman empires as well as the medieval manor or the ruler and ruling classes under various forms of capitalism. Structures are also analyzed in the form of **groups** and **classes** and their economic interests so that attention is directed to the struggle between economic classes. The **behavioral approach** focuses on the individual and the small group as the unit of analysis, with attention to motivations, perceptions, attitudes toward authority, and other considerations.

The distinctions among these approaches reveal the many tendencies employed in the study of comparative inquiry. The mainstream of the social sciences has tended to use the structural or structural-functional approach, labeling it middle range in theoretical orientation. There also has been a tendency to pursue narrow, micro orientations through the behavioral approach. Disillusionment with the failure of behaviorism to deal

with the issues and problems of society and with the tendency of structuralism to deal with segments of systems without relating them to the
whole society has led many professionals to emphasize the normative approach.

An important debate has ensued over whether our comparisons must
be carried out in field research that incorporates the history and culture of
particular situations or be empirically based around formal or abstract
models in which data are tested and manipulated. This debate may be
cast in terms of normative or empirical theory or subjective or objective
analysis. The bottom line in these distinctions lies in the question whether
social science is really scientific. Is it possible, for instance, to cast a science out of human behavior and to be able to predict behavior? During
the 1950s and 1960s behavioral science attempted to answer in the affirmative with survey data of individual preferences. That tradition carried
on into the 1980s and 1990s with an emphasis on formal theory carried to
the extent that it was unclear in many disciplines, political science and sociology, among them, whether one needed to be an area specialist as well
as a scientist. Whereas an older generation of scholars may have conducted comparative research abroad in particular countries, today a
younger generation, caught up in statistical data and abstract theoretical
models, may be less inclined to go to the field. The fact is that travel to the
field not only permits familiarity and sensitivity to other cultural situations but also mitigates the ethnocentrism and bias that can be associated
with presumably scientific work.

Classificatory arrangements and frameworks are useful in the search
for theory. A **typology** divides and orders information and facts along the
lines of classifications and frameworks, often in subtle ways, so as to allow the use of quantitative techniques. The use of models in the study of
comparative politics has broader implications. A **model** brings disparate
parts together and demonstrates relationships. Models tend to simplify
representations of the real world. They can facilitate understanding but
they do not explain. They help comparative specialists bring order to the
mass of information available to students of comparative politics.
Models, like typologies and classifications, are limited, however. They are
mental constructions, not theories, although they are often distorted to
signify theoretical advancement. In contrast, a **paradigm** is a scientific
community's perspective on the world, its set of beliefs and commitments—conceptual, theoretical, methodological, instrumental. A paradigm guides the scientific community's selection of problems, evaluation
of data, and advocacy of theory. This book identifies the mainstream and
alternative paradigms of comparative politics.

Divergent lines of thinking in comparative politics affect these aspects
of theory and inquiry. Those people influenced by Max Weber, for in-

stance, tend to stress the notion of **ideal types** or situations. The ideal is projected as a possibility that might be realized through time. For example, U.S. democracy often is recognized as an idealized political type that given time might be realized by a less developed society, a process that implies a unilinear progress through which societies evolve. When backward societies are not able to advance, the ideal may become confused with reality. In contrast, Marxists might relate theory to real situations, not ideal types, and seek an explanation of underdevelopment in the historical interplay of social forces in relation to production.

This discussion has emphasized the traditional terminology of social science, but many of these terms are applicable both to the mainstream and alternative lines of thought that are delineated throughout this book.

THEORETICAL DIRECTIONS

Since 1953 the major theoretical trends in the comparative field have tended to cluster around such concepts as state and system as institutional frameworks, class and group in society, individual and collective preferences in culture, capitalist and socialist development, and representative and participatory democracy.[2] These themes constitute chapters in this book, pursuant to my intention of identifying the major contributions in the field of comparative politics and explaining how each has become a central thrust in the field and what its relationship is to political economy.

Institutional Frameworks

During the early 1950s the traditional concern with the state was supplanted by the influence of systems analysis. Three writers were particularly influential in using the political system as a macro unit in comparative politics. David Easton in *The Political System* (1953) and other works set forth a concept of political systems graphically illustrated in a box with its inputs of demands and supports and outputs of decisions and policy. Influenced by the functionalist anthropologists Bronislaw Malinowski and A. R. Radcliffe-Brown (1952) as well as by the sociologists Max Weber (1949) and Talcott Parsons (1951), Gabriel Almond first offered a simplistic classification (1956) that included non-Western and newly independent nations. He then set forth categories of structure and function, relating them to all systems in the introduction to *The Politics of*

---

[2]See Bill and Hardgrave (1973) for an earlier introduction to comparative political theory. Also, Rustow and Erickson (1991) provide a useful mix of theoretical and practical experience.

Developing Areas (Almond and Coleman, 1960). Later he related his conception of system to culture and development. Finally, Karl Deutsch in *The Nerves of Government* (1963) drew heavily upon the cybernetic theory of Norbert Wiener in postulating a systematic model of politics.

Almond and other comparativists convincingly argued in the late 1950s that the notion of the state had been long obscured by a multitude of conceptualizations and should be replaced by the political system, which was adaptable to scientific inquiry in the emerging age of computers. Despite his effort to construct the parameters and concepts of a political system, Easton recognized that political science owed its existence to the traditional emphasis on the state. These two political scientists, however, insisted, well into the 1980s, on the importance of the political system as the core of political study. Alternative work appeared with the publication of Ralph Miliband's *The State in Capitalist Society* (1969) and Nicos Poulantzas's *State, Power, and Socialism* (1978), and they engaged in a debate over whether the state was instrumentally dominated by a ruling capitalist class or potentially autonomous through its structural apparatuses. This sort of debate led to the call by the political sociologists Peter Evans, Dietrich Rueschemeyer, and Theda Skocpol (1985) in *Bringing the State Back In* for more attention to the question of the state, signifying that despite the objections of Almond and Easton, the comparative mainstream had come full circle and restored a focus on the state to its important place in the study of politics.

Class and Group Formations

From the 1920s, studies of elites and ruling classes absorbed the attention of political sociologists and political scientists who examined community power. During the 1950s C. Wright Mills in *The Power Elite* (1956) looked at the question of power and who rules and noted a concentration of power at the community and national levels, only to be attacked by Robert A. Dahl in *Who Governs?* (1961) and others who relied on a pluralistic conception of politics. Comparativists tended not to be distracted by the pluralist-elitist debates of the early 1960s, and even Dahl, who turned to Europe, noted a relationship between pluralism and socialism as one means of achieving democracy. William Domhoff in *Who Rules America?* (1967) described a network of social, political, and economic power in the United States and was able to replicate Dahl's study of New Haven and show in *Who Really Rules? New Haven and Community Power Reexamined* (1978b) that perspective on power as concentrated or pluralistic largely depends on the methods and questions employed in empirical study.

Comparative inquiry moved in at least two directions. One looked at elites and masses in several nations, whereas another turned to questions of class struggle and an analysis of a ruling capitalist class (bourgeoisie) and a subordinate working class (proletariat). Theories of class stemmed from a number of traditions, including the attention to the circulation of elites evident in Vilfredo Pareto's *Sociological Writings* (1966), the idea of a governing class in Gaetano Mosca's *The Ruling Class* (1939), and the concern with ruling class in the work of Marx. Among the criticisms of this literature was the attention on power structure alone; an ignoring of mass behavior; an emphasis on stratification studies without examining the economic, especially capitalist, basis of class; and an undue stress on working class as agency in changing conditions of capitalism and socialism when in fact other popular forces (ecological, feminist, pacifist, and so on) had emerged to push reforms and changes.

Individual and Collective Preferences in Culture

The cultural thrust in comparative study, conspicuously prominent during the 1960s, emanated from traditional work on culture in anthropology, socialization and small group studies in sociology, and personality studies in psychology. The concept of political culture was related to nations or national cultures. In this sense political culture represented a recasting of the older notions of national character. Political culture related to systems as well. **Political culture** consisted of beliefs, symbols, and values that defined situations in which political action occurs. Types of political culture characterized systems; for example, parochial, subject, and participant political cultures. These types of political cultures reflected the psychological and subjective orientations of people toward their national system. The pioneer comparative effort to construct a theory of political culture was Gabriel Almond and Sidney Verba's *The Civic Culture* (1963), which was based on a survey of the attitude of citizens toward their nation in the United States, Great Britain, Germany, Italy, and Mexico. Their study built on the proposition, set forth earlier in the work of Almond, that the ideal political or civic culture could be found in an Anglo-American model of politics. Lucian Pye and Verba elaborated on the theory and brought together essays by prominent specialists in *Political Culture and Political Development* (1965). Most of the work on political culture focused on two subareas, political socialization and communication, in which attitudes and opinions of individuals could be surveyed and analyzed. But there also have been attempts to relate political culture to the politics of specific nations, such as Pye's *Politics, Personality, and Nation Building: Burma's Search for Identity* (1962).

Since cultural characteristics tend to reflect the conservation of values, attitudes, and norms, political cultural studies inevitably emphasized stability and patterns of continuity in political life. Research questioning this approach and concerned more with the prospects for societal change could utilize the approach to study how power holders maintain control or how indigenous peoples oppose outside penetration, for example, the cultural resistance of Africans in Angola or Mozambique to the commercialization and colonization schemes of the Portuguese during the colonial period. The notion of culture also was incorporated in the idea of the new man, or person, the selfless and self-sacrificing individual who was willing to work for the betterment of socialist society.

Capitalist and Socialist Development

A concern with development was prompted by the emergence of many new states in the Third World. Almond and Coleman (1960) directed attention to areas outside Europe and the United States. Eventually Almond tied his ideas about political system and political culture to development, the result being a book with G. Bingham Powell, *Comparative Politics: A Developmental Approach* (1966) in which the two consciously began to work out a model of concepts and stages that characterized development; their work appeared at a time when many theoretical approaches to development were advocated.

One of these approaches was represented by Almond, Pye, and others, who built on traditional notions of formal and representative **democracy**, premised heavily on the Anglo-American experience, and recast them into a more sophisticated and sometimes abstract terminology around political development and the notion of progress through stages. A stage theory of development appeared in A. F. K. Organski's *The Stages of Political Development* (1965), a work modeled after that of the economist Walt Rostow (1960). These works set forth a series of stages through which nations evolve along a linear path from traditional to modern life. A second approach focused on conceptions of nation building and combined old notions of nationalism—those of Hans Kohn, for example—with interpretations of development, as in Karl Deutsch's *Nationalism and Social Communication* (1953); Rupert Emerson's *From Empire to Nation* (1960) and Kalman Silvert's *Expectant Peoples: Nationalism and Development* (1963) applied nationalism and development to the areas of Africa and Latin America. Studies of **modernization** represented another perspective on development, represented by Marion J. Levy's *Modernization and the Structure of Societies* (1966), an ambitious effort to apply **structural-functionalism** to a theory of modernization, and David Apter's *The Politics of Modernization* (1965), a provocative attempt at model building. Another approach to development included studies of change and order under capitalist societies, a prominent example being Samuel P. Huntington's *Political Order in Changing Societies* (1968), which continued to be influential into the 1980s.

Criticism of these approaches emphasized their ethnocentrism and failure to address the lack of development in backward nations; instead the theories concentrated on solutions through the diffusion of capitalism and technology from the advanced to the less developed nations. Theorists focused on the Third World to work out a theory of underdevelopment. The idea that the diffusion of capitalism promotes underdevelopment and not development in many parts of the world was embodied in André Gunder Frank's *Capitalism and Underdevelopment in Latin America* (1967), Walter Rodney's *How Europe Underdeveloped Africa* (1972), and Malcolm Caldwell's *The Wealth of Some Nations* (1977).

Three Brazilian social scientists presented theoretical understandings that substantially influenced developmental theory everywhere. Theotônio dos Santos (1970) worked out the idea of the "new dependency" to explain the traditional relationship of nations in these areas to the advanced capitalist countries, especially the United States; this form of **dependency** was especially characteristic of the multinational firms in the period after the Second World War. A variation of this theme appeared in Ruy Mauro Marini's (1978) notion of "subimperialism," a situation in which some Third World countries could serve as intermediaries for imperialist nations in the exploitation of other countries. Finally, Fernando Henrique Cardoso (1973) advocated the idea of associated dependent development, whereby some capitalist growth was possible in dependent countries. Although these ideas appeared as radical alternatives to the North American literature on development, soon they became absorbed in the mainstream of political science, despite the objections of Almond and Weiner and Huntington (1987) and other comparativists who ultimately responded to criticism that had largely discredited their earlier theories.

Today many political economists assume that the problems of capitalism have been transcended in an era beyond industrialization (postindustrialization), capitalism (postcapitalism), and socialism (postsocialism). Although some specialists believe that exploitation of the Third World can be overcome by a newly emerging globalism, others argue that globalism is but a façade for traditional-style imperialism. What is clear in this debate is that most of the world has succumbed to integration with an evolving and pervasive capitalism in all its monopoly and dominant forms and that as we enter the twenty-first century, U.S. hegemony has dramatically reappeared, with Japan in disarray and Europe struggling to unify itself. Those still concerned about development and its negative impacts on people and the environment have turned their attention to sustainable development and finding ways for peoples to be self-sufficient while preserving nature and ecology.

Representative and Participatory Democracy

Since the time of Aristotle and Plato democracy has evolved as a major theme in comparative literature. Most writing, especially that on the advanced capitalist societies, has cast democracy in liberal and republican terms of formal and representative political institutions, usually separated into executive, legislative, and judicial activities, along with a competitive political party system. The command socialist regimes that appeared after the Russian Revolution and particularly at the end of the Second World War were cloaked in constitutional arrangements that in theory alluded to formal and representative forms approximating and in some cases transcending those of traditional Western democracies but in practice relegating most decisionmaking to bureaucrats and technocrats in the state apparatuses or to privileged officials of vanguard socialist and communist political parties. Revolutionary situations in some Third World countries (notably in Cuba, Nicaragua, Vietnam, and China, as well as Angola and Mozambique) were associated with attempts to extend democracy socially by providing for basic needs of people, economically by egalitarian distribution of income and wealth, socially through extension to women and minority groups, and politically through mass participation in vanguard parties or pluralistic institutional frameworks. Although most of these experiments failed and only the formal representative political party and electoral systems came to be identifiable with democracy, in fact a variety of alternative approaches can be identified in the search for new theories and practices of democracy, as suggested in a useful synthesis by Matthias Stiefel and Marshall Wolfe (1994). They identified a number of dimensions to participation, including encounters between excluded peoples and those elements of society that enforce the exclusion; efforts among poor and marginalized peoples to work through movements and organizations; individual experiences told through biographical accounts; involvement through programs or projects proposed by government agencies, voluntary organizations, or international bodies; incorporation of participatory schemes as a component of national policy; and resistance to antiparticipatory structures and ideologies. Among the approaches to participation they emphasized pluralist democracy, modernization, government processes, self-reliance among the poor, legitimation and power, revolutionary and postrevolutionary mobilization, consciousness raising and self-liberation, social movements, trade unions and other collective actions, worker management, and defense of the natural order (22–34).

   This list of approaches to participation broadens the perspective on the prospects for democracy. For example, Stanley Aronowitz (1994) in an assessment of this question in the United States, advocated a radical participatory democracy as opposed to socialist currents of identity representation, including the popular new social movements organized around feminist issues, ecological concerns, and so on. Principally concerned with the rise and fall of socialism in the United States, Aronowitz noted that identity politics has been limited in recent years to a small but growing number of African Americans and a few white women such as Betty Friedan and Catharine MacKinnon who have entered the public debate. In Aronowitz's view two ideological factions have emerged: one faction in the wing of the redistributive left, including trade unions, with economic justice as its goal; the civil rights movement and single issue groups in housing, education, welfare, and social security; and liberal democrats and socialist parties; and another faction comprising the **new social movements** of feminism, black nationalism, and ecology. He related the rise of identity politics to the decline and fall of the socialist left in the 1980s. He offered a definition of radical democracy as a unifying concept for the disparate social movements, exemplified early on as a concept in the French Revolution of 1789 and in the Paris Commune of 1871, with principles such as insistence on direct popular participation in crucial decisions affecting economic, political, and social life and institutions; democratic management in state ownership of enterprises; changes in work time, in size of enterprises and social institutions, and so on; and plural universalism whereby the power to make decisions rests on those affected by them. Radical democracy thus evolves as "a universal . . . that is hostile to the tendency of modern states to centralize authority . . . entails limiting the power of representatives by genuine self-management of leading institutions to their control by a bureaucratic/political class . . . refuses the imperative of hierarchy and privilege based upon economic power" (1994: 64–65).
   Although this search for a radical democracy has usually been associated with socialism, the fall of the command socialist regimes in the former Soviet Union and Eastern Europe led some progressives to affirm the victory of capitalism not only in the present century but for the twenty-first century as well. The economist Robert Heilbroner (1993), for example, outlined the obstacles to and the dynamics of socialism and expressed pessimism over the prospects of a participatory economic democracy under either capitalism or socialism. A more optimistic future appeared in the vision of Michael Albert and Robin Hahnel (1991a, 1991b) of a society that maximizes participation rather than competition and antagonism. Norms of overall consumption could be relevant to all persons, a system of voting would shape productive flows, social constraints

would affect choices of voters rather than emanate in the planning process itself, and all members would be encouraged to undertake some work on a regular basis outside their principal tasks.

*   *   *

Now I turn to the two chapters that make up Part 1 of this book. The first exposes the politics of comparative inquiry by examining a number of important issues and contradictions that confront students and scholars alike. Awareness of these concerns makes us conscious that preconceptions and ideological preferences taint much of the thinking. The second identifies historical roots and fundamental preferences and traces mainstream and alternative preferences in the search for a paradigm. Five chapters follow in Part 2, each focusing on one of the theoretical themes identified above. In these chapters I use a dialectical process in which dichotomies of theory are set forth to confront readers and students with the need to recognize different ways of comprehending problems, thinking about solutions, and sorting out personal preferences.

1

THE POLITICS OF
COMPARATIVE INQUIRY

In his 1969 presidential address to the American Political Science Association (APSA), David Easton spoke of the relevance and action of the new revolution under way in American political science, and he identified as its objects of criticism the disciplines, the professions, and the universities. In his 1981 presidential address to the same association, Charles Lindblom stated that he believed that although the dissenting perspective had few adherents in the American political science profession, many students, including the brightest, were exploring it independently. In a 1970 presidential address, Karl Deutsch queried why political scientists had failed to provide policy solutions during the U.S. debacle in Vietnam, the impression being that the discipline was avoided by activists concerned with policy changes.

Although such issues occasionally appear, controversies and debates in the social science disciplines tend toward internal academic concerns and are less likely to address the ongoing dissatisfaction with the failure of professionals to relate to the contemporary world. Newspaper coverage of the 1998 APSA convention reported, for instance, that political scientists in attendance could not find in their models and statistical data any satisfactory explanation for the tumultuous events surrounding the sex scandal and impeachment proceedings involving President Clinton.

Some critics argue that the academic disciplines, known for conservatism, are intimately linked to the U.S. political and economic system, which they seek ethnocentrically to describe. Mostly outside the disciplines, a questioning of the establishment and traditional practice has led to a change in outlook. In his retrospective account, Todd Gitlin reminds us that "invisible from the outside, there were questions, endless questions, running debates that took their point from the divine premise that everything was possible and therefore it was important to think, because ideas have consequences" (1987: 7). In another view of the sixties, James Miller (1987) writes "of passionate debate, during sit-ins, in marches, at violent confrontations—at times when people, discovering discontents and ideas and desires in common, sensed, often for the first time and sometimes in the teeth of danger, that together they could change the world" (317). Illusions of democracy in the United States were shaken not only by events in Vietnam but by the Watergate crisis, which exposed flaws in the political system and brought down the Nixon presidency, and by the Iran-Contra scandal during the Reagan and Bush administrations, which revealed corruption and the practices of a "hidden government." U.S. military interventions in the Dominican Republic in 1965, in Grenada in 1983, and in Panama in 1989 were but repeated manifestations of the gunboat diplomacy of the past century and constituted an effort to restore an image of American supremacy throughout the world. All these developments implied that ideology and politics were very much alive in American life.

Thus the present chapter turns to issues of society and politics that affect the professions and society at large. It questions the ideological foundations of American political science and economics and inquires about the relationship of the disciplines to the universities, government, and the corporate world. What are the implications, for instance, of the familiar situation in which the teacher-scholar also assumes an advisory role to government, contributes to the shaping of government policy, or participates in decisions determining research funds for studies that reinforce that policy? What about the relationship of political science to the government and policymaking? What about the links between social science and government policymaking? What about the connection of university research to the government and the educational foundations? This brief exposition is intended to confront and awaken the reader to the fact that all has not been well with mainstream social science in the United States, little can be taken for granted, and there is room for scholars and students to be active in rectifying the situation. The following political issues for debate are taken up one by one in the sections of this chapter:

The American Legacy
Dissent in Academia
Prevalent Beliefs and Values
Ideology and Politics
Ideology Revisited
Politics and Science
Scholarship and the Establishment

THE AMERICAN LEGACY

American social science has been characterized by Dorothy Ross as liberal and practical with shallow historical vision and technological confidence: "It is modeled on the natural rather than the historical sciences and imbedded in the classical ideology of liberal individualism" (1991: xiii). These values can be related to "the national ideology of American exceptionism, the idea that America occupies an exceptional place in history, based on her republican government and economic opportunity" (xiv). Political scientists since the beginning of the twentieth century have focused on Western historical experience, but "their categories of analysis and prescriptions, like the topics themselves, followed their inherited tradition, with its antimajoritarian conception of liberty, its desire to expand elite governance, and its focus on institutional analysis" (Ross, 1991: 298).

A further insight into this background of political science was suggested by John Gunnell, who turned to such founders of the discipline as John Burgess and others, who "were racists and imperialists" and "not very interesting" even though they were decisive in shaping the discipline. Burgess alluded to most of the world as inhabited by barbarian populations and argued that there was "no human right" to the status of barbarism. Only the "political" nations were capable of helping the "unpolitical populations" by imposing organization on them "by any means necessary." Gunnell referred to a prominent figure during the 1930s and 1940s, Charles Merriam, who had pressured Gabriel Almond to delete parts of his doctoral dissertation that dealt with wealth and power in the United States because of references to the Rockefellers, who were benefactors of the Social Science Research Council and the University of Chicago (Gunnell, 1990: 36).

This background may assist students who desire to delve into the perspectives that shape contemporary thinking about the world at large. The social sciences today do not rely entirely on the legacies of the past, however. Indeed changes, albeit slow, are evident every day, but they are largely shaped by past experience; note, for example, the criticism by present-day postmodernists of grandiose industrialization schemes during the twentieth century. Those desiring to challenge prevailing assumptions need to account for established practices and not be frustrated if proposals and ideas for change become absorbed in the dominant institutional life.

DISSENT IN ACADEMIA

The realities of society have awakened some of us to an awareness of the underpinnings and ideological premises that buttress academia. Students are exposed to the ideology and mystique that pervade the relationship of political science and economics to university professors, government officials, business interests, and the military. During the sixties, several radical social scientists contributed to this awakening. Todd Gitlin (1965) challenged the ideological premise in political science that power is pluralistically distributed among a variety of groups and institutions so that no one can dominate the others. With historical roots in North America after the Second World War, this premise of pluralism affirmed the mistaken belief that there were no power elites, that power is widely distributed in communities, that power is observable and may be investigated in case studies of decisions by formal political bodies, and that the power system allows for change. James Petras (1965) referred to various ideological schools: One school espoused stability and maintenance in the name of equilibrium and balance, premised on limited commitment and participation so that consensus dominates political action and conflict remains minimal; another school emphasized group interactions of society but viewed politics as a balance of various forces contending for power and decisionmaking; a third school envisaged the role for the autonomous politician as the political broker, mediator, or statesperson in the resolution of issues; and a fourth school focused on political parties as organizers that make the political system accountable to the electorate and ensure popular participation. These various threads made up an ideology with an emphasis on stability and maintenance, equilibrium and balance, consensus and pluralism, autonomy and participation. Finally, Marvin Surkin (1969) affirmed that we must "unmask the guise by which the most prevalent modes of thought, their institutional expression, and their ideologies keep us from grasping their real social meaning." He argued that social science in general and political science in particular are increasingly becoming ideological in "the service of the dominant institutions of American society" (575).

Since the 1960s dissent in political science has manifested in the New Caucus for a Political Science, through its newsletter, *Caucus Forum*, and its journal, *New Political Science*. Bertell Ollman explored the conflict in studying an alternative mode of thought, say, Marxism, and the anxiety experienced when contradictions appear between the alternative and the dominant mode of thinking one has grown up with: "One of the reasons they cling to their ideology, therefore, is because it is 'comfortable,' and when studying Marxism makes what they believe increasingly untenable, many students experience real anxiety" (1978: 9). Mark Kesselman attributed the paucity of Marxist political studies, especially in the United States, to the lack of systematic political analysis in the writing of Marx, who died before elaborating a projected volume on the state. Kesselman believed that Marxist political science in the United States is weak because "capitalist hegemony has been so secure" (1982: 115).

Dissatisfaction with the economics profession also appeared during the 1960s with the establishment of the Union for Radical Political Economics (URPE), with its journal, *Review of Radical Political Economy*, and a popular weekly, *Dollars and Sense*. Thousands of radical professors and students joined in search of alternative theory and methodology as well as ways to link economic analysis to the issues of the day. A typical exposition of this positioning appeared in Howard Sherman's *Foundations of Radical Political Economy* (1987), in which he criticized conventional conservative and liberal as well as dogmatic Marxist views and argued for a nondogmatic view of the social sciences that is progressive and humanist in its attention to comparative and historical analysis and to radical political economy.

The mainstream remains vigilant, interested in but wary of Marxist contributions. Gabriel Almond (1990b, 1990c) recognized the ideological divisions in political science as split among political choice advocates, political econometricians, humanists, and radical political theorists. He separated political scientists into ideological (right and left) and methodological (soft and hard) dimensions, and he identified their ideological inclinations with four schools of thinking. At the soft extreme of the methodological dimension are descriptive clinical studies and political philosophical studies that use empirical evidence and logical analysis; at the hard extreme are the quantitative, econometric, and mathematical modeling studies involving theories of voting, coalition making, decisionmaking, and so on. At the left side of the ideological dimension are the Marxists, critical political theorists, and others who refuse to separate knowledge from action and advocate socialism; at the right side are the neoconservatives who favor free market economy, limits on state power, and anticommunism.

These ideological differences among colleagues and between professors and students, political dissension in academic departments, and personal value preferences may impact on student performance. For example, throughout the 1990s there have been tensions over a changing "discourse" as proponents of postmodernism insist on a detachment from ideas associated with capitalist modernization and all its impact on individuals and society at large. Thus arose the belief that we would be better off working at home rather than in the factory and producing through informal economic practices rather than on assembly lines.

Since relatively small numbers of women hold positions in academia, especially in economics and political science, or in practical politics, gender has become a controversial issue. Gender also has much to do with male dominance and machismo, and historians have begun to use it to analyze how powerful men have imagined masculinity in their political roles. Gender becomes associated with the worldview of individuals, and masculinity thus can be studied in the life and actions of powerful men.

The terms gender and sex are used interchangeability in the literature, but different meanings are apparent in relating women's liberation to class, race, and ethnicity. Gender often is conceived within institutional life, such as gender in the workplace or in the household. Gender also involves gay and lesbian movements and their struggle for political, social, and democratic rights and against sexism and homophobia.

These divisions should make clear the possibilities for students to assume a skeptical stance, open their thinking to a variety of views, and search for and build a personal framework for inquiry and understanding.

PREVALENT BELIEFS AND VALUES

Any allusion to ideology in political science or the other social sciences most certainly must take into account the thesis posited by Thomas Kuhn in *The Structure of Scientific Revolutions* (1970) that scientists inevitably adopt a structure of beliefs, values, and myths about the objectivity of their work; guiding them is a paradigm, or basic ordering, about the fundamental character of reality. Usually their students are inculcated with a similar mode of thinking.

In their search for a scientific paradigm, political scientists, for instance, may skirt important substantive questions as they quantify and attempt to remove the personal biases of the observer while their scientific inquiry focuses on the routine and repetitive processes of government and their techniques and methodology manipulate reality for the sake of efficiency. They tend to seek a boundary between the political and other activities of society.

Economists and other social scientists manifest similar disciplinary preferences, for example, a concentration on economic questions to the exclusion of the political. A focus on political economy opens up the possibility of bridging disciplines but does not necessarily ensure attention to societal problems. Such refinement of what is political frequently has occurred in response to the demand that a science must emerge from the study of politics. Thus the formal theorists with their methodology and quantitative techniques believe they are helping to shape a technocratic and depersonalized modernizing society.

How do such preferences affect our understanding of the real world? During the Cold War after 1945, international affairs were divided into a dichotomy of democratic and benevolent capitalist nations on the one hand and the monolithic communist nations on the other. Thereafter this focus shifted to a concern with the "three worlds" of development, the consequence of many studies that moved beyond viewing the Third World neutrals as naïve and easily manipulated. The collapse of state bureaucratic regimes and their command economies in the Soviet Union and Eastern Europe in 1989 also deflated the image of the communist threat, and debate during the ensuing decade revolved around the prospects for meaningful democracy in a world that appeared to be more harmonious on the surface, yet actually was fragmenting in the face of ethnic and nationalist aspirations for independence and autonomy.

The dilemma of democracy stemmed from a general assumption that American society is correct and good, that an alternative arrangement is unrealistic. The prevailing ideology in American political science drew on a "civic culture" in Anglo-American society and pluralism in the U.S. democratic process. This ideology consists of the beliefs that the United States is good, that progress is inherent in the evolution of U.S. institutions, and that political relations with other nations have the purpose of protecting and extending freedom and ensuring economic prosperity on a mutual basis. Furthermore, progress depends on the functioning of a free market in which firms compete for profits and workers compete for wages. The market is dominated by large, competing corporations, marginally regulated by the government, which efficiently produce, according to consumer demand, the best quality goods and services and the highest standard of living for the general population. The basis of individual freedom is the right to own private property, and civility is the basic standard of morality. Disrespect for authority threatens this order; thus the United States must defend itself from the penetration of outside forces, such as international **communism,** for example, during the Cold War, which envisaged a worldwide conflict between good and evil. At the same time, as the wealthiest and most powerful country on earth, the United States would manifest its civilizing traditions among the peoples of the world, especially those in the less developed countries.

This perception of U.S. hegemony probably is held by a majority of people in the United States today, yet its fundamental premises have been challenged on many fronts. During the U.S. involvement in Southeast Asia, racial discrimination against blacks, Chicanos, Puerto Ricans, and other minority groups at home was linked with war, imperialism, and exploitation abroad. Inequality for women in the workplace was conspicuous, with wages for women lower than those for men working similar jobs; and in the universities women held only a small percentage of the available academic positions.

These examples suggest that there is a politics that shapes perspectives. Politics and traditional preferences also ensure the continuity of mainstream practices in academia. Certainly changes are taking place, especially among progressive researchers and teachers—whose contributions, however, do not easily gain the recognition, prestige, or tenure they deserve. Women have neither exercised much influence nor been well represented. African American, Asian American, Latino, Native American, and other non-Anglo scholars have been ostracized from the profession, especially when they challenged established views. Mainstream journals and publishers have not been receptive to new ideas or alternative frames of reference.

Interpretations of society and politics generally are rooted in prevailing assumptions. Critical observers frequently search for discrepancies and abuses of government or private power groups. Dissenting conclusions too often manifest in clichés or unsubstantiated generalizations that lack the historical perspective and understanding needed for effective action. For example, the government may be corrupt; the middle class shallow, self-serving, and amoral; the dominant class conspiratorial; and the working class compromised. The powerful may be seen as powerful and oppressing the weak at every opportunity; and racism is seen as ingrained in the heart of the United States. Students must learn that such a perspective may indeed reflect reality, but it should be accompanied by the uncovering of supporting evidence and interpreted in the light of society as a whole.

IDEOLOGY AND POLITICS

Some social scientists have stressed that traditional ideologies are no longer relevant to a contemporary technological and modernizing society. They see instead a harmonious society of varied and diverse political forces, which bargain and strive for consensus in their actions. Daniel Bell, for instance, argued in *The End of Ideology* (1962) that in advanced societies there has been an exhaustion of belief patterns and extremist political movements. Bell attributed the existence of ideology to the revolutionary impulses of the past century and a half, manifested in particular by Hegel and Marx, who sought the transference of ideas into action. But Bell believed that ideology, once it becomes "a road to action, has come to be a dead end" (393; see generally 393–407), and in a reassessment many years later he reaffirmed that "ideology has become an irretrievably fallen word" (1988: 331).

In line with the demise of ideology has been the transformation of social science into a science premised on the success of the natural sciences. Thus the behavioral sciences evolved, neutral in character and acceptable to both natural and social scientists seeking to find some unit of measurement, whether it be money for the economist or the vote for the political scientist. This perspective of social science is rooted in the industrialization and technology of a society characterized by bureaucracy, specialization, and the division of labor.

These trends have affected the universities and education in general. For example, some critics, especially progressive academics concerned with these trends, come to view knowledge as a commodity, something detached from those who produced it, that can be sold in the market. One consequence may be alienation as the intellect becomes detached from the self and fact is distinguished from value. The specialist in society and in the university may ignore the whole process of learning, and the cumulative acquisition of knowledge becomes the assembly line of the modern university.

Prophecies of the end of ideology were intended to mitigate the cultural contradictions of capitalism and lead to the thesis of "postindustrial society" as a vision also promoted by Daniel Bell, along with Seymour Martin Lipset and others. This view envisioned an improvement of living standards; a closing of gaps between classes through mass education, mass production, and mass consumption; and a diminishing of ethnic, linguistic, regional, and religious loyalties along with a marginalization of total ideologies. Francis Fukuyama (1992) suggested that liberal democracy constitutes the final step in the ideological evolution of humankind.

Many of these ideas have been criticized as idealistic or as defenses of the capitalist order. In capitalism ideology actually permeates politics. For example, the victories of the environmental movement may have been at the expense of workers, and slow-growth activism may have saved nature at the expense of poor people, as attested frequently by the political economist James O'Connor in the journal he edits, *Nature, Capitalism, Socialism*. Often ideology is a reflection of powerful men, as in the case of the confirmation hearings of the Supreme Court justice Clarence Thomas, a black jurist accused by the law professor Anita Hill of sexual harassment, whose nomination was confirmed by male peers; in Oliver Stone's film *JFK*, which revived the conspiracy theory of the New Orleans district attorney and judge Jim Garrison, suggesting that the assassination of President Kennedy may have been tied to his desire to avoid introducing U.S. troops in Vietnam, a position opposed by the Joint Chiefs of Staff; or in an all-white jury's acquittal of white police officers involved in the Los Angeles beating of a black man, Rodney King. These and other examples may help students in recognizing ideological influences that influence major political events.

IDEOLOGY REVISITED

The term **ideology** apparently originated among post-Enlightenment theorists and ideologues, who used it with reference to a "science of ideas" for discovering truth and dispelling illusions. Marx and Engels gave the term a different meaning in *The German Ideology,* in which ideology was concerned with **false consciousness,** or any set of political illusions produced by the experiences of a social class; only through the struggle of classes would true consciousness be achieved. Such struggle would involve a recognition of the misconceptions that relate to the failure of individuals to understand their alienated relationship to their surroundings. Thus progressive advancement toward a classless society would eliminate all mythologies and superstitions and ensure a benevolent society, universal in scope and acceptance. Without fundamentally altering this definition, Karl Mannheim in *Ideologie und Utopie (Ideology and Utopia)* distinguished two meanings: the particular conception of ideology as "conscious disguises of the real situation" and the more inclusive total conception of "an ideology of an age or of a concrete social group" (1929/1936: 55–56) such as a class. Mannheim considered that ideas exposed as distortions of a past or potential social order were ideological whereas those realized in the social order were utopian.

Contemporary social science may distort these specific meanings of ideology. For instance, ideology is used pejoratively to describe totalitarian regimes, lending credence to declarations that ideologies become exhausted in a modernizing world. But this stance may overlook the fact that the wealthiest society the world has known is able to tolerate inequalities, not by totalitarian force but by subtle internal controls based on beliefs, values, and ideas to which most people willingly subscribe. For example, ideology, in the sense understood by György Lukács, Marx, and others, is so deeply rooted in the consciousness of the U.S. people that they experience great difficulty in comprehending—indeed they tend to accept—the subtle forces that envelop their everyday actions. Simply stated, this is false consciousness shaped by the media and forces of capitalist society. It is not even clear that the revelation of U.S. policy failures in Vietnam or the Watergate and Iran-Contra scandals awakened the people to the reality. Nor did Americans become concerned over needless bombings in the Sudan and Iraq, events timed to divert attention from the sex scandal and impeachment trial of President Bill Clinton but widely criticized abroad. Even as such events are exposed, the illusions of a democratic order carry on.

Ideologies have evolved in a past and continuing association with the process of industrialization and the consequent economic and social problems that accompany that process. Ideologies tend to address themselves to utopian goals, to the resolution of the problems of human existence. And in the light of the contemporary world they tend to be defined in unrealistically optimistic terms, whether they profess a free market or a classless society. Modern ideologies flourished in the era of rapidly

changing economic and political developments that accompanied industrialization, especially in Europe and the United States. With the growth
of technology, it is often argued, conditions stabilized and a democratic
consensus prevailed, resulting in the decline of universalistic, humanistic,
and intellectually fashioned ideologies in the Western world. In contrast,
it is sometimes believed that the persisting mass ideologies of the Third
World are parochial, created by political leaders seeking economic development and power. Many who argue that ideologies have reached an end
in the modern world persist in the belief that the resulting political order
in the nations of the Third World will be led by new elites in a totalitarian
arrangement lacking democratic institutions. The way out would be for
the Western world to intervene and impose representative democracy, as
illustrated by U.S. intervention in Panama in 1989 and in Haiti in 1994.
Skeptics recognize that such drastic measures usually fail to get at the
root of problems shaped by social inequality, wide gaps in income levels
among peoples of poor countries, weak health services, and inferior
schooling. The dilemma was captured by *Mother Jones* (May 14, 1989: 13)
in a quote from Susan Sontag referring to a new era of capitalism in the
wake of the industrial revolution and welfare state capitalism: "There's a
new polycentric, post-nationalist, hyper-capitalist international society
being formed. In this world in which materialism has almost a new dimension, it's so hard to get people to think about questions of injustice."

POLITICS AND SCIENCE

Mainstream social scientists may have avoided overtly becoming involved in the major decisions of society, but intellectuals have been constrained by their academic institutions, dependent on private and public
foundations for funding their research, and conditioned more to conform
than to rebel. Thus they no longer are the "public intellectuals" that
Antonio Gramsci believed were essential to shaping decisions in everyday life. Russell Jacoby (1987) emphasized this position in his exposition
of the decline of the public intellectual in North America.

At another level, however, intellectuals and the government are able to
manipulate information and events and cover up illegal activities with
relative ease. A couple of examples illustrate the difficulty of exposing
these practices. Nearly fifty years after the event, the historian Jon Wiener
revealed that Talcott Parsons, one of the most influential American sociologists of the twentieth century, while associated with Harvard University
also worked with U.S. Army intelligence officers to smuggle Nazi collab-
orators into the United States as Soviet studies experts. Also, and especially after the Second World War, ties between U.S. universities and the
CIA were prevalent, including subsidies to student, academic, research,

and journalistic organizations. Finally, in July 1970 President Nixon approved a plan based on a memo by his aide Thomas Huston and endorsed by the FBI director, J. Edgar Hoover, and other intelligence officials. This plan, which culminated in the Watergate scandal, included electronic surveillance of individuals and groups, covert opening of mail, surreptitious entries and burglaries to gain information on progressive groups and intellectuals, and recruitment of campus informants.

The linguist Noam Chomsky once referred to the failure of social scientists to counterbalance government policies and actions by emphasizing the traditional values of democracy. He believed that social scientists with access to money and influence surrender their independent judgments, neglect teaching, and distort scholarship. They become a technical intelligentsia interested in stability and order. Researchers often camouflage their partisan allegiances and contempt for human beings by professing themselves to be discoverers of truth, unchanging forces of history, or masters of objective laws of science.

The experiences of economics and political science are not unlike those of other disciplines in which dissident intellectual movements emerged, including the Union of Radical Sociologists and its journal *Critical Sociology*. The dissent extended to area specialists and such alternative publications as the *Review of African Political Economy, Bulletin of Concerned Asian Scholars, Latin American Perspectives, NACLA (North American Congress on Latin America) Report,* and *Middle East Report.*

SCHOLARSHIP AND THE ESTABLISHMENT

It is apparent that the university is not always neutral with respect to the major questions of society. The university depends on society for support, and it caters to those needs that society seeks to promote by providing university support. Given this mutual relationship between the university and society, knowledge becomes a commodity, something detached from those who produce it and something that can be sold in the marketplace. Thus, the student learns to exercise intellect in a detached way rather than to use intellect in a dialogue between self and the outside world. Reflecting the society around it, then, the university becomes a bureaucratic industry, oriented toward specialization and division of labor. Many academics today tend to be specialized and restricted to limited tasks, less learned than in the past, and not concerned with the whole or with what the final product looks like. Scholarship thus has become a profession rather than a vocation. The pressure to publish in quantity in mainstream journals obscures critical thinking and mitigates controversy and debate. This tendency carries over to students, whose intellectual development may be downplayed. Students' intellectual abilities—

curiosity, analysis, aesthetic appreciation, and creativity—are not usually emphasized in relation to objectives of confronting complexity and creative thinking.

One important issue that persistently runs through the social sciences, especially in the United States, is over whether our comparisons must be carried out in the field or relegated to formal or abstract models. As discussed in the introduction to this part of the book, the bottom line is whether social science is really scientific and whether analysis is subjective or objective. Those on the side of science point to a distinction between an older generation of scholars who have conducted research outside the United States in specific national and cultural situations and a younger generation caught up in statistical data and abstract theoretical models. Younger social scientists may avoid the trouble of fieldwork altogether, but it is clear that whatever its pretenses at objectivity, scholarship has always been subjective and ideological to some measure. Although one dominant faction of academics may convince most of us to follow its lead, our struggle should be to open up social science theoretically and to ensure pluralism and democratic outcomes.

Government and corporate intrusion into academic and cultural life has been pervasive. The recruitment by intelligence agencies of student and faculty operatives to report on activities in and outside the United States has undermined comparative inquiry, especially in the United States, about the Third World. Congressional reports have identified CIA contracts with universities, some of which involved classified work. These reports disclosed that the agency had sidestepped a presidential ban against such links to individual academics, several hundred of whom were providing leads, arranging contracts, and producing books.

It is also alleged that the corporate ties of university to business serve the needs of the capitalist world, in particular U.S. capitalism at home and abroad. Universities and factories alike produce goods and services packaged to contain a U.S. view of the world. University research also is dependent on private foundations. The nonprofit foundations serve a network of research and policy organizations that influence Washington, for example the Council on Foreign Relations and its prestigious quarterly, *Foreign Affairs*.

The argument has been presented that ideology is relevant. Ideological assumptions about industrialization, progress, stability, and order permeate the policies and actions of the university, the government, and the corporate world. Ideology permeates academic life, as academics tend to be ideological in that their values and beliefs are often tied to property, money, and influence, reflecting the capitalist world around them. They may disguise their preferences, allegiances, and biases in professionalism and in scientific objectivity, thus appearing as apolitical and conservative.

Progressive and concerned scholars and students have reassessed these positions, challenged the ruling professional power structure, promoted a sense of ethics in scholarship and teaching, and exposed government penetration and control of much academic research and publication and the implications thereof for comparative inquiry.

2

THEORETICAL PATHS

Theory may be associated with the search for a paradigm. A **paradigm** is
a scientific community's perspective of the world; its set of beliefs; and its
conceptual, theoretical, and methodological commitments. The paradigm
guides a scientific community's selection of problems, evaluation of data,
and advocacy of theory. Thirty years ago, Thomas Kuhn's analysis of paradigms caught the attention of social scientists. In *The Structure of
Scientific Revolutions* (1970), he argued that the scientific community tends
to work within paradigms based on past scientific achievements. The
concepts, laws, and theories of science are found historically in prior experience, not in the abstract, and they become the basis of scientific learning and initiation into professional life. They shape and condition
thought. The paradigm to which one subscribes guides research by direct
modeling and abstracted rules. Paradigms establish the limits of what is
possible, the boundaries of acceptable inquiry. A successful paradigm
then enables a scientific community to determine criteria for the selection
of problems to be used for finding solutions. Scientists working with a
successful paradigm, however, might be unable to perceive possibilities
beyond their own assumptions or they might deflect attention from competing modes of scientific activity.

We need to question whether these Kuhnian assumptions have relevance for the social sciences and for students of politics and political
economy. Is there in fact a dominant paradigm that guides our thinking,
and what are the prospects for a new scientific revolution? These questions are particularly important in light of my insistence that we be skeptical of established thinking and open to alternative possibilities.

The present chapter focuses on this problem of paradigm and identifies
many perspectives. Its intent is to compare and contrast dominant ways
of thinking and their influence on social science, in particular political science and political economy. In the twentieth century, for example, inquiry

in political science, especially in comparative politics, evolved in a traditional mold of descriptive, legal, and configurative studies, with attention to the formal institutions of individual countries; this tradition was strongly influenced by Western experience, in particular that of England and the United States. During the 1950s behaviorism took hold as both a reaction to traditional studies and a means of empirically molding the study of politics with rigorously scientific and logical models of focusing on political questions. In the late 1960s and the 1970s a postbehavioral alternative to the behavioral revolution was envisaged. In line with the dissatisfaction and protest of that era, postbehaviorism promised relevancy and action along with attention to urgent problems of society. Variants of postbehaviorism have been expressed in other forms, such as postmodernism, postpositivism, post-Marxism, postcapitalism, postsocialism, and so on, which became part of the debates and discourses among intellectuals, continuing into the decade of the 1990s. Distinctions among the three main frameworks are identified in Figure 2.1.

The question is whether any of these frameworks ever constituted a paradigm. Was a scientific revolution occurring through the replacement of one framework by another through time? Kuhn suggested four phases in the scientific revolution: (1) the *preparadigmatic phase,* during which a number of approaches or schools are in competition and no single theory predominates in the scientific community; (2) the *paradigmatic phase,* in which a scientific community adopts a paradigm; (3) the *crisis phase,* in which the dominant paradigm is challenged and revised in competition with new and old paradigms; and (4) the *phase of the scientific revolution,* represented by the shift of the scientific community to different paradigms. The frameworks described earlier do not precisely fit the notion of paradigm, but clearly they have been employed in the search to find a dominant paradigm.

At the height of behaviorism in 1968, Sheldon Wolin argued that no scientific revolution had taken place in political science and no extraordinary theoretical paradigm yet existed, although an ideological framework of guiding assumptions had made its mark on the discipline. The reader may find the paradigmatic phases identified by Kuhn useful for identifying these assumptions and understanding the following brief examination of historical roots and fundamental premises.

Two significant modes of thought have influenced contemporary social science. One mode, **positivism,** grew out of the classical British empiricism associated with David Hume and elaborated by the French philosopher Auguste Comte. Positivism is the basis of contemporary social science concerned with knowledge derived from objective observations of real experience. The other mode, **historicism,** grew out of a German academic debate in the nineteenth century that influenced Hegel, Marx, and other thinkers.

FIGURE 2.1   Frameworks for Comparative Inquiry

Traditionalism	Behaviorism	Postbehaviorism
Prescriptive	Nonprescriptive	Problem Oriented
Qualitative	Quantitative	Qualitative & Quantitative
Eurocentric	Anglo-American	Third Worldist
Descriptive	Abstract	Theoretical
Static	Static	Dynamic
Historical	Ahistorical	Holistic
Conservative	Conservative	Radical

Sometimes referred to as perspectivism, subjectivism, relativism, and instrumentalism, historicism dealt with history. The German sociologist Karl Mannheim considered historicism an extraordinary intellectual force that epitomized "worldviews" and permeated everyday thinking.

POSITIVIST THOUGHT AND ITS ROLE IN SHAPING THE MAINSTREAM

Positivism assumes the possibility of a science based on sensory experience and independent of time, place, and even circumstance. Such is the foundation of empirical science, which stresses laws, concepts, and theories that differ from metaphysical accounts of the world as well as from nonempirical endeavors in logic and pure mathematics. Thus generalizations about the external world are meaningful only if they are constructed from or tested by the raw material of experience. Knowledge based on experience is objective. One can know only what one can see, touch, or hear.

Positivists have criticized historicists for theorizing about broadly conceived questions, for utilizing data to illustrate rather than to test their theories, and for failing to tie theory to data. The historicists may have postulated overly ambitious theories of history rather than engaging in careful testing of hypotheses or application of concepts, and certainly their predictions of the imminent universality of democracy were premature. The positivist reaction to historicism, especially that emanating from German academia and influencing North American political scientists at the turn of the twentieth century, moved the study of politics toward abstract, formal legal, and configurative studies and evolutionary theory.

The European experience also produced a school of political sociologists who were broad ranging in their theory and dedicated to formulating a science of politics. These early political sociologists in turn influenced contemporary social scientists to use the behavioral approach in

FIGURE 2.2 Early Thinkers and Ideas of the Mainstream		
Positivists	*Political Sociologists*	*Behaviorists*
Hume	Mosca	Parsons
Comte	Pareto	Easton
Spencer	Michels	
	Weber	

comparative inquiry. The theoretical and conceptual contributions of these three schools constitute what we call the mainstream paradigm in comparative politics today (see Figure 2.2).

The Early Positivists

The ideas of three thinkers are rooted in positivist thought and influential in the study of contemporary politics. David Hume, a precursor to positivism and its conception of science, reasoned in his *Treatise of Human Nature* (1739–1740) that knowledge based on experience is objective and that statements are factually meaningful only if verified through empirical observation. Hume believed that it is best to accept the authority of those who actually govern, as long as the existing rulers are not oppressive. Government should be stable, power depends on obedience, and a social order based on inequality may be useful and acceptable.

Auguste Comte, a founder of modern sociology, was concerned in his *Cours de philosophie positive* (1830–1842) with formulating a new science of society. He conceived of a system based on three stages of philosophical thought: theological, metaphysical, and positive. The third stage represented observation and understanding of facts with empirical certainty. Comte believed that progress is dependent on the consolidation of authoritarian order and emanates from the stages of evolution.

Herbert Spencer, a philosopher of evolutionism influenced by the Darwinian theory of natural selection, in his *Social Statics* (1851) and *The Man Versus the State* (1854) diverged from Comte's notion of authoritarianism by advocating that the state should play a minimum role in society and not be permitted to intervene in private enterprise. He envisaged that equilibrium was the key to the evolution of a perfect society.

The Early Political Sociologists

A number of important thinkers were deeply interested in constructing a science of political and social life. Influenced by positivism, they did not limit their study to formal distinctions among types of governments. Instead, they constructed broad theories of politics, and they were especially interested in questions of power and rule.

Gaetano Mosca, a Sicilian political theorist and practitioner, was one of the first to build a science of politics based on a distinction between elites and masses. Mosca focused on the **ruling class,** defined as the people who directly participate in government or influence it. As elaborated in *The Ruling Class: Elementi de scienza política* (1896/1939), Mosca depicted the ruling class as a political class that represents the interests of important and influential groups, especially in parliamentary democracies. He described divisions of the ruling class as well as of the lower strata of civil servants, managers, and intellectuals. He argued that participation emanates from competition among the segments of the ruling class and that this class undergoes changes in composition through the recruitment of members from the lower strata and through the incorporation of new social groups in a process he characterized as the **circulation of elites.**

Vilfredo Pareto, an Italian aristocrat and liberal, also wrote on the circulation of elites in *Cours d'économie politique* (1896–1897) and other works, but he distinguished more sharply and systematically than did Mosca between the rulers and the ruled in every society. He referred to governing elites and nongoverning elites, arguing that correlations could be found in the degree of political and social influence and position in the hierarchy of wealth in all societies. He conceived society as a system of interdependent forces moving together in **equilibrium.**

Roberto Michels, a German sociologist who became a naturalized Italian, was influenced by the ideas of both Mosca and Pareto. Although he criticized classical theory, which viewed governments as divided among democracy, aristocracy, and tyranny, Michels argued that in fact governments are always led by the few. In *Political Parties* (1915) he advanced the thesis that democracy and a large bureaucracy engendered by the complexity of an advancing society are incompatible. He differed with his predecessors over the assumption that competitive struggle within the political class would allow access to political power. He showed the impossibility of ending the division between rulers and ruled in a complex society, and he argued that class struggle would culminate in new oligarchies.

Finally, Max Weber, a German liberal and political sociologist, wrote prolifically on many methodological and theoretical subjects. He examined the question whether the German bourgeoisie could assume the leadership of the nation. In *The Protestant Ethic and the Spirit of Capitalism* (1920/1958), he examined the implications of the motivations and drives of the entrepreneur in capitalist economies. In his work on economic and social history, he analyzed the evolution of Western civilization as a developing rationality brought about through the impacts of capitalism and

technology and science, as well as the gradual specialization of bureaucracy. Weber referred to **ideal types,** or conceptual formulations, which
describe and classify phenomena that approximate empirical probability.
Ideal types served as the basis for his analysis of authority—traditional,
charismatic, and legal. These types were similar to stages in the development of bureaucracy, which he envisaged as evolving in a rational manner. He also looked at the question of class as related to the unequal distribution of powers and opportunity, but his principal concern was with
groups and status.

The ideas of the early political sociologists influenced mainstream social science. They served as the intellectual foundation of comparative
inquiry and were incorporated into political science. In particular, they
influenced the study of parties and pressure groups and turned investigation toward informal rather than formal political institutions and toward
beliefs about political competition, distribution of power, and conceptions of pluralism. The themes in the work of Michels and Weber continued in the writings of Arthur E. Bentley and David Truman. The notion of
ruling class in Mosca and Pareto led to a series of studies of power dispersed through community politics, exemplified by Robert Dahl in *Who
Governs?* (1961). The Marxist notion of ruling class was more comprehensive, defined as an economic class of property owners and employers
who rule politically. Among the political sociologists, only Michels understood history as a series of class struggles. Later C. Wright Mills in *The
Power Elite* (1956) and G. William Domhoff in *Who Rules America?* (1967)
were to approximate this conception.

In their endeavor to formulate a science of politics, the early political
sociologists constructed broad theories and sought data through empirical investigation. They were not entrapped by legal-formal and configurative studies and thus were willing to examine information institutions
and processes. They were influenced by evolutionary theory, the notion
that progress is achieved through stages in a developmental process.
Although they acknowledged the division of labor and the specificity of
institutions as societies reached advanced stages, in general they determined the parameters of mainstream social science, for example, refuting
the prevailing nineteenth-century conception of the closed ruling class by
showing the continual circulation of elites and of classlessness by insisting on the inevitability of hierarchical structure in most societies.

The Early Behaviorists

After the Second World War, as old empires collapsed and new nations
were born, comparative inquiry rapidly expanded to the study of the
non-Western world. Totalitarianism in Germany and Italy, authoritarian-

ism in most of the socialist nations, and the highly differentiated Third World shattered the traditional belief in the conception of representative democracy, and it soon became apparent that comparative study could no longer sustain the inevitability of Western ideal political forms. Inquiry thus branched out into areas and aspects of politics previously little studied, accompanied by the recognition that the study of politics should be more scientific. New concepts and methods and rigorous testing procedures became commonplace in the effort to systematize the study of political behavior and make it a science. In particular, quantitative procedures were incorporated for the testing of theory.

Behaviorism was especially influenced by sociology and cultural anthropology. Two levels of analysis were conspicuous. The first level consisted of the introduction of broad frameworks of analysis. In sociology, Talcott Parsons, in *The Social System* (1951), attempted to build a systematic theory of action. Influenced by Weber, Parsons elaborated a structural-functional level of analysis and the functional prerequisites of social systems. Later he identified five sets of pattern variables: affectivity versus affective neutrality, self-orientation versus collective orientation, universalism versus particularism, achievement versus ascription, and specificity versus diffuseness. He believed that human actions were profoundly influenced by physical, chemical, and biological properties; boundary-maintaining systems; and culture and shared symbolic patterns. In the presentation of a broad framework, Parsons showed the interrelationship of all social phenomena. At the same time he set forth new categories that permitted analysis at a second, narrower level, at which political phenomena would be subject to rigorous qualitative analysis.

Parsons's attention to systems stimulated David Easton, in political science, to set forth a systematic theory of politics based on stability and equilibrium. His elaboration of structural-functional categories influenced not only his fellow sociologists, such as Marion Levy and Robert Merton, but also Gabriel Almond, one of the major figures in comparative politics. His attention to pattern variables moved Almond and later Sidney Verba to the study of political culture. His theory of action provoked Almond and others to relate their concern with system and culture to the study of development.

The emphasis on abstract political analysis in early positivism impacted on political studies in several ways. It influenced the separation of content from form in political thought; it accounted for the isolation of political thought from the study of formal political institutions in political science; and it led to a stress on hard facts and superficial and mechanistic interpretations. Evolutionism in politics turned to the rise of the state in its primitive form and its passage through stages to more complex forms.

HISTORICIST THOUGHT IN THE SEARCH FOR AN ALTERNATIVE PARADIGM

Historicists take exception to positivist thought, arguing that data based on sensations are not acquired in unbiased situations. The mind is active, not passive, and it selects and shapes experience according to prior awareness. One cannot determine if the source of experience corresponds to the perspective of the objective world. Furthermore, the historicist assumes various views, not a single view of the world. Truth is relative to the worldview characteristic of the epoch or culture to which one belongs. Worldviews therefore are temporal and relative, not absolute.

Historicism has influenced social science and the study of politics. Science, it is argued, must be understood in terms of history, a view close to that held by Kuhn, who believed that the scientific community is governed by a prevailing paradigm and that this paradigm represents the historical perspectives of the scientific community at a given moment. The mainstream positivist and the alternative historicist movements were involved in a hundred-year struggle for a paradigm of which behavioralism and postbehavioralism were recent manifestations. The early historicists, political sociologists, and contemporary postbehavioralists provided the principal influences of historicism on social science and the study of politics. (Figure 2.3 catalogues early and later historicists.)

The Early Historicists

Historicist thought, especially as it influences the radical study of politics today, is rooted in the work of several German thinkers.

Georg Hegel, a philosopher and nationalist, delineated a conception of the authoritarian state. In *The Science of Logic* (1812–1816), he embraced the experience of many generations and civilizations, both past and present. His search for truth involved a process of stages through which he elaborated his triad of thesis, antithesis, and synthesis, with synthesis representing a new level of understanding. Hegel distinguished three powers in the state and tried to fit them in his dialectical scheme. One

FIGURE 2.3 Progressive Thinkers	
Early Historicists	*Later Historicists*
Hegel	Mannheim
Marx and Engels	

power was to determine the universal will (legislative power), another to settle particular matters in conformity with the universal will (executive power), and the third to will with ultimate decision or finality (sovereign power). Sovereign power, which symbolized the unity of the state, relates to the other two powers as synthesis relates to thesis and antithesis. Here his conception of state was unclear and different from that of Marx, who characterized Hegel's thought as idealist and as a defense of the Prussian state. So too was Hegel's conception of social classes. He divided society into three classes: the agricultural class, those who work or derive income from land; the business class, or all who work in commerce and industry; and the universal class of magistrates and civil servants. Unlike Marx, Hegel failed to distinguish landowners from peasants or employers from employed; nor did he differentiate merchants from industrialists, or owners of property from workers who have nothing other than their labor to sell.

Karl Marx and Friedrich Engels were German thinkers who differentiated the roles of various classes in the process of production and in their relations to the state. They fused a materialist conception of the world with dialectic thought to form a world outlook that envisaged a struggle for emancipation of the working class and a transformation of society. In *A Contribution to the Critique of Political Economy* (1859/1904), Marx argued that the relations of production and the development of the forces of production constituted the real foundation (the infrastructure) on which the legal or political structures (the superstructure) are based. Class and class struggle emanated from relations and forces of production. One's class depends on ownership of property and the type of property owned. The proletarian owns his or her labor, which can be sold to others; the slave does not own his or her labor; and the serf is obliged to work for the lord for a certain period. The capitalist, in contrast, owns the means of production, which allows the appropriation of a large portion of other people's work. Thus these classes are unequal, and an exploitation of class by class is evident. A society divided by class requires a state or an organized hierarchy to govern it. This state serves the interests of or can become an instrument of class rule. If a society becomes classless, the state will disappear.

Later Historicist Influences and Trends

Another German thinker, the sociologist Karl Mannheim, was deeply committed to historicism. He believed that all thought is socially determined and historically variable, as expressed in his conception of "particular" and "total" ideologies in his *Ideologie und Utopie* (*Ideology and Utopia*, 1929/1936). All thinking, including scientific inquiry, relates to a particular perspective and to the thinker's epoch and culture. This perspective provides an individual with beliefs and values as well as with concepts for the interpretation of experience. Ideology evolves from perspective. Ideology comprises beliefs and assumptions about the world that are accepted but not fully verified. Additionally, one's outlook is bound by inherited knowledge and beliefs as well as by social position. This approach differed considerably from that of positivist social scientists, who based their models on the natural sciences, formulated empirical generalizations into systems, and emphasized rigor and quantification.

A contemporary current of ideas, labeled the "new historicism," offers support for the belief that historical investigation and interpretation should not judge past understanding on the basis of present values but rather seek to understand particular authors and ideas in terms of the context in which they experience and write about politics.

COMPETING PARADIGMS

The competing efforts of positivists and historicists influenced social science, especially the study of U.S. politics. Samuel Huntington (1974) identified three competing models, or paradigms: progressive, pluralist, and consensus. Early in the twentieth century, a progressive interpretation of history, with an emphasis on class conflict and economic interests, appeared in the works of Charles Beard, Frederick Jackson Turner, and others. Later the pluralist character of U.S. politics, with a role for multiple groups and interests in shaping of public life, was seen by Arthur Bentley and, still later, David Truman and Robert Dahl. The progressive historical and the pluralist interpretations dominated thinking until the Second World War, when a consensus view of U.S. politics, taking Alexis de Tocqueville as prophet, was established through the writings of Louis Hartz, Daniel Bell, Seymour Martin Lipset, and others. The consensus interpretation influenced many historians to abandon their progressive emphasis and turn to models of equilibrium and stability. This led Daniel Bell to argue that nineteenth-century ideologies such as liberalism and socialism no longer had relevance in contemporary society and to suggest that the conflicts and tensions of capitalism and socialism were being transcended by new patterns of life in the form of postindustrialization.

These early perspectives evolved into a plethora of interpretations on contemporary society: the critique of postmodernism by Fredric Jameson, the idea of postsocialism in the thought of Alain Touraine, and post-Marxism in Ernesto Laclau and Chantal Mouffe. The notion of postliberalism was advanced by Samuel Bowles and Herbert Gintis (1986), who criticized contemporary liberal and Marxist political theory and sought space for a radical democratic synthesis in which representative democ-

racy can be applied to the economic sphere to ensure a more equal distribution of income and resources. Capitalism and democracy are incompatible, they argued, and the welfare state does not give citizens the power to
participate in the economy. Although this thinking about "post" formulations of society was chastised by Boris Frankel (1987) in a critical
overview, debate carries on around such conceptions as postpositivism,
postimperialism, and so on.

The movement toward the formulation of a mainstream paradigm has
been traced from its positivist tradition, especially the logical empiricism
that captivated many positivist thinkers of the late nineteenth century
and the behaviorists of the mid-twentieth century. In part, this paradigm
evolved as a reaction to the noncompetitive, descriptive, parochial, and
static traditional approach, with its emphasis on formal and legal aspects
of government. The mainstream paradigm also incorporated a critique of
traditional political thought, including Marxism and approaches interrelating fact and value in comparative analysis. The paradigm assimilated
some liberal premises, for example, the separation of religion from government. Secularism in politics emanated from the tradition of John
Locke and later of John Stuart Mill that every person has the right to hold
and profess an opinion, as long as the opinion is not seditious. Finally,
capitalism has also shaped the mainstream paradigm, according to Jeffrey
Lustig (1982), who argued that contemporary times are dominated by collectives rather than individuals: "These collectives are organized, however, in line with the requirements of a capitalist society, according to in-
dividualist principles . . . hoarded, fenced off, and exchanged for profit, as
people attempt to preserve privacy within association, and to assert control over elements of cooperation" (246). These premises reinforced the
pluralist and consensus interpretation of U.S. politics in the twentieth
century.

Historicism takes the position that science can only be understood in
terms of history. In this section I have traced the movement toward the
formulation of an alternative paradigm from its historicist origins and an-
tipositivist reactions to the postbehavioralism of the mid-twentieth century. The search for an alternative paradigm also draws on historicist assumptions from Marxist thought. Although political science does not
depend on Marxism—even if a Marxist paradigm has established itself in
the social sciences, as Michael Harrington (1976) affirmed—Marxists continue to challenge the dominant ideas of the discipline in their search for a
new paradigm.

A comparison of the mainstream and alternative paradigms is delineated in Figure 2.4.

Six general characteristics distinguish these paradigms in their interpretation of advanced, especially capitalist, societies. First, the mainstream

FIGURE 2.4   Paradigm Comparison

Mainstream Paradigm	*Alternative Paradigm*
Positivist Tradition—Liberal Thought Behaviorism	Marxist Tradition—Historicist Thought Postbehaviorism

paradigm tends to be analytically ahistorical, constrained by its micro and compartmentalized view of society, and its focus on problems is delimited by disciplinary boundaries. In contrast, the alternative paradigm is holistic in interpretation, with a macro view of society and an interdisciplinary analysis. Second, whereas the mainstream paradigm focuses on stable systems, the elements of which are in equilibrium, the alternative paradigm examines the state and a hierarchy of constituencies in conflict with the masses of society. Third, the mainstream paradigm envisages an ideal civic culture of participation and interaction among diverse groups that compete for power and influence in decisionmaking, whereas the alternative paradigm offers, for example, a class analysis of society. Fourth, both paradigms relate to authority, but the mainstream stresses the centralized order in an increasingly specialized society and the alternative emphasizes centralized authority with a broad and general base. Fifth, the mainstream views rulers as diffused and rationally dispersed among many centers of power or as representative of broad segments of population, and the alternative paradigm sees rulers as dominant, concentrated socially, and unified in political and economic interests. Finally, the mainstream defines development as evolutionary, generally unilinear, materialistic, and progressive, whereas the alternative understands development to be revolutionary, multilinear, and attentive to the basic needs of all people.

Historical debates around these divisive issues can be identified in another manner, as suggested in Table 2.1. In search of a paradigm reaching beyond positivism, Sjolander and Cox (1994) provided a synthesis of the debates that have shaped the field of international politics; the table shows the somewhat similar positions in that field and in comparative politics. Three chronological periods are depicted. In the second quarter of the twentieth century, the major concern in the study of international politics was between, on the one hand, idealists in the mold of Woodrow Wilson who believed in a vision of a unified global society moderated by international mechanisms such as the League of Nations and later the United Nations and, on the other, realists like Hans Morgenthau and Henry Kissinger who adopted a statist, power-centered conception of

TABLE 2.1   Major Debates and Turning Points

	International Politics	Comparative Politics
First Debate (1920s to 1950s)	Management of global conflict (idealism) vs. international relations of states (realism)	Euro-American configurative traditional studies vs. structural-functional and system comparisons
Second Debate (1960s to 1980s)	Behavioralist, scientific, and positivist neorealism vs. intellectual pluralism and critical assessment of paradigms	Behavioral, scientific, and positivist attention to aggregate data vs. postbehavioral normative and historical comparisons in a theoretical context
Third Debate (1980s to 1990s)	Positivist, including rational choice, conceptions vs. postpositivism; break with earlier ideas through reflexive theorizing	Positivist, including rational choice, conceptions vs. historical single- and multiple-case and postpositivist studies within a theoretical context

SOURCE: Adapted from Sjolander and Cox (1994).

global politics. Whereas attention on international issues incorporated a global perspective, inquiry in comparative politics focused on such issues as the formation of nation-states, constitutions, and governmental activities in Europe and the United States. Investigation in both fields initially tended toward description and later incorporated theory and methods that sought to provide a more systematic basis to understanding. With the rise of behaviorism in the 1950s, attention focused on the choice of scientific method and value-free research, a dominant movement that was challenged by the postbehavioral revolution of historicism and normative theory that accompanied dissent during the 1960s. By the 1980s, and continuing to the present, the search for a paradigm evolved through a third controversy, involving, on the one side, the refinement of the positivist approach and attention to rational choice models and, on the other, the formulation of a postpositivism and incorporation of critical theory.

Marxist and Non-Marxist Political Economy

The discussion thus far has focused on the origins and strains of thought that have shaped the intellectual traditions of social science and, in particular, political science. Not only the content but also the weaknesses and contradictions of mainstream thinking have been exposed in an introductory manner. The efforts of some scholars who considered alternatives also have been identified. Both the mainstream and alternative scholars have studied questions of political economy and, inevitably, the counter-paradigm that Marx developed in his criticism of bourgeois social science and political economy. Now it is essential to examine some of the epistemological foundations that have shaped the traditions of political economy, from classical to modern times, in particular the contributions of Marx and the distinctions between Marxist and non-Marxist thought so that we can clearly perceive the methodologies and values on which our investigations are based. Understanding of these distinctions can be enhanced by delving into Daniel Fusfeld's *The Age of the Economist* (1966) and Ronald Meek's *The Labour Theory of Value* (1956).

In his political and economic studies, Marx began to elaborate a conception of the state. Early in the 1840s, he shifted attention from jurisprudence to material interests: "I was led by my studies to the conclusion that legal relations as well as forms of state could neither be understood by themselves, nor explained by the so-called general progress of the human mind, but that they are rooted in the material conditions of life" (Marx, 1859/1904: 11). In *The German Ideology* (1845–1846), Marx and Engels related their conceptions of the state to the productive base of society through successive periods of history. They examined the interests of the individual, the individual family, and the communal interests of all individuals. Division of labor and private property tend to promote contradictions between individual and community interests so that the latter takes on an independent form as the state separates from the real interests of individual and community. In showing this separation of state from society, Marx and Engels argued that we should not look for categories in every period of history—that would be idealistic. Instead we must be able to explain the formation of ideas from material practice.

In a famous passage in the preface to *A Contribution to the Critique of Political Economy* (1859/1904), Marx depicted a distinction between *base* and *superstructure*: "The sum total of these relations of production constitutes the economic structure of society—the real foundation, on which rise legal and political superstructures and to which correspond definite forms of social consciousness" (11). The base or economic structure of society serves as the real foundation on which people enter into essential relations over which they exercise little control, whereas the legal and political superstructure is a reflection of that base, and changes in the economic foundation bring about transformations in the superstructure. This synthesis appears to reduce societal relationships to a dichotomy of categories and to simplistic formulations, and it has been attacked as determinist, dogmatic, and static; yet it also yields the essential concepts of Marxism as well as a departure point for comprehending the relationship of politics and economics. We turn to these concepts below (many of which were mentioned in Chapter 1 and all of which appear in the glos-

FIGURE 2.5   Concepts of Political Economy

Social Formation

Base or Infrastructure (Economy)	Superstructure (Politics)
Mode of Production	State
Forces of Production	Juridical Apparatus
Means of Production	Ideological Apparatus
Relations of Production	Repressive Apparatus

sary), but the dubious reader should also read extensively in Marx's writings to capture the depth and insight that his orientation to political economy provides us.

Drawing from Marx's distinction between base and superstructure, Figure 2.5 delineates the essential concepts of political economy.

The concepts cluster under social formations in accordance with the development of particular societies and peoples at different periods in history. They are schematically divisible along economic and political lines. On the economic side, the **mode of production** is the mix of productive forces, means of production, and relations of production. The **forces of production** comprise the productive capacity, including plant and machinery, technology, and labor skill. The **relations of production** consist of the division of labor that puts productive forces in motion. The **means of production** include the tools, land, buildings, and machinery with which workers produce material goods for themselves and society. On the political side, the state is constituted by the legal forms and instruments, such as police and army, that maintain class rule. These can be characterized as **apparatuses**—repressive, ideological, legal, and so on.

These concepts, of course, are not mutually exclusive and should be utilized in relation to each other. The methodology of political economy includes many other concepts. **Necessary production**, for example, is that portion of labor that satisfies the basic human needs for food, drink, shelter, and so on. **Surplus production** evolved with inventions and new knowledge that made possible increases in the productivity of labor. Surplus production led to the division and specialization of labor. Changes in the forces of production affected relations of production so that revolution and class struggle became possible at certain junctures of history.

Dialectics may be employed in the search for a theory of political economy. Hegel's dialectic was idealist and mystical and set forth rigidly as a system. Marx's dialectic was intended to be a flexible method of analysis, not a dogma or a complete and closed system. The "vulgar" Marxist assumption promoted by Stalinists and others that dialectics inevitably leads to scientific truth, however, should be rejected; so also should the view of materialist Marxists who proclaim that dialectics is unscientific. Marx believed that dialectics should be combined with a materialist, not an idealist, view of history.

Dialectics allows for the building of theory on new facts as well as for the interpreting of facts in relation to new theory. Dialectics needs be conceived as a set of universal laws that solve all problems and relate to all knowledge of past and present history. There is no precise formula for dialectical inquiry, but some guidelines can be employed. For example, look at the interconnections of problems to all of society and avoid dealing with problems in isolation. Approach problems in a dynamic, not a static, way by examining their origin and evolution. Identify opposing forces, their relationship, and conflict. Explain the relation of quantitative to qualitative changes and vice versa. Ask if one aspect may be eliminated when it has eliminated or negated an opposing aspect or if a new aspect may supersede or include an old aspect. Such guidelines, even in abstract form, may lead to questions that can be asked about everyday problems. These guidelines serve as the foundation for a scientifically viable method in the sense indicated by Marx, who emphasized that the study of political economy requires concreteness, unity of many elements, and synthesis. A category or concept treated in isolation leads to abstraction, and the method of political economy must combine abstract definition with concrete synthesis.

Marxist theory seeks to be holistic, broad ranging, unified, and interdisciplinary, in contrast to the ahistorical, compartmentalized, and often narrow parameters of mainstream thought. Recognition of these differences allows us to make some distinctions between the Marxist and non-Marxist influences that have shaped the epistemological strains of political economy over the past century. This use of Marxism intends to be open and flexible, since Marx himself considered Marxism to be unfinished and in a state of flux, subject to change and adjustment based on reality and practical experience.

To summarize the argument to this point: First, inquiry should be holistically and historically oriented rather than limited to segments and current affairs. Synthesis and overview help in the search for an understanding and explanation of the problems and issues of society. Second, the study of politics should be combined with economics. Distinctions between politics and economics often lead to confusion and a distortion of reality. Dialectics as a methodology may lead to dynamic and integrated analysis. Third, contrasting methodologies—mainstream and alternative—are identifiable in the study of political economy; these methodologies generate sharply different questions and explanations. Distinguishing between Marxist and non-Marxist criteria allows for understanding differences between these methodologies and pursing inquiry along one or the other line of thought. Marxism thus should be seen as a methodology rather than an ideology, and it is to be hoped that some of the polarization that the term evokes thereby will be diffused. It is also essential to put aside dogmatic and inflexible interpretations, acknowledge the failure of much scholarly work to clarify concepts and theory, and note the tendency to rely on fuzzy notions of politics and economics as well as on impressionistic observations and descriptions. With this backdrop in place, discussion can turn to the epistemological origins and currents of political economy as they illustrate the differences between the two lines of inquiry.

ORIGINS AND EVOLUTION OF POLITICAL ECONOMY

The following are the major periods and trends of political economy identifiable through history:

FIGURE 2.6   Schools of Political Economy

Schools

Petty Commodityism
Mercantilism
Classical Liberalism
Utopian Socialism
Marxism
Marginalism
Neoclassicalism
Keynesianism
Post-Keynesianism
Neo-Marxism

This section is intended as a general overview of the major thinkers, trends, and influences that have shaped these conceptions of political economy. It serves as a guide to the past and as a foundation to help those seeking a contemporary understanding of political economy. Most historians of political economy date the origins of political economy to **petty commodity production**: Once commodity production responds to markets and money appears, then fluctuations in prices occur. Some producers fall into debt, and primitive communal relations begin to dissolve.

Theories of the Ancient and Middle Ages

Petty commodity production seems to have first emerged in ancient China and Greece. Mang-Tsze in China and Plato and Aristotle in Greece attempted to analyze the instability that accompanied petty commodity production and to find ways to overcome it on behalf of the communal society. They recognized the impact of the division of labor on commodity production and were able to distinguish between use value and exchange value. Aristotle in particular identified this dual concept of commodity. Mang-Tsze believed that agricultural labor was the source of value, and Plato came close to offering a theory of labor value.

The expansion of petty commodity production in the European Middle Ages stimulated the scholastic theologians Albertus Magnus and Thomas Aquinas to delve into the value problem. Aquinas, for instance, sought a fair price, thereby justifying the merchant's profit and defending the established commercial order. Eventually this medieval conception of a just price lost its significance in the face of international trade and money. John Duns Scotus, another scholastic thinker, worked with a theory of exchange value based on labor, and Abd-al-Rahman-ibn-Khaldun, an Islamic philosopher, elaborated a historical-materialist view of history (Mandel, 1968: 2: 697).

The Mercantilists

The principal concern of political economy in Europe between the fourteenth and seventeenth centuries was the nature of wealth in an impersonal system of markets. This was a period marked by the discovery and conquest of new geographical areas; new flows of capital to and from the New World; and the rise of monarchs and merchants who promoted nationalism, undermined local barriers to commerce, and benefited from foreign trade and the erosion of the power of the old order of church and nobility.

Mercantilist writings of the period pragmatically analyzed how nations produce wealth, with attention to a credit balance of payments, a favorable trade balance, manufacturing, and fertile soil. The early mercantilists described economic life in terms of a circulation of commodities, whereas writers in the later seventeenth and eighteenth centuries addressed questions about the social surplus product that became evident with the growth in manufacturing and technology in agriculture. Two strains of political economy appeared, as described by Mandel (1968). One, the British school, was represented by William Petty, who in *Political Arithmetic* (1651) analyzed the agricultural origins of surplus value. The French Physiocratic school, including, for example, Pierre Boisguillebert,

represented the other strain. In *Détail de la France* (1695), Boisguillebert
concentrated on agricultural labor as the only source of value. François
Quesnay, a leading Physiocrat, argued in *Economic Table* (1758) against the
mercantilist assumption that wealth springs from trade and industry and
placed emphasis on the surplus produced in agriculture. He advocated
that taxes be paid by the landowners, not the small farmers, merchants,
and manufacturers, who were considered to be productive. Finally,
Nicholas Barbon, in *A Discourse of Trade* (1690), related the value of a commodity to the cost of making goods and emphasized communal profit.
Ronald Meek (1956) argued that Barbon represents a transition from mercantilism to the classical approach of Adam Smith and others.

The Classical Liberals

The legacy of the liberals carries on today in very influential ways. They
believed that private property should be protected and that the production of wealth was based on the incentive to work that the right to property instilled in the individual. Individual initiative thus must be free of
mercantilist constraints. These ideas emanated from English thought, in
particular the advocacy of free trade in the writings of Dudley North and
John Locke's notion that production is the consequence of individual effort to satisfy human needs and that the workers should be able to use or
consume their own products.

Adam Smith consolidated these ideas into classical political economy.
In his *Inquiry into the Nature and Causes of the Wealth of Nations* (1776), he
brought together the major themes of commodity, capital and value, and
simple and complex labor. He was the first to formulate a labor theory of
value, whereby the amount of labor can be identified in the value of commodities. He identified the laws of the market, with an "invisible hand"
to explain the drive of individual self-interest in competition. He envisaged a competitive market equilibrium.

David Ricardo, in *Principles of Political Economy and Taxation* (1871), was
both a disciple and a critic of Smith, and he contributed refinements to political economy. Ricardo advocated the accumulation of capital as the basis for economic expansion. He believed that governments should not intervene in the economy, a principle he applied to the international
political economy, arguing that a division of labor and free trade policies
would benefit all nations. He related Smith's ideas of orderly growth and
market equilibrium to the international economic system. He also noted
the conflict between the interests of landlords (opposed to the community) and capitalists (favorable to the community). His thought influenced
socialist interpretations of political economy, in particular his propositions
that the value of any commodity is purely and solely determined by the

quantity of labor necessary for its production and that social labor is divided among the three classes of landowners, capitalists, and workers.

Among other classical liberals were Thomas R. Malthus and Jeremy Bentham. In *Principles of Political Economy* (1820), Malthus contributed a theory of population to political economy, arguing that population reproduces faster than food production so that unless population growth is checked, the masses will face starvation and death. In *Introduction to the Principles of Morals and Legislation* (1789), Bentham viewed human selfishness as natural and desirable but believed that individual and public interests should coincide. Government action was acceptable if not undertaken in response to the narrow interests of special groups, and individuals should be allowed freedom in a framework of moral and legal constraint.

The Utopian Socialists

The insights of Ricardo into labor and production and the gloomy prognosis of Malthus stimulated a group of utopian socialists in their criticism of capitalism. Robert Owen pushed for labor reforms, including a shorter workday and the ending of child labor. He promoted village cooperatives in his utopian scheme. Claude-Henri de Rouvroy, Comte de Saint-Simon, an aristocrat later relegated to conditions of poverty, believed that the workers deserved the highest rewards of society, and the idlers, the least. He argued for the reorganization of society. John Stuart Mill manifested socialist leanings in his *Principles of Political Economy* (1848), in which he retraced the path of Smith and Ricardo but placed emphasis on production rather than on distribution. Pierre-Joseph Proudhon, another utopian socialist, was a critic of the orthodox economics of his time.

Marxists

Transcending the theories of the utopian socialists and of the classical liberal thinkers, Marx worked out a theory of surplus value as well as a synthesis that allowed for an explanation of class struggle. He developed theories on the prices of production and the tendency of the rate of profit to fall. His early work attacked the utopian socialists, whereas his later work was directed toward all his predecessors but in particular the classical liberal economists Ricardo and Smith. In *The Poverty of Philosophy* (1847) Marx exposed the "metaphysics" of Proudhon's political economy and argued that one should instead examine the historical movement of production relations. He insisted that the production relations in a society form a whole and that the society can only be explained in terms of all relations simultaneously coexisting and supporting one another.

The Marginalist Neoclassicists

The marginalist theory of value and neoclassical political economy were formed in response to the popularization of Ricardo's thought, the impact of the utopian socialists, and the influence of Marx. The onslaught on Marxism was linked with efforts to bring about the demise of the labor theory of value as it had evolved through Smith, Ricardo, and the classical thinkers. The neoclassicists attempted to be rigorous, detailed, and abstract. They emphasized equilibrium and thus were often criticized for not accounting for the disturbances that affect equilibrium, for proposing a static framework, and for not dealing with structural crises.

The Keynesians

After the start of the Great Depression, John Maynard Keynes, in his *General Theory of Employment, Interest, and Money* (1936), moved political economy from an apologetic stance on capitalism to a pragmatic one. Rather than justify capitalism in theory, it was now essential to preserve it in practice by mitigating the extent of periodical fluctuations. Keynes's follower Paul Samuelson and others have continued in this macroeconomic tradition to the present period.

The Post-Keynesians

The post-Keynesians emphasize realism with attention to the relevance of economic problems. They stress explanation rather than prediction; focus on history and institutions; and argue that a free market economic process is fundamentally unstable, production rather than exchange is at the base of analysis, and disequilibrium and change over time rather than equilibrium and stability are essential. Post-Keynesianism draws its intellectual inspiration from Keynes and Michal Kalecki.

The Neo-Marxists

Followers of Marx carried on in a Marxist tradition. Engels edited and published the second and third volumes of Marx's *Capital*, followed by Kautsky's editing of Marx's *History of Economic Doctrine*. Later efforts to expand on Marx's earlier contributions included Kautsky's treatment of capitalism in agriculture, Rudolf Hilferding's *Das Finanzkapital* (*Finance Capital*, 1910), Rosa Luxemburg's *Accumulation of Capital* (1913), and Lenin's *Imperialism: The Last Phase of Capitalism* (1917). The Stalinist period dampened interest in Marxist theories of political economy, but after about 1960 there was a revival of interest, promoted by the work of Paul

Baran, Leo Huberman, Harry Magdoff, and Paul Sweezy along with the
writings and teachings of hundreds of other Marxists throughout the
United States and other parts of the world.

*   *   *

This examination of various schools helps to sort out the differences between methodologies that follow a Marxist direction, including radical
political economy, and those influenced by classical liberalism, including
the public choice and mainstream approaches that avoid Marxist influences. Distinctions in theory, method, and concept tend to reinforce this
dichotomy. As long as contrasting values are recognized and premises are
set forth explicitly, both methodologies may be useful in the study of political economy. Attention to capitalist accumulation allows for an examination of political as well as economic issues. Study of capitalist accumulation with an emphasis on precapitalist and capitalist formations and
modes of production makes possible an integration of inquiry that
heretofore has led economists to investigate questions relating to the material base of society and political scientists to be concerned with issues of
the idealized political superstructure. Some might argue that economists
should deal primarily with theories of imperialism and dependency, and
political scientists, with theories of the state and class, but all these concerns need to be assimilated by the political economist. The solution
would seem to be the reconstitution of economics and political science as
political economy.

PART TWO

Dichotomies of Theories

The following five chapters each focus on a theme important to comparative inquiry. The first examines institutional frameworks of state and system; the ensuing chapters look at four dimensions relevant to the social sciences: social (class and group formations), cultural (individual and collective preferences), economic (capitalist and socialist development), and political (representative and participatory democracy). Different perspectives and various theoretical currents are associated with each of these themes in all the social science disciplines, but especially in political science and political economy. This discussion juxtaposes major ideas in an effort to give direction and make sense of their complexity and diversity as well as to allow the reader an opportunity to envisage a variety of perspectives and to find a particular preference and orientation.

For example, to distinguish some of the conceptualizations of two great thinkers, Marx and Weber, the dichotomies sketched in Figure II.1 may be useful.

These differences in conceptualization do not necessarily imply categorical distinctiveness, which in practice may be illusory. There are indeed points of convergence, but the differences may reveal how Marxian and Weberian thought has influenced major themes in comparative inquiry.

Marx, for example, offered an important conception of the state and its ruling class. Through time and struggle, he believed, society would evolve toward two hostile classes, the capitalist bourgeoisie and the working proletariat (although a multitude of classes appear throughout periods of capitalism). The first elements of the bourgeoisie sprang from the merchant class in towns established in feudal times. Eventually a manufacturing bourgeoisie pushed aside the guild masters. A modern bourgeoisie emerged along with modern industry and ensured not only its economic dominance but its political control over the modern state, so

FIGURE II:1   Conceptual Differences

Concept	Marx	Weber
Capitalism	Exploitative and wasteful	Efficient and rational
State	Disappears with classless society	Strengthens with capitalism and bureaucracy
Classes	Dominant and popular interests in conflict	Competitive and diffused

that the state became the instrument of the ruling bourgeois class. Under capitalism, the state becomes instrumental in maintaining the property relations of the wealthy minority. The state does not stand above class as long as classes exist, but it is always on the side of the rulers. Thus the class that rules economically, that is, owns and controls the means of production, also rules politically.

Weber, in contrast, looked at differences between material and ideal interests, implying a multiplicity of interests and many competing forces. He defined the state as a human community, legitimized by its monopoly of physical force in a given territory. He focused on bureaucracy and its routinization, harmony, efficiency, and order in the organization of the state. Impersonal detachment and relations ensured the rationalization of state activities. Concerned that class is an economically determined concept, Weber suggested that status groups exist and are stratified but can be rearranged within economic classes according to market demands for change. Thus persons are more interested in the fortunes of their status group than in the overall fortune of the class to which they nominally belong. The conceptions of Marx and Weber differ sharply. Marx interpreted the state as monolithic and tied to the interests of the ruling class, whereas Weber viewed the state as sanctioning a plurality of interests. Marx viewed all forms of dominance under the capitalist state as illegitimate; Weber looked to the legitimate forms of dominance. Marx advocated the abolition of the state and its classes, but Weber envisioned the enhancement of the state through the legitimization of its activities. Marx understood changes in the state and ruling class as reflections of historical materialism and the conflictual interplay of social relations and forces of production that have characterized various epochs; Weber concerned himself with the resolution of conflict through the rationalization of the bureaucratic order. Weber combined state force and violence with legitimacy, but Marx offered a broader definition in which the state can be nothing but a subtle instrument of coercion to suppress the lower strata.

FIGURE II:2 Political Economy and Imperialism	
Non-Marxist	*Marxist*
Underconsumption (Hobson)	Finance Capital (Hilferding)
Withering of imperialism	Monopolization of banks and
(Schumpeter)	corporations (Lenin)

Such differences can be illustrated on another level. If we identify the major theories of imperialism, we might distinguish between those concerned with political expansion through war and conquest, on the one hand, and those based on economic premises. Theoretically this dichotomy of political and economic imperialism might be more appropriately conceptualized within political economy, with a distinction between Marxist and non-Marxist theories of imperialism, as shown in Figure II.2.

At the turn of the century the English liberal J. A. Hobson offered an interpretation of imperialism that shaped ensuing non-Marxist conceptions and also influenced some Marxist conceptions. He argued that the drive to invest capital abroad was dependent on underconsumption at home and that if an increase in domestic consumption occurred, then there would be no excess of goods or capital and therefore no need to promote imperialism abroad. Joseph Schumpeter identified many types of imperialism, ranging from the empires of antiquity to modern experiences rooted in precapitalist economies, and he predicted imperialism would disappear in a rational and progressive era of capitalism. Rudolf Hilferding used a Marxist analysis in his focus on finance capital to explain the dominant role of banks in their concentration into powerful monopolies in combination with industrial capital. Lenin began with Hobson's description of imperialism but characterized it as bourgeois social reformism; he built on Hilferding's notion of finance capital in his characterization of imperialism as monopoly capital, or the highest stage of capitalism. Comprehension of the origins and manifestation of these and other theories at the end of the nineteenth century and throughout the twentieth century helps in analysis of development in the period after the Second World War, in particular in recognizing the Marxist and non-Marxist interpretations that pervade the literature on development, underdevelopment, and dependency. These examples serve to introduce the chapters that follow. We shall discover that both Marxist and non-Marxist influences appear in the mainstream and alternative theories that run through the literature and that conceptualization may obscure meaning and confound the reader. Thus the effort to distinguish and contrast different theories may allow for sorting and simplification. My principal task is how to introduce comparative politics and political economy to the introductory student. The traditional country-by-country approach has been partially transcended by turning to concepts and theories that give the student a context for coping with descriptive and historical detail. My attention to dichotomies of concepts, theories, and ideas is intended to open up and challenge students to think about the subject matter and not feel that its parameters have been predetermined or limited. That is, the questions are, for the most part, not closed, and inquiry should be an on-going and challenging task. I hope that this approach will help students overcome what often, especially in introductory courses, is a passive rather than active experience in the classroom. North American students in addition tend to be somewhat parochial and uninterested in other societies and cultures—which are after all the basis of comparative inquiry. There is much to learn and comparative inquiry surely will lead to more perceptive understanding of one's own situation. Critics argue that students lack interest simply because of the introductory character of a course, but my personal experience suggests to the contrary that introductory students can be more motivated than others to discover new knowledge and to think deeply about issues, assess different conceptual frameworks, and judge contrasting theories in their academic endeavors.

3

INSTITUTIONAL FRAMEWORKS

STATE AND SYSTEM

The study of politics and political economy has involved interest in the state in theorists ranging from Aristotle and Plato to Machiavelli to Gramsci. This chapter identifies some of the ideas around the concept of state, assesses a variety of theories on the state, and affirms that the state is a central focus of politics. Parallel to and sometimes in opposition to the concept of state, theories of system have also long interested scholars. This chapter delineates these theories and shows their influences and limitations. The social sciences employ concepts of both state and system to emphasize political institutions and their impact on society and economy.

Examples reveal the schisms over the concepts state and system. First, important theoretical differences are evident in the thought of Karl Marx and Max Weber, who provided a foundation and shaped subsequent social science. Marx believed that the contradictions of each society undermined order and stability, whereas Weber looked for the qualities of stability and order in a modern productive society. Neither thinker developed a definitive theory of the state: Marx, focused on the state in his critique of Hegel and in his studies of mid-nineteenth-century France, conceived of the state as a kind of superstructure of political institutions and ideological activity that reflected changes in the economic base, the intensification of contradictions, and the subsequent struggle among social classes. Weber was interested in the state and its legitimacy and power through force and coercion, and he looked for the qualities of stability and order in a modern productive society, saw historical change as gradual, and noted that evolutionary progress depended on the fundamental conditions of each society. Both also were interested in systems. Marx classified societies into economic systems based on mode of production and relations of production manifested through social classes: feudal, bourgeois, and proletarian. Weber classified societies as political systems of authority: traditional, charismatic, and rational-legal.

A second example of divergence is evident in political science, which since its inception in the nineteenth century has emphasized the concept of state: "Its adoption was most essentially a function of the Germanization and disciplinization of political science" (Gunnell, 1990: 125). By the 1950s mainstream comparativists, influenced by Gabriel Almond, proclaimed in *The Politics of Developing Areas* (Almond and Coleman, 1960) that the state was imbued with many meanings and could not be operational in the then-current comparative investigation, part of the problem being the proliferation of newly emerging countries of the Third World as the old colonial empires of Europe collapsed after the Second World War. They believed that the state, conceived in its Weberian sense with attention to "the legally empowered and legitimately coercive institutions," could be assimilated in the concept of political system, together with institutions, including political parties, interest groups, communication media, family, school, church, and so on (Almond, 1988: 855). During the mid-1980s a campaign—in the mainstream but emanating from political sociology—was mounted under the rubric "bringing the state back in" to social science (Evans, Rueschemeyer, and Skocpol, 1985), and interest in the role of the state prevailed into the 1990s.

Although the concept of the state was retained by conservative political scientists disillusioned with behaviorism and interested in preserving a more traditional emphasis on formal institutions of government, it also was emphasized by progressive political scientists during the 1960s and 1970s whose perspectives drew from Marx and initially appeared outside the United States. Particularly significant was the debate over an instrumentalist conception of state in the work of the British political scientist Ralph Miliband and a structural conception in the writing of the Greek political sociologist Nicos Poulantzas.

SYSTEMS THEORIES

The idea of system might relate to an entity such as a legislature, political party, or labor union, but usually the term connotes nation or state. Classifications of systems reveal a variety of viewpoints and interpretations (see Figure 3.1), situated in the classical theoretical literature by different political and economic experiences and in the contemporary world by the emergence of many new nations, the amassing of information and data, and the discovery of many technological advances that accompanied increased complexity. Scientists and social scientists alike have attempted to bring order to this complexity by utilizing the term.

FIGURE 3.1	Classifications of Systems			
Aristotle	*Almond*	*Apter*	*Binder*	*Coleman*
Monarchies	Anglo-	Dictatorial	Traditional	Competitive
Aristocracies	American	Oligarchical	Conventional	Semi-
Democracies	Continental	Indirect	Rational	competitive
	Europe	Representation		Authoritarian
	Totalitarian	Direct		
	Pre Industrial	Representation		

The classification of systems has caught the attention of comparativists ranging from Aristotle, who conceived of societies in terms of monarchies, aristocracies, and democracies, to Gabriel Almond, who offered a breakdown of Anglo-American, continental European, totalitarian, and preindustrial systems. The myriad of typologies include the following: F. X. Sutton broke societies into agricultural and industrial systems; James S. Coleman wrote of competitive, semicompetitive, and authoritarian systems; and David Apter divided the world into dictatorial, oligarchical, indirectly representative, and directly representative systems. Fred W. Riggs analyzed fused, prismatic, and refracted systems, and S. N. Eisenstadt offered a comprehensive classification of primitive systems, patrimonial empires, nomad or conquest empires, city-states, feudal systems, centralized bureaucratic empires, and modern systems; the last he divided into democratic, autocratic, totalitarian, and underdeveloped categories. Leonard Binder differentiated among three types: traditional, conventional, and rational systems. Edward Shils referred to political democracies, tutelary democracies, modernizing oligarchies, totalitarian oligarchies, and traditional oligarchies. Arend Lijphart compared majoritarian and consensus models of democracy.

These examples illustrate ways of organizing our thoughts about reality and facilitating the use of a variety of approaches rather than relying on a single method. There is no doubt that the idea of system has implanted itself firmly in social science theory, but it has not resolved the doubt and uncertainty that also pervades social science. The obsession of social scientists with theories of systems is largely attributable to the desire to be able to predict accurately and thereby change things for the better. Although social scientists may emulate classical Newtonian physics in the search for general laws that have universal application and attempt to transcend the logical positivism of Auguste Comte and others who applied science to the study of social life, it is clear that the origins of contemporary systems theories emanate from many different sciences, including the fields of biology, cybernetics, and operations research (see Figure 3.2).

FIGURE 3.2   Contemporary Theories of the System

Discipline	Proponent
Biology	Bertalanffy
Communications	Wiener
Anthropology	Malinowski
Economics	Leontief
Sociology	Parsons, Merton, Levy
Political Science	Easton
Psychology	Laszlo

In biology Ludwig von Bertalanffy was the major influence in combining scientific and philosophic views to formulate a conception of system called general systems theory. Bertalanffy and his colleagues founded the Society for General Systems Research and a journal, *Behavioral Science*, as well as a yearbook. Their basic conception differentiated physical science (which deals with closed systems isolated from their environment) from biology (which concerns itself with open systems of living organisms or cells). These writers sought to apply the conception of open system to society and to explain the nature of human history by seeking laws that apply to all systems, including those of the living organism or society. They aimed to integrate natural and social science and devise an exact theory of the nonphysical fields of science.

Cybernetics is the systematic study of communication and control in all kinds of organizations, and scientists have attempted to apply communications engineering to social phenomena. In *The Human Use of Human Beings* (1954) Norbert Wiener, for example, determined that the performance of machines may be corrected and guided by information in a sort of feedback process similar to the functioning of living individuals. He drew an analogy between the nervous system and the automatic machine, in that the performances of both are governed by means of communicating information. He argued that the network of communications extends everywhere, so that world society can integrate into an organic whole, and he felt that his concept of cybernetic control through feedback could be a model for legitimizing government operations. The political scientist Karl Deutsch played out this theme in his *The Nerves of Government* (1963).

Operations research was an outgrowth of attempts to apply a systems approach to the use of radar installations and the prediction of military outcomes during the Second World War. The statistical and quantitative techniques of wartime became useful later in industry, and eventually operations research was applied to the solutions of social problems, especially in education, urban areas, and health services. With the shift from military to civic applications, operations research eventually became known as systems analysis.

Systems theory in political science is indebted to these influences and to contributions from economics, sociology, and the other social sciences. History, too, has exerted some influence. Neoclassical economics has contributed to systems theory, especially in its search to find equilibrium in economic activities. Even today, however, much economic problem-solving is dominated by piecemeal and incrementalist schemes and techniques that determine linear cause-and-effect relationships and are restricted to mechanistic systems that do not account for the processes of change and lose touch with social reality. Efforts to transcend this limitation emerged with computer simulation and input-output analysis such as that developed by Wassily Leontief, who sought to analyze the relations among all segments of an economic system; his analysis was used in the former Soviet Union for planning at the national level. This analysis can be limited to short time periods and thus tends to be static.

Game theory and formal modeling also have been used in the generation of mathematical explanations of strategies, especially for marketing in business firms. Game theory and formal modeling have been widely used in political science analysis of electoral strategies and international confrontations. Both political scientists and economists apply game theory to the testing and implementation of rational choice theory and the construction of formal models designed to test hypothetical and real situations. Rational choice theory assumes that the structural constraints of society do not necessarily determine the actions of individuals and that individuals tend to choose actions that bring them the best results. The political scientist emphasizes bargaining with allies and opponents in a fashion modeled after the economist's attention to exchange, especially through competitive market systems.

In sociology, the idea of system evolved in the work of Talcott Parsons, whose action frame of reference derived from Max Weber and influenced macro theory. His conceptual scheme was set forth in *The Social System* (1951). His work influenced notable sociologists such as Robert Merton and Marion Levy.

Three major tendencies are discernible in the literature on systems theory. One trend, sometimes characterized as global or grand theory and ahistorical in its thrust, emanates from the physical sciences and culminates in the contributions of David Easton in political science. A second trend, known as structural-functionalism, is holistic but tends toward ahistorical and middle-range analysis, with roots strongly embedded in two academic traditions: the work of the anthropologists Bronislaw Malinowski and A. R. Radcliffe-Brown and of the political scientists Arthur Bentley and David Truman. Both traditions converge in the important writings of Gabriel Almond, who significantly influenced comparative political science. A third trend involves alternative understandings of systems theory, including understandings that reach toward global theory and historical and holistic synthesis, including Marxist formulations.

Systems Theory as Grand Theory

Systems theory in political science is commonly associated with David Easton and his search for a general systems theory of politics. Easton attempted to evolve a theory of systems, based on the work of the political scientist Charles Merriam and others. Merriam had written about "systematic politics," a notion similar to the sociologist Karl Mannheim's projection of a "systematic sociology." Merriam used a variety of disciplines, including biology, sociology, anthropology, economics, and philosophy, in his investigation of the action patterns of institutions. He described what he called the whole life process, in which he included government and politics and the evolutionary quality of political effort achieved through reason, reflection, and experiment.

Easton attempted to build an empirically oriented political theory through a series of writings. The first of these works, *The Political System* (1953), presented a case for a general theory of politics. The second work, *A Framework for Political Analysis* (1965), set forth the major concepts for the development of such a general theory. A final work, *The Analysis of Political Structure* (1990), extended his argument that structure must be taken into account in political analysis. A synthesis of his major ideas follows.

Easton's quest for theory involved the formulation of a general framework, a focus on the whole system rather than merely on its parts, an awareness of environmental influences on the system, and a recognition of the differences between political life in equilibrium and in disequilibrium. Political life is in disequilibrium, a status suggesting not only change or conflict but a countertendency to equilibrium that envisions a normal outcome of what might be. This outcome is contrasted with what actually transpires, and the differences can be explained. Scientific knowledge, Easton believed, is theoretical and based on facts, but facts alone do not explain events and must be ordered in some way. The study of political life involves the political system as a whole rather than solutions for particular problems. Theory must combine with reliable knowledge and empirical data: psychological data on personalities and motivations of individuals and situational data shaped by environmental influences.

Easton (1981) rejected the concept of state, referring to the confusion and variety of meanings, although later, in a reaffirmation of systems, he felt compelled to contend with the contribution of Nicos Poulantzas on the state. Likewise, he understood power as only one of many significant concepts useful in the study of political life. Power, however, related to the shaping and carrying out of authoritative politics in a society. Power rested on the ability to influence actions of others, and control of the way others make and carry out decisions determines policy. Easton referred to policy as "a web of decisions and actions that allocates values" (1953: 130). Thus the concepts of power, decisionmaking, authority, and policy shaped Easton's idea of political life as the authoritative allocation of values for a society.

These concepts are illustrated in his rudimentary diagram of the **political system**, reproduced in Figure 3.3, which incorporates attributes of the system such as units and boundaries, inputs and outputs, and feedback. The diagram suggests that the concept of systems permits a separation of political life from the rest of society, which Easton called the environment, demarcated by a boundary. Outputs (political actions or decisions) are shaped by inputs (demands and supports) fed into the political system. Outputs emanate in the form of decisions and policy actions, then are fed back into the environment by satisfying the demands of some members of the system. Easton referred to open and closed systems, with political life representing an open system, receptive to influences from its environment. Boundaries distinguish political systems from other systems (economic, social, and cultural) and delimit what is included or excluded in inquiry. He argued that political systems tend to persist in the face of frequent or constant crises.

Easton placed himself in the mainstream of general systems theory, which he adapted to political science. He thus joined the interdisciplinary tradition of seeking to understand the whole system and set forth a grand theory in the building of a paradigm in the sense used by Thomas Kuhn in *The Structure of Scientific Revolutions* (1970). Easton's work was influential in political science, although most students today overlook the fact that he awakened in political scientists the need to analyze complex interrelationships of political life. He shared the characteristics of many thinkers of the behavioral movement, including the rejection of traditional concepts such as state and power and the incorporation of concepts such as inputs, outputs, and feedback, along with emphasis on theory construction. Yet it is clear that he failed to construct a theory of politics relevant to empirical analysis. His excessive preoccupation with stability, maintenance, persistence, and equilibrium is similar to the outlook of biology, but the theory does not adequately deal with political change. Its abstractions may lead to misperceptions about real situations and people,

FIGURE 3.3   Easton's Diagram of a Political System

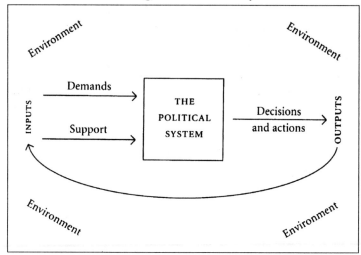

SOURCE: Reprinted from David Easton, *A Framework for Political Analysis* (1965: 112), by permission of the University of Chicago Press.

for example, the attention to the demands of interest groups on the government may obscure the more important demands of the government and ruling classes on people. His theory yielded some generalizations but few if any testable hypotheses. Furthermore, the ideological underpinnings of the framework were associated with his preoccupation with an intellectual crisis and the imminent waning of democratic liberalism. The desire to establish a true science of politics led Easton to relegate the discipline to the status of an applied science or reforming discipline.

This attempt at grand theory led Easton to empirically study the political socialization of children and to move his analysis from the grand scheme of things to a micro level in which individual attitudes could be identified and assessed. His insistence on systematic inquiry at this level coincided with the behavioral movement, which looked at individual attitudes, values, beliefs, and other qualities. He may have facilitated, or at least his efforts coincided with, the building of rational choice models and theories as alternatives to functionalist or structural-functional theory, examples being Anthony Downs's *An Economic Theory of Democracy* (1957), James Buchanan and Gordon Tullock's *The Calculus of Consent* (1962), and William Riker's *The Theory of Coalitions* (1962).

Rational choice theory is normative theory concerned with behavior and assumes that all individuals are rational in choices and action. Game theory may examine the logic of choices and their consequences within constraints set by the rules of the game. Difficulties with this approach appear when the behavior of an individual actor is projected to a society as a whole or when narrowly defined modes are used to predict and explain the behavior of real individuals in complex situations. Rational choice theorists have tried to overcome this limitation by emphasizing culture, history, and institutions, that is, the context in which choice occurs.

Systems Theory as Structural-Functionalism and Middle-Range Theory

Systems theorists like David Easton caught the attention of Gabriel Almond, who also influenced comparative politics during the 1950s and 1960s. Almond referred to systems as the interdependence of parts, inputs and outputs, boundary, and environment—all aspects of the Eastonian framework. For the concept of "political," Almond cited Easton's definition of "authoritative allocation of values" but emphasized Weber's idea of legitimacy. Almond fused these ideas with the terms structure and function, and he stuffed Easton's simplified black box with specific functional and structural categories by designating a variety of inputs and updating and modifying outputs in terms of a classical division of powers representative of the executive, legislative, and judicial branches of government. Almond also drew from the thought of Talcott Parsons, especially Parsons's macro theory of social systems and structural-functionalism. Like Parsons, Almond attempted to relate systems to culture. In modified form he also assimilated Parsonian aspects of functional prerequisites, structural differentiation, and specialization, and he was interested in the cultural secularization of developing systems.

Almond's conception of the political system was initially expressed through ideas drawn from Easton relating to totality, stability, and equilibrium. He focused on such concepts as roles (in his view the interacting units of a political system) and structures (representing the patterns of interaction). He introduced the concept of political culture (embedded in a particular pattern of orientations to political action). His system was elaborated through a set of structures and functions in a conscious effort to avoid the formalities of government institutions in areas where changes are widespread. In an anthology of essays coedited with James S. Coleman (1960), he revised basic concepts of comparative politics: the political system replaced the state and the legal and institutional apparatus employed by traditional political scientists; in addition, function substituted for power, role for office, and structure for institution. These concepts were incorporated in his thesis that all political systems (including advanced and backward nations) have universal characteristics: All political systems have political structures, the same functions are performed in all political systems, all political structures are multifunctional, and all political systems are mixed in the cultural sense. Almond modeled his system around a framework of inputs (interest articulation, interest aggregation, and political communication), outputs (rule making, rule application, and rule adjudication), and feedback. The inputs represented processes of participation, expression of political interests and demands for action, and the coalescing of those interests and demands as articulated by political parties and interest groups. The outputs effectively were government functions corresponding to the traditional use of three separate powers in government similar to the Western European and U.S. governments.

Almond conceived this approach as "middle-range" theory and emphasized "interdependence" within two macro structural-functional formulations. In part he drew this conception from his predecessors, the anthropologists Radcliffe-Brown and Malinowski and the sociologists Parsons and, especially, Parsons's followers Marion Levy and Robert Merton. Interdependence linked inputs and outputs, boundary, environment, and other concepts. He also was influenced by a form of micro structural-functionalism emanating from the traditions of pluralism and liberalism that sprang from *The Federalist* and incorporated in contemporary political science through the work of Arthur Bentley, David Truman, and Robert Dahl.

Almond's structural-functional formulation has been criticized as deterministic or ideological, conservative or restrictive, or simply false. The emphasis on the equilibrium of functional systems may lead to exaggeration of the cohesiveness of such systems, vague descriptions, lack of analysis, and confusion in analysis of ideal and observed situations. Preference for the status quo may result in ideological bias. A concern with consensus may obscure attention to change, and emphasis on tradition may equate Anglo-American democracy with the modern political system, against which all other political systems must be compared without recognition of variation and defects.

Alternative Systems Theory

Easton recognized the limitations of systems in equilibrium. Almond, in the image of Parsons, combined his formulation of systems with perspectives on action. These efforts, however, were not sufficient to counter criticisms of systems theory. The systems literature deals with general observations and makes scant reference to the real world. It has had, for example, no tangible impact on shaping U.S. politics.

A further problem was absorption of many social scientists, Almond in particular, in their ideal of an Anglo-American model of politics, thus limiting the possibility of alternative perspectives. Marx, for example, was also concerned with the idea of system, which he conceived as a political economy in which changes were the consequences of class conflict according to the material forces of production. Easton, in his early work, recognized the "scientific approach" of Marx, in particular his mastery of tools of inquiry and historical and dialectical materialism. He was aware of an emphasis on the laws and goals toward which society tended to evolve into **socialism** and eventually into **communism**. Moreover some of these ideas found a place in systems theory.

Evolutionary thinking, for example, was present in eighteenth-century thinkers such as Montesquieu, who in *The Spirit of Laws* (1748) discovered order in the histories of all nations, noted interconnected laws, and attributed change to material causes; and Condorcet, whose *Outline of the Intellectual Progress of Mankind* (1795) attempted to apply the uniform and natural laws of the universe to society and identified ten stages in the history of civilization. These early efforts set the basis for interpretations of evolutionism during the nineteenth century: Herbert Spencer in *The Man Versus the State* (1854) argued that the state should play a minimal role in society and that through evolution equilibrium would result in the perfect society; Auguste Comte in *Cours de philosophie positive* (1830–1842) advocated a science of society, based on a system of three stages of philosophical thought (theological, metaphysical, and positive) and stressed that progress is dependent on the consolidation of authoritarian order and emanates from stages of evolution; and Charles Darwin in *On the Origin of Species by Means of Natural Selection* (1859) offered a materialist explanation of the origin of the species and emphasized progress through struggle.

Darwinism and evolutionary ideas influenced Engels, who in *Dialectics of Nature* (1883) examined the achievements of the natural sciences during the nineteenth century. Engels criticized metaphysical and idealist conceptions in the natural sciences and drawing on Marx's use of Hegelian dialectics, offered a dialectical materialist explanation of natural science. Engels emphasized the general evolutionary connections in nature, interrelating all matter, organic and inorganic. He attacked the piecemeal arrangement of science proposed by Comte and others. He traced the patterns of changing science through historical periods. He argued that humans react to nature and change it, creating new conditions for themselves. Thus causality relates to the actions of the individual on nature rather than to a deterministic process based on laws in nature itself. Engels believed that nothing takes place in isolation and a holistic, not segmented, view of system is essential. Everything affects and is affected by every other thing. An individual makes the environment serve his or her purposes and can bring about devastating social consequences, leading to the division of the population into different classes and to antagonisms between ruling and oppressed classes.

Contemporary theorists qualify their evolutionary approach. In *The Rise of Anthropological Theory: A History of Theories of Culture* (1968), Marvin Harris admonished us to beware of the myth of unilinear evolutionism that runs through most classical evolutionary theory. He argued that society and culture may skip steps in a sequence or evolve divergently—that is, evolutionary theory need not incorporate deterministic notions about progress and perfectibility, which are often imbued in the traditional literature with racist connotations. Harris believed that Marx and Engels depended on a functional model of sociocultural life. Marxist functionalism not only denies the maintenance of a sociocultural system but accommodates dysfunctional ingredients, so that conflict and change are assimilated in a model that is evolutionary, not dialectical.

Whereas Harris criticized the dialectics of Marx and Engels as "vague" and "romanticized," the sociologist Al Szymanski (1972) combined functionalism and dialectics. He attacked the inherently conservative nature of the prevailing functional theory, for example, in the thought of the renowned anthropologist, Bronislaw Malinowski, who saw society as responding to basic biological needs and avoided the study of class societies in which needs other than biological needs develop and must be preserved. In contrast, Marx grounded his functionalism on an explanation of the contributions major institutions make to capitalism, and he envisaged profit maximization as facilitated by the state as the managing force of the bourgeoisie. Thus functionalism can be effectively employed in analysis when interpreted dialectically. Marx employed functionalism as an essential part of his methodology in an effort to advance social science. Unlike most conventional functionalists, Marx was able to understand the contradictory nature of society.

Drawing on Marx and Engels, Szymanski related dialectics to functionalism. Dialectics, he believed, is a method for understanding the physical and social world. It involves a moving back and forth between abstractness and concreteness, between theory and reality. He referred to three principles of dialectical functionalism: First, things tend to interrelate with one another, to form systems, and they must be understood as parts of a greater whole. Second, although things are interdependent, they also have internal contradictions. Third, things tend to change as a consequence of contradictions in the system, and change is the essential aspect of dialectical functionalism. For example, in maximizing profits through monopoly capital, the capitalist system tends to undermine its early practice of free competition.

In an attempt to relate these radical conceptions to mainstream conceptions of system, Sanford (1971) offered a progressive revision of the structural-functionalism of Almond and G. Bingham Powell (1966), imbuing it with "a radical and existential ideological bias" (1971: 27). Retaining Almond and Powell's categories, Sanford attempted to transcend the limitations of liberal pluralism by drawing on the "systematic" discussions of the Russian Marxist Nikolay Bukharin and the writings of the U.S. Marxists Paul Baran and Paul Sweezy. Sanford showed that the state and its ruling classes would break through groups and organizations, isolate individuals, and undermine the autonomy of the subsystem. His approach revealed cleavages, tensions, and conflicts that allow for differentiation of social classes and domination of some classes over the masses of people and the competing groups and interests emphasized in the literature on pluralism.

In yet another effort to combine classical Marxism with new perspectives of social science, Pablo González Casanova tried to understand system as a whole and its holistic perspective as historical in orientation. He believed that even a discredited structural-functionalism might be incorporated in a theory based on dialectics: "History as struggle emphasizes human political categories with dialectical relations, with reciprocal actions, which are not simple relations of cause and effect, since in the midst of historical regularities a series of novelties or surprises are generated both in the structure and sequence of historical development" (1973: 234).

Systems theory was used in the former Soviet Union and in Eastern Europe. During the 1960s it was popular in the former German Democratic Republic. Its major proponent, Georg Klaus, showed how technological concepts of the West could be easily assimilated into Marxism-Leninism, in particular functionalism and cybernetic systems theory. He envisaged a cybernetics theory of dynamic and self-regulating systems characterized by connections with the environment, a conception formulated in terms of the biological organism and assuming maintenance, stability, and control. Klaus considered information to be the link between cybernetics and dialectical materialism and information to be tied to organization. Cybernetics systems theory thus precisely defines categories of historical and dialectical materialism, rationalizes automation, assists economic planning and increases labor productivity, and facilitates autonomous control in organizations. Klaus also established connections between cybernetics and dialectical logic. The terminology of Western systems theory (function and structure, inputs and outputs, and feedback) was employed in the East German formulation. The feedback system of a socialist society would ultimately replace the control of society by the state. Mass participation and consciousness would replace the central regulating institutions of a socialist society. In the end it was not clear whether this experimental application of systems theory in a socialist country served to mystify, challenge, or defend the interests of the German technocratic bureaucracy.

This review of systems theory suggests possibilities and limitations. Mainstream theories suffer from generalization, vagueness, and lack of relevance to everyday societal problems. Critics of systems theory suggest that inquiry fails to take into account the human condition. The use of systems theory in the search for science may be distorted by the implications of biological determinism in analogies drawn between animal and human behaviors. A further complaint is the failure of many systems advocates to conceive system in international terms, an especially important relationship in light of the ever dominant and challenging international capitalist order. Long ago Marx and Lenin and their followers perceived the necessity of this focus, and some contemporary thinkers have also conceptualized system in an international context. Two examples reflect the effort to resolve the problem of tying system to the international order. Immanuel Wallerstein (1974) examined capitalist agriculture and the origins and evolution of the European world economy since the sixteenth century. He abandoned the tendency, prevalent in social science today, to focus on the sovereign state or the national society, favoring instead a **world systems theory**. Like Wallerstein, Samir Amin (1974) combined all the social sciences in a historical and holistic perspective, using an explicit Marxist framework and building a radical paradigm of understanding. Writing in the midst of the Cold War, he set forth the thesis that the world was not divided into two markets, one capitalist and the other socialist, but that only one, the capitalist world market, was prevalent. This theory of accumulation on a world scale was based on a theory of capitalist formations between the center and periphery of a world system.

STATE THEORIES

Historically the study of politics has incorporated an understanding of the **state**, and since its inception in the nineteenth century, political science has prominently focused on the concept. Its evolution can be traced through four phases. The early influences in American political science date to the late-nineteenth-century work of German political scientists and Theodore Woolsey, who became a major American theorist of the state. During the late 1950s Gabriel Almond and other important comparativists replaced the concept state with **political system,** arguing that the state was imbued with so many meanings it could not be used effectively in current comparative investigation. Then during the late 1960s and the 1970s alternative theories of the state, based on a Marxist conception, caught the attention of political science. Finally, mainstream political sci-

FIGURE 3.4   Contemporary Theories of the State

Mainstream	Alternative
Pluralist Capitalist	Pluralist Socialist
Institutionist	Instrumentalist
Corporatist	Structuralist
Bureaucratic Authoritarian	Feminist

ence came full circle with a recognition of the need to return to the state during the early 1980s. The drive to "bring the state back in" reversed the trend initiated twenty-five years earlier.

The discussion to this point hints at the many theories of state that permeate the literature (see Figure 3.4). Most of these theories draw from the experience of advanced capitalist countries, and space does not permit us to delve into particular situations, especially the collapse of states in weak countries, such as Angola, Sierra Leone, and Somalia in Africa or the breakup of Yugoslavia and Czechoslovakia around historical ethnic and cultural preferences. Nor do I examine the policies of neoliberalism in both strong and weak countries in which regimes have sought to dismantle or trim the state or privatize public activities. It is clear, though, that the state continues to exercise a major role everywhere, regardless of the debates around state weakness or prospects for state autonomy and the preoccupation with the market, decentralization, subnational and communal movements, and the appearance of nongovernmental organizations and social movements. The following discussion provides a sketch of contemporary theories of the state; I encourage readers to delve into them further through the detailed syntheses available in Jessop (1982, 1990), Carnoy (1984), and Chilcote (forthcoming).

Mainstream Theories of the State

Pluralist Capitalist Perspective   The demands and interests of competing groups and individuals filter through a political marketplace. According to the liberal tradition of U.S. social science, the competition is pluralist, the marketplace capitalist. Two views prevail. On the one hand, neutral state agencies mediate conflict that emanates from party and group competition; on the other, agencies of the state function as the bases of political power, and competition among the agencies for funding determines their relationship to parties and interest groups. The former position approximates the notion that the state should not be necessarily seen as a coherent entity separate from society, nor should the complexity of the state lead to rejection of the concept altogether, even if the prevailing understanding today is that the character of modern society is represented by a distinction between state and society: "The state should be addressed as an effect of detailed processes of spatial organization, temporal arrangement, functional specification and supervision and surveillance, which create the appearance of a world fundamentally divided into state and society" (Mitchell, 1991: 95).

The latter position can be illustrated by a framework for analyzing a multidimensional society. Michael Mann (1986), for example, dispensed with orthodox ways of looking at society, such as systems theory, structuralism, structural-functionalism, and so on. He focused on four overlapping and intersecting power networks (ideological, economic, military, and political) and applied a Weberian methodology of ideal types to an analysis of the development of Europe into the eighteenth century. This approach thus builds pluralistically around various power networks while skirting systems theory and most of the statist currents in mainstream and alternative thinking.

Institutional Perspective   The institutional perspective is prevalent in the mainstream acceptance of the state and state theory as central to the study of comparative politics. Stephen Krasner (1988) used an institutional approach to understand the sovereign state, asserting that the "range of options available to policy makers at any given point in time is a function of institutional capabilities that were put in place at some earlier period" (67). Thus the sovereign state has come to be the form of political organization acceptable to the modern world, a position he defended against utilitarian or functional approaches that see outcomes as the consequence of individual choice. James Rosenau (1988) supported the trend to reinstate the concept of state, because of the "diminished effectiveness of whole systems" and "a deep disillusion with systems analysis," and he asserted that "the state is deeply embedded in our terminology and is unlikely to yield to efforts to replace it" (22).

Corporatist Perspective   The idea of **corporatism** emerged conspicuously in the fascist regimes of Europe: in Germany, Italy, Portugal, and Spain, in particular, where the state was conceptualized on a horizontal level, mediating between labor and capital to mitigate conflicts and disruptions. Political scientists like Philippe Schmitter turned to Portugal in search of a model that would serve comparative analysis. Schmitter modified the traditional understanding of corporatism and associated the amorphous complex of agencies representing the state and civil society in the corporatist system as somewhat analogous to the interest group activity conspicuous in less authoritarian societies in North America and Western Europe. In research on Brazil, he demonstrated how interest groups function under an authoritarian regime. Thus, in his view, the authoritarian corporate state tolerates a degree of pluralism similar to the experience of democratic societies. Planning at the national level usually involves corporatist compromises between labor and capital worked out through the intervention of the state. This perspective represented a shift from a traditional to a "societal" or "liberal" understanding of corporatism.

Schmitter eventually came to the view that contemporary conditions have so changed that national negotiations are of decreasing importance; this is due to policies aimed at improving productivity and international competitiveness and to the shift of interest conflicts from class-based cleavages to social movements based on issues of gender, environment, consumer protection, and so on. He also noted the displacement of workers from traditional industry to services and public employment as a result of international competition. Ultimately he recognized that corporatism may soon be dead: "I have become less and less concerned that corporatism . . . will survive, much less be as much an imperative for the future of capitalism" (1989: 72).

Bureaucratic Authoritarian Perspective **Bureaucratic authoritarianism** originated in Guillermo O'Donnell's (1988) study of Argentina during the military intervention but was relevant to authoritarian situations elsewhere in Latin America. This work influenced further study of state structure and intervention in nondemocratic settings, in particular of the expanding role of the state in the process of capital accumulation in Latin America. Under bureaucratic authoritarianism, state intervention becomes decisive under authoritarian conditions and serves as an impulse to the developmental process, especially with the exhaustion of the import substitution model of industrialization in which state and national capital are unable to work in isolation from international capital.

In a comprehensive review of the literature on these theories, William Canak (1984) showed that the peripheral state has become irrelevant because the increasing internationalization of production undermines industrial structures in every nation, whether it is in the core of advanced nations or in the periphery of underdeveloped nations. Furthermore, as the size of state expenditures and the extent of state intervention increase similarly in both core and peripheral nations, and international capital becomes decisive on a global and national level, the legitimization of the state increasingly becomes questionable. In a seminal work on these developments, *Dependency and Development* (1979), Fernando Henrique Cardoso and Enzo Faletto showed that in Latin America nations dependent on the advanced capitalist nations were not necessarily incapable of achieving capitalist development. Once national and state capital combine with international capital, capitalist development is possible even under conditions of dependency. Cardoso observed this possibility under the military dictatorship in Brazil during the 1970s, but with his election as president of Brazil in 1994, due largely to a coalition with neoliberal forces, he was able to more aggressively implement policies that opened up his country to massive foreign investment, privatization of state enterprise, and a streamlining of state agencies and services. Although many observers noted these actions as a shift from a progressive theory of **associated dependent capitalist development** to neoliberal practices, the need to reform the state was seen quite differently by the political economist who was one of Cardoso's ministers, Luiz Carlos Bresser Pereira. Pereira argued that the "crisis of the state" was a product of the excessive and distorted pattern of state growth during a cyclical period of expansion. The implementation of reforms and privatization would not lead, he argued, to a minimal state as envisaged by neoliberals but, on the contrary, to a reorganized state ready to intervene and grow with new vigor: Reforms must "recognize that the objective should be to restructure the state in order to strengthen it, not to make it weaker" (1993: 1350).

Alternative Theories of the State

Most of the new thinking expands on the conceptions of Marx but also draws on the thought of Hegel, Engels, and Lenin. Marx evolved his initial notions through a detailed assessment of Hegel. In his *Critique of Hegel's Doctrine of the State* (1843/1975b) Marx agreed with Hegel that a fundamental contradiction existed between the state and the civil society of citizens. Marx, however, separated forms of the state from an ideal or abstract conception and rooted them in "the material conditions of life." Marx noted that in ancient Greece the state and community were combined in a polis and there was sense of unity between the people and the state and between private and public interests. In medieval times there was also less separation than later occurred between the state and civil society "because civil society was political society; because the organic principle of civil society was the principle of the State" (1843/1975b: 137). Under capitalism the state separates from civil society, and there is an estrangement between public and private life; additionally, there is an estrangement of individuals from each other as the civil society fragments into private interests competing against each other. Under such conditions the state legitimizes the right of individuals to pursue particular interests through the possession of private property. Private property promotes inequality, enhances disunity among people, and undermines the equality and general intent of the community at large. Private property dominates contemporary society.

In *Origins of the Family, Private Property, and the State* (1884), Engels traced this relationship between the state and civil society as capitalism evolved through the centuries. At a certain stage of development, he believed, contradictions appear in the form of classes of conflicting economic interests. Mitigating these contradictions and moderating the conflict is the state: "a power, apparently standing above society . . . arising out of society, but placing itself over it, and increasingly alienating itself from it" (Engels, 1884/n.d: 140).

In *The German Ideology* (1845–1846), Marx and Engels focused on the impact of coercion in the process of production and in economic relations. They noted that once coercion shifts from the economic base of society, it tends to concentrate in the state or the political superstructure: "The social organization, evolving directly out of production and commerce . . . in all ages forms the basis of the state and the rest of the ideological superstructure" (quoted in Draper, 1977: 252).

What then distinguishes the state in modern history from tribal communities? In *Manifesto of the Communist Party* (1848/1958), Marx and Engels referred to the "executive" of the state as a committee for managing the affairs of the bourgeoisie; as such the state serves the economically dominant class. The modern state is distinguishable through a number of functions: It holds power over a territory rather than a kinship group, it wields power through institutions or instruments of coercion that separate it from collective society, it imposes taxes on the citizens to ensure its financial basis, and it wields power through a bureaucracy that stands apart from and above the society as a whole.

A dominant or ruling class may not necessarily be monolithic, as sometimes believed, especially in a competitive capitalist society in which conflicting and antagonistic individual and group interests may exist. Although the state may ensure the domination of the ruling class over all society, it also acts in the interest of the ruling class, whereas the other interests of society are subordinated to the interests of the ruling class. The state also may mediate the differences and conflicts that are found within the dominant or ruling class.

Building on a theory of the state elaborated by Marx and Engels, Lenin in *State and Revolution* (1932) emphasized the oppression of one class by another: "The state is the product and the manifestation of the *irreconcilability* of class antagonisms. The state arises when, where, and to the extent that the class antagonisms *cannot* be objectively reconciled. And, conversely, the existence of the state proves that the class antagonisms *are* irreconcilable" (8). Lenin also insisted that state power must be destroyed through revolution and that compromise and reformist solutions will not resolve class antagonisms:

> If the state is the product of the irreconcilable character of class antagonisms, if it is a force standing above society and increasingly separating itself from it, then it is clear that the liberation of the oppressed class is impossible not only without violent revolution, but also without the destruction of the apparatus of state power, which was created by the ruling class and in which this "separation" is embodied (1932: 9–10).

How to solve this dilemma? Lenin believed that under the capitalist state the standing army and police were the active instruments of power rather than armed power organized by the people. Struggle against the state and its instruments of power must therefore be carried on by the people in the form of the proletariat. As the development of production evolves to a high stage, classes will not be necessary, and the proletariat will be able to seize power and transform the means of production from private to state property. Bourgeois democracy will become proletarian democracy, the majority will suppress the oppressive minority, and the functions of the state will devolve on the people until there is no need for such power and the state disappears altogether.

Lenin outlined these ideas as evolving through several stages in the developmental process: first, a bourgeois society with capitalism at the base; second, the early transition away from capitalism under the revolutionary dominance of the proletariat; third, the emergence of socialism, an early form of communism, in which the means of production no longer are the private property of individuals but belong to the whole society, even if the inequalities of capitalist society are not altogether eliminated; and fourth, "full" communism in which bourgeois inequalities are eliminated, the state has been replaced by the rule of all society, and people work voluntarily according to their abilities and are recipients according to their needs.

An alternative theory of the capitalist state suggested the possibility of various means of democratically gaining control over the state. Whereas Lenin saw hegemony as a strategy for revolution in which the working class and its representatives win the support of the majority, Antonio Gramsci, an Italian Marxist and contemporary of Lenin, extended the concept to the capitalist class and its possibilities for gaining state power. He believed hegemony could be achieved through alliances between classes and other social forces rather than through revolutionary force.

This brief overview of concepts and theories of the state leads us to four alternative perspectives: pluralist socialist, instrumentalist, structuralist, and feminist.

Pluralist Socialist Perspective Openings to representative and formal democracy in countries long dominated by authoritarian rule, either in fascist capitalist or existing state socialist regimes, frequently were accompanied by the view that pluralism could be compatible with a socialism in which the state filters the demands and interests of competing individuals, groups, and classes. For example, a "socialist pluralism" was the central concern of many leftist Portuguese intellectuals after the fall of the fascist dictatorship in April 1974.

A pluralist socialist perspective has not been elaborated in any definitive theoretical form, but important elements of a theory are available that help toward an understanding. The first is a "critical" exposure of the mystification of the state and emphasis on ideology and false consciousness as a means of liberating individuals and groups from the oppression of capitalism. This emphasis on the human condition dates to the early writings of Marx and his criticism of Hegel's conception of the state as being above particular interests and classes and acting as a mediator ensuring orderly competition among individuals and groups while preserving the collective interests of society within the state itself. Marx saw the state as a political expression of class structure embedded in production. The Hegelian-Marxian view was adopted by Herbert Marcuse and others representative of the Frankfurt school.

During and since the 1960s economists and political scientists delved into the conflict between the state and social classes. Conflict implies struggle among classes, class fractions, and groups. The German political scientist Claus Offe, for example, emphasized the class character, structure, ideology, process, and repression of the state and its mechanisms. The North American economist James O'Connor (1973) looked at crises of corporate profitability and state bankruptcy as a means of understanding the relationship of class struggle to the contradictions in the accumulation process.

Instrumentalist Perspective Marx and Engels alluded to the executive of the state as a committee representative of the interests of the ruling classes. Lenin referred to the standing army and police as instruments of state power. In *The Theory of Capitalist Development* (1942), Paul Sweezy characterized the state as an instrument in the hands of the ruling classes. Such views are tied to the idea that the state is the "instrument" of the ruling or dominant class. The instrumentalist perspective thus focuses on the class that rules and on the ties and mechanisms such as the state police that link the state instrumentally to the ruling class. Critics of **instrumentalism** charge that not only is pluralism evident in most societies and the state often relatively autonomous, but we need to focus on institutions and social and political groupings rather than classes as defined by their relationship to production.

Structuralist Perspective   The structuralist thesis assumes that the functions of the state are determined by the structures of society rather than through the activity of those who occupy positions of power in the state. Structuralists examine the constraints and contradictions of capitalism within the structure in which the state is embedded. Structure, rather than struggle by individuals and classes, is of principal concern.

During the 1960s and 1970s the French philosopher Louis Althusser provided a foundation for **structuralism** in an essay on the ideological state apparatuses (1971). Elaborating on the political side of this structuralism, Nicos Poulantzas (1973, 1978) argued that the bourgeoisie is unable as a class to dominate the state; rather, the state itself organizes and unifies the interest of this class. His position countered instrumentalism and led to a debate with Ralph Miliband, whose *The State in Capitalist Society* (1969) reflected an instrumentalist approach. A principal criticism of structuralism is that it cannot explain class action that arises from class consciousness.

Feminist Perspective   **Feminism** allows for a look at gender relations as an aspect of a power relationship and challenges traditional ways of studying the political by focusing on patriarchy and the domination of women by men. Gender has much to do with male dominance and machismo, and historians have begun to use it to analyze how powerful men have imagined masculinity in their political roles. For example, the image of President John F. Kennedy was associated with such qualities as courage, toughness, and youth. His perception of masculinity may have been essential to his individual worldview and conception of power. Male perceptions of masculinity and power may account for the predominant role and privileges most men hold over women in society.

Feminism implies ideological struggle against the degradation of women and against male dominance. Within the movement, four principal perspectives appeared (Giele, 1988): liberal feminist theory with an emphasis on equality, individual rights, justice, and freedom; Marxist feminist theory with attention to the exploitation and oppression of women; radical feminist theory with a focus on the differences between the sexes as the principal cause of women's oppression; and socialist feminist theory, which advocates the restructuring of reproductive relations by socializing such private family activities as housework and child care.

The terms gender and sex may be used interchangeably in the literature, but different meanings are apparent in relating women's liberation to class, race, and ethnicity. Gender often is conceived within institutional life, such as gender in the workplace or in the household or in the bureaucratic apparatuses of the state.

Parallel with the familiar neglect of feminism is the fact that feminists have not elaborated a theory of the state but have instead focused on theories of gender. Feminists tend to favor a participatory style of politics and thus do not focus on the impersonal and bureaucratic nature of the modern state, nor do they delve into how through the state and its apparatus men sustain male power in both the public and private sectors. Criticizing traditional feminist approaches and Marxist theory, Catharine MacKinnon, in *Toward a Feminist Theory of the State* (1989), contended that there is no feminist theory of the state. She exposed the conjunction of feminism and Marxism as a method in a search for an understanding of the state. She emphasized the differences between the two, noting that Marxists criticize feminism as bourgeois in theory and practice and as serving the dominant class and that feminists view Marxism as male-dominated theory. Whereas the Marxist method is dialectical materialism, the feminist method is consciousness raising. In MacKinnon's view, feminism becomes Marxism's ultimate critique as Marxism serves to criticize classical political economy.

*   *   *

This discussion has revealed an important paradox. Marx and Engels distinguished between state and society in order to clarify the interrelationship of political and economic life. They envisaged the possibility of a stateless society in modern times, a notion deemed unattainable by most students of politics. Consequently many contemporary political scientists have downgraded the concept of state and replaced it with system. Although this practice may obscure the conditions of enforcement and constraint that society holds over individuals in the capitalist world today, we need not be deluded by such distractions. One of the proponents of the systems approach, David Easton, reminded us of the origins of his political science and acknowledged its debt to Marx by showing that the distinction Marx drew between state and society allowed political science to emerge as a discipline separate from the other social sciences.

During the 1980s, both mainstream and alternative approaches brought state theory to center stage, whereas systems theory dwindled in its perceived importance in comparative politics and political economy. A comparative assessment appears in Figure 3.5, with attention to the strengths and weaknesses of systems and state theories.

Systems theory has been employed for classification of national political systems and country analysis, which is helpful in historical comparisons and overview, and it has been applied at both macro and micro levels, allowing for holistic interpretation as well as attention to individual

FIGURE 3.5   Comparisons of System and State Theories

System Theory	*State Theory*
Advantages	
Classification facilitated	Focus on essence of politics
Macro and micro theory possible	Attention to state within political economy
Equilibrium framework	Theory and institutions combined
Consensus and stability facilitate analysis	Economic basis in evaluation of state
Disadvantages	
Fails to deal with human condition	Definitional impreciseness
Theory not operational	Multitude of conceptions
Equilibrium obscures change	Stateless society unrealistic
Deterministic, ideological	Emphasis on policy implementation

preferences. Although both macro and micro theories appear in the literature, they tend not to be operational in real situations and case examples. In short, they are abstractions, often deterministic, ideological, and conservative. Systems theory emphasizes equilibrium, which facilitates investigation of diverse phenomena and allows the observer to maintain controls over political complexities; this tends to exaggerate the coherence and cohesiveness of a system and to obscure attention to structural changes, revolutionary developments, and violence. Systems theory may ignore the human condition and the activities and preferences of people in shaping political outcomes.

State theory, in contrast, focuses on the state and its agencies and apparatuses, the essence of contemporary politics, particularly in advanced capitalist countries. It allows for attention to the political dimension of political economic study, and it combines theory with institutional analysis. It also incorporates the economic foundations of society as essential in the evaluation of society. Mainstream approaches, however, usually stress institutional development, ignoring class and other forces that may promote conflict and change. Historically, diverse conceptions of the state have appeared in the literature, suggesting that a multitude of approaches may obscure focus on the state. Prospects for a stateless society are unrealistic in light of the importance of the state in modern capitalist and existing socialist societies.

The confusion over various approaches to state and systems impact on the present generation of political scientists, who wrestle with the question of what is political and what is political science. Marx and Engels answered with a definition of politics in terms of the power of the state, the superstructure that represents a bourgeois society and reflects the economic needs of the class controlling production. Marx and Engels linked the state to the class structure of society. Although some political sociologists and other social scientists have used this conception in their work, most tend to steer clear of Marxism, preferring instead to distinguish politics from economics and to avoid questions of power and coercion, class and class struggle.

4

THE SOCIAL DIMENSION

CLASS AND GROUP

Social class is a rather common term in sociology but is less used in other disciplines, especially mainstream economics and political science. In a North American setting **class** usually implies the stratification of society into upper, middle, and lower classes, usually distinguishable by such variables as income, education, and status. The concept of class has not been emphasized in theories emanating from the main traditions of political science, whether formal-legal, institutional, behavioral, or rational choice, especially when these have involved study of the United States and Western Europe. Class theory has been elaborated and employed in progressive circles in political science and economics, and it is now rather commonplace in the overlapping disciplines of political anthropology, political economy, and political sociology. In international circles class frequently is incorporated in political analysis, especially in comparative politics, and in economic analysis, in the fields of comparative and international political economy, development, and labor studies. Of course, class has been a central concept in the political science and official Marxism of socialist states (until 1989 in the Soviet Union and Eastern Europe, and still in the late 1990s in China, Cuba, North Korea, and Vietnam). Historically class was worked into the theoretical discourse of social democrats, democratic socialists, and communists everywhere, and class has been significant in analyzing the major revolutionary experiences of the Third World since the Second World War (in Angola, Cuba, Mozambique, Nicaragua, and many other countries).

In large measure, these developments can be explained by the influence of liberal capitalism, which has been pervasive in the advanced industrial societies, accompanied by theoretical constructions that tend to neglect class as an important aspect of socioeconomic and political change. In contrast, studies in and of less advanced societies often concern the state and its apparatuses. This leads directly to the issues posed by class, class analysis, and class struggle. Thus this conceptual history recognizes the origins and evolution of class in political science. How theorists and practitioners use class in their interactions with society also helps in understanding various interpretations and meanings in the discourse and practices of the political community.

In a general sense, class is often thought of as a grouping. This is so even in the orthodox Marxist literature and sometimes in stratification theory. **Group** is the term most commonly employed in mainstream political science, often in a manner that obscures attention to social classes and their economic interests. The mainstream draws on the thought of James Madison, who envisioned competing interests in the struggle for power, and Arthur Bentley and David Truman, who wrote about group and interest theory. They believed that references to individuals must account for group relationships, shared attitudes, and interests.

For more than a generation, Truman's *The Governmental Process* (1951) was a standard text in this area. Acknowledging his debt to Madison, Robert Dahl in *Who Governs?* (1961) used group and interest group theory as a foundation for his ideas on pluralism. In *Pluralist Democracy in the United States* (1967), Dahl described a political order with a wide dispersion of power and authority among government officials, private individuals, and groups. Power, he believed, was segmented, not organized in a clear hierarchical pattern. Peaceful management of conflict, consensus, and participation flowed from this order. Most of the attention in the literature on pluralism focused on the United States, where a wide diversity of equally powerful groups was assumed to exist. But in replicating Dahl's study of New Haven, William Domhoff (1978b) showed how a differing methodology and questions could produce different findings about power. Other critics have noted that even in a group-oriented society like the United States only half of the people belong to voluntary associations, and such associations are only peripherally involved in politics. Pluralists also assumed that state policies reflect accurately the demands of diverse interest groups, yet critics have commented that only certain policies can be implemented under capitalism and class society. For example, policies to reduce inflation or unemployment might be acceptable, but other policies might be perceived as socially and economically disruptive and therefore unacceptable.

The present chapter explores these theoretical differences between class and group in an effort to show their strengths and weaknesses. It begins with the theoretical underpinnings in the thought of Marx and Weber and their early contributions to class and group theory. It also identifies major currents and issues in group and class theory.

THEORETICAL FOUNDATIONS

Comparative inquiry may transcend the inclination to favor group over class analysis. This section offers a general historical overview of the concept class and concentrates, first, on the origins and influences of class theory since the nineteenth century; and second, on a variety of approaches that have prevailed throughout the twentieth century. I show that even during particular periods of interest in class (for example, the intense activity around socialism in the 1930s and the emergence of the New Left in the 1960s) the discourse on class has tended to be overlooked or misappropriated by mainstream political science. Nevertheless, class continues to be incorporated in influential alternative thinking.

By grasping how Marx viewed the nature of class, we can better understand how the concept class has been appropriated and misappropriated in political science. In the brief last chapter of the third volume of *Capital*, Marx referred to the three big classes of landowners, industrial capitalists, and workers. He analyzed the struggles between these classes but also acknowledged the existence of other lesser classes composed of bureaucrats and professionals, the petty bourgeoisie, the peasantry, and so on. The advance of capitalism would be accompanied by the struggle of a bourgeoisie of modern capitalists and owners of the means of production with modern wage workers who sell their labor in order to live.

The relevance of Marx's attention to class can be seen through an examination of the use of the term in two principal writings. *Manifesto of the Communist Party* (Marx and Engels, 1848) presents a structural class theory of testable propositions and predictions, whereas *The Eighteenth Brumaire of Louis Bonaparte* (Marx, 1852) offers a historically oriented interpretative scheme relevant to changing political events. In the *Manifesto*, Marx and Engels may have focused on a simplistic model of two classes so as to demonstrate how modern capitalism would evolve, and they appear to have assumed that intermediate classes would gradually meld with the proletariat. In his own historical writing on mid-nineteenth-century France, however, Marx developed a multiclass approach that reflected a complex understanding of class analysis, one that identified the importance of other classes alongside the bourgeoisie and proletariat. Furthermore, he envisaged the state as attaining autonomy and dominance over civil society at a time when bourgeois power was undermined by working-class insurgency and the strength of the proletariat was weakened by bourgeois repression. A schematic comparison of the two approaches might take the form shown in Figure 4.1.

FIGURE 4.1   Two Theories of Class

Structural Theory of Class	*Historical Theory of Class*
Abstract	Concrete
Two-class model	Multiclass model
Class polarization and struggle	Class alliances and fractions
State as instrument of ruling class	State as autonomous
Outcome of proletarian revolution	Unpredictable outcome and classless society

Adapted from So and Suwarsono (1990: 52).

Although it is important to appreciate the richness of Marx's approach to class in order to make sense of class analysis, Marx was not the only theorist who shaped the discourse of class. An understanding of the historical usage of class in social science necessitates also looking at Max Weber. More than other thinkers, these two have influenced class analysis in the social sciences, and the divergence in their understandings of class has divided intellectuals both theoretically and methodologically.

Weber's attention to class is found mainly in his *Wirtschaft und Gesellschaft* (partially published in English as *The Theory of Social and Economic Organization*, 1947), in which he argued that economic interests in the market led to the creation of classes. He identified four essential social classes: the working class, the petty bourgeoisie, the propertyless intelligentsia and bureaucratic specialists, and the educated privileged classes that control property. He also conceived of **status groups** within these classes, stratified and hierarchically ranked according to the demands of the market and reflecting a diversity of interests and preferences. As markets change, status groups are rearranged within a class so that a lower status group might be elevated to a higher level and others might drop in ranking. Status groups and the individuals within them are mobile and in flux; individual talent and initiative may bring about change in individual and group positions in society (Weber, 1958: especially 181–187).

For Weber the concept of class does not have to be tied to the concept of mode of production; instead categories of stratification are linked to market societies. Furthermore, the Weberian conception of class is not based on polarized antagonistic relations. Finally, it does not deal with problems of material interests, experiences, and possibilities for collective actions. Thus Weberians face less constraint in applying occupational categories to their analysis than do Marxists.

Weber's attention to class recognizes broad categories of class, yet implies attention to individuals and groups, competition through mechanisms of the market, and the possibility of autonomy in a complex society. Marx's emphasis on class usually is understood in a structural context, especially in his later and mature work, but he too was sensitive to individuals and especially to the human condition. In the *Economic and Philosophical Manuscripts* (1844), he developed an analysis of the alienation of labor and showed that under capitalism the worker cannot be satisfied in production for someone else. Marx desired to expose the **false consciousness** that accompanies the capitalist era and reflects the nature of the state that the bourgeoisie adopts for the protection of its property and interests. This concern with consciousness and alienation is also found in the seminal work of György Lukács in *History and Class Consciousness* (1923) and in the writings of the Frankfurt school, including Erich Fromm, Herbert Marcuse, and Jürgen Habermas.

Historically classes have evolved through transformations in society. A bourgeoisie arose from the merchant class in European towns established during the feudal Middle Ages. Then manufacturing replaced production in closed guilds, and a manufacturing class supplanted the guild masters. Modern industry soon took the place of this early manufacturing, along with the invention of machinery, the expansion of markets, and the rise of a new bourgeoisie. Accompanying this process, serfs and peasants evolved eventually into rural and urban wage labor.

This sketch of history, however, deserves elaboration, for society is more complex, as evident in Figure 4.2, than the often-portrayed dichotomy of dominant bourgeoisie and subservient proletariat; this complexity is emphasized in the *Manifesto* and in the diverse categories, including the three great classes of landlords, industrial capitalists, and workers, set forth at the end of *Capital*. In the *Eighteenth Brumaire* Marx analyzed French politics of the middle nineteenth century in terms of a multitude of classes, including an aristocracy of monarchy and high finance, large industrialists, merchants, middle class, petty bourgeoisie, proletariat, and lumpen proletariat.

Even though he distinguished among four classes (property class, bureaucrats and intellectuals, petty bourgeoisie, and working class), Weber emphasized status groups that allowed mobility between classes. This led mainstream social science to stratify society into upper, middle, and lower classes. This stratification usually involves describing each class type by income, occupation, and education and may result in analyses in which class conflict is overlooked or believed to be insignificant so that the concept class eventually may become blurred.

The discussion thus far has revealed a larger number of class categories: bourgeoisie, petty bourgeoisie, middle class, proletariat, peasant,

FIGURE 4.2   Class Categories in the Thought of Marx and Weber

Marx & Engels Manifesto	Marx Capital	Marx 18 Brumaire	Weber Wirtschaft
Bourgeoisie (Capitalists)	Landowners Industrial Capitalists	Monarch Landowners Financial Aristocrats Industrialists	Property Class Bureaucrats and Intelligentsia Petty Bourgeoisie
Proletariat (Workers)	Workers Petty Bourgeoisie Intermediate (Bureaucrats and Professionals) Peasantry	Middle Class Petty Bourgeoisie Peasantry Lumpen Proletariat	Working Class

and so on, yet a close look at each category is necessary. The **bourgeoisie**, for instance, consists of owners of capital who purchase means of production and labor, but it may be distinguishable by property relations, say, as large landowners or a monopolistic bourgeoisie or large owners of industry and banking capital who may have ties with foreign capitalists and own factories, insurance companies, banks, and large commercial companies. This bourgeoisie may comprise nonmonopolistic owners of industrial and commercial property or owners of small industrial and commercial enterprises or small and middle-size farms. The bourgeoisie could be distinguishable by the type of capital or means of production possessed, for example, an agrarian bourgeoisie of modern landowners who run farms with modern machinery and pay salaries to workers; an industrial bourgeoisie; a commercial bourgeoisie; a banking bourgeoisie; and so on. The bourgeoisie might be further identified by the amount of capital owned, as in a large, medium, or small bourgeoisie.

Likewise, the category **petty bourgeoisie** might be broken into small capitalists who directly or indirectly control their means of production but do not possess capital. They may reside either in urban areas (as owners or tenants of small artisan industries and businesses or as independent professionals) or in rural areas (as sharecroppers, tenant farmers, and so on). Small petty bourgeois firms can develop into large capitalist enterprises. Some small firms are run by craftspeople. Some firms employ unskilled, low-wage workers. This potential diversity does not mitigate the ideological role of the petty bourgeoisie: "The small-business sector has a key symbolic role to play in the maintenance and reproduction of a capitalist society." Three key elements define their ideology: a belief in "independence," a distrust of large complex organization, and a preference for tradition and continuity: "beliefs which stress the value of a passionately held, rugged, competitive individualism founded on the belief in the moral goodness of hard work and individual achievement" (Clegg, Boreham, and Dow, 1985: 82).

The category **proletariat** includes workers who do not own any means of production and who sell their **labor power** for money. They may be urban workers or farmhands who earn wages.

Other differences arise from questions of who rules and the nature of power, issues that comparative studies of politics have examined from ancient times to the present. The legacies of Marx and Weber have influenced thinking on the concentration or dispersion of power, leading to debate and polemical discourse. Intellectuals have tended to side with Weber in their attention to pluralism and individual choice but emphasize Marx in their views of structure and collectivity. The remainder of this chapter demonstrates that this Marxist-Weberian dichotomy is not always clearly manifest in these respective positions. The following analysis delineates how the thinking of these two men influences overlapping tendencies among the principal twentieth-century contributions to theorizing and understanding group and class.

PERSPECTIVES ON GROUP

North American political science has traditionally emphasized the idea of group and group interests, political parties, subsystem autonomy, structural functionalism, and other conceptual formulations that tend to obscure class and class analysis. Although this tendency persists, in the 1990s interest in rational choice preferences of individuals in society has also diverted attention from class. Yet there are other explanations for the traditional emphasis, including ideological, political, and methodological considerations, as the following discussion makes clear.

Contrasting ideological perspectives helps to clarify the role of individual and group in politics. One mainstream view, represented in *The Civic Culture*'s five-nation survey by Gabriel Almond and Sidney Verba (1963), drew on the experience of representative democratic systems, of which the Anglo-American model is a prototype, and suggested that political life is shaped by individuals who behave in passive, subject, or participant ways through political parties and interest groups rather than social classes. An alternative view, in E. P. Thompson's *The Making of the English Working Class* (1963), argues that history can be rescued from "below" through a focus on class consciousness and the creativity and initiative of the mass of people. In the process, Thompson resurrects the concept of class in opposition to mainstream social scientists who deny its usage as a relationship and process. These different views help to elucidate the mainstream emphasis on pluralism through group interests and pressure and explain how a focus on class tends to be relegated to a secondary status. Four perspectives illustrate this position.

Elitism and Anticlass Bias

The central premise of the **elitist theory of democracy** is that in every society a minority makes the major decisions, an idea that dates back to Plato. The political sociologist Vilfredo Pareto in his *Sociological Writings* (1966) emphasized distinctions between elites and nonelites and proposed the idea of a **circulation of elites**, implying two meanings: One elite may take the place of another, and individuals may move from a low to a high stratum in society. Pareto divided this high stratum into a **governing class,** or elite (those who directly or indirectly govern), and a nongoverning elite. He transcended such Marxist categories as ruling class by stressing governing class, or elite, rule. Pareto drew examples of the rise and decline of elites from the Italian experience but was nevertheless criticized as overly general, sometimes polemical, and not well grounded in historical example.

Pareto's contemporary, Gaetano Mosca in *The Ruling Class: Elementi di Scienza Politica* (1939) preferred to use such concepts as ruling class, governing class, and political class, but his understanding did not differ radically from that of Pareto; he argued that two classes of people exist in all societies, a class that rules and a class that is ruled. Mosca believed that the small ruling class monopolizes power and benefits from its position, in contrast to the more numerous and dominated majority, but he also assumed that the majority, once discontented, can influence the ruling class and even depose the ruling class and assume its functions. In emphasizing this circulation of ruling classes, Mosca gave importance to the rise of new interests, a position closer to Weber than to Marx.

This European analysis influenced North American thought in two ways: first, by the emphasis on power in a centralized bureaucracy rather than in citizen involvement in electoral politics; and second, by the implications of elite circulation for a pluralist analysis, in particular the notion that new classes replace old classes, new groups may gain access to a ruling class whose ranks are open, and politics rather than economics may be determinant. Rule is characterized by moderation and co-optation, thereby mitigating the possibility for radical confrontation and structural change. Both tendencies lead to analysis of groups and individuals rather than social classes and to analysis premised on a breakup rather than concentration of power.

Diverse Interests in Pluralism

Pluralism assumes a polity composed of diverse interests and the dispersion of power. For mainstream political scientists this model is derived from a particular theoretical reconstruction of Anglo-American politics, one that draws on liberal economic and political thought, especially that of John Locke and Jeremy Bentham, who focused on property rights and individual initiative; on the writings of James Madison, who stressed competing interests in the struggle for power; and on the perspectives of Arthur F. Bentley and David Truman, who devised theories of interest groups and pushed for an interpretation of the politics of modern industrial states devoid of class analysis.

In *The Process of Government* (1908), Bentley perhaps best captured this understanding by insisting that class was not a viable category of scientific analysis. He argued that in the modern nations political life comprised groups freely combining, dissolving, and reformulating according to their particular interests. Influenced by this attention to groups and interests, even thinkers who conceptualize capitalism as the economic basis for a pluralistic society interpret the division of labor in capitalist society in terms of competing "interests" between owners and producers. Thus class distinctions are at least implied in their work, even if these distinctions are ignored in much of the pluralist literature. Dorothy Ross in *The Origins of American Social Science* (1991) relied on these interpretations to demonstrate her thesis that American liberalism has evolved into an exceptional and pervasive ideology.

Acknowledging his intellectual debt to James Madison, Robert Dahl formulated a theory based on a wide dispersion of power and authority among government officials, groups, and individuals. He understood the structure of power as segmented, not organized into a hierarchical pattern. He envisaged society as comprising polyarchies in which barriers to political opposition are not substantial and subsystem autonomy and organizational pluralism prevail in a milieu of consensus and order, constraints on violence, and equilibrium. Dahl later elaborated on his theory, arguing that socialist economies can be highly decentralized and pluralistic. Although he acknowledged conflictive pluralism, Dahl deemphasized the importance of orthodox interpretations of class as tending "vastly to underestimate the extent to which ideological diversity among elites leads to fragmentation rather than solidarity . . . 'class' in its various manifestations is only an element, albeit nearly always a significant one, in a fragmented pattern of cleavages and conflicts that is persistently pluralistic" (1978: 193).

A more explicit effort to confront the problem that pluralism tends to ignore a Marxist perspective of class is in the work of Ralf Dahrendorf, especially his *Class and Class Conflict in Industrial Society* (1959). His synthesis of Marxist class theory confirmed the difficulty of incorporating a Marxist view in a theory of pluralism. He resolved the problem by constructing ideal types of class in a "postcapitalist society" in which authority does not necessarily depend on wealth and prestige, conflict between classes and groups is dissociated, and pluralism of institutions and interests allows for widespread participation in decisions. This example illustrates that the fundamental problem with pluralism can be the idealization of a politics that does not always reflect real conditions. Under capitalism, an emphasis on bargaining and resolution through consensus may cause one to overlook contradictions inherent in class society. For instance, the view that state policies reflect accurately the demands of diverse interest groups was undermined by the manipulations of the Nixon, Reagan, and Bush administrations during the Watergate and Iran-Contra scandals. Likewise, idealistic impressions of pluralism within socialism that suggested the possibility of classlessness, for example, in the former Soviet Union, overlooked the coercive activities of a dominant party and secret police as well as the class nature of a strongly centralized bureaucracy.

The Post-Marxist Conception of Class

During the late 1950s Daniel Bell advocated an "end of ideology" and predicted a "postindustrial society" with improved living standards; a closing of gaps between classes; and a diminishing of ethnic, regional, and other loyalties. These ideas influenced other academics to speculate on the future and to blur traditional notions of the bourgeois order, of the dilemmas of capitalism and socialism, and of class struggle. This discourse was criticized as idealistic or a defense of the capitalist order, especially in the United States, and it provoked Samuel Bowles and Herbert Gintis to seek space for a radical democratic synthesis between a liberalism that "shelters the citadels of domination," and a Marxism that obscures "nonclass and noneconomic forms of domination" (1986: 17–18). They envisaged a postliberalism in which democratic personal rights displace property rights. They argued that Marxism reduces institutions to class terms and emphasized conflictual pluralism obscured class interests, diminishing the role of the state and playing down the internal contradictions of capitalism that affect relations of production and often lead to class struggle.

This thinking also appears in the work of some European Marxists and former Marxists, such as Ernesto Laclau and Chantal Mouffe, who have insisted, "It is no longer possible to maintain the conception of subjectivity and classes elaborated by Marxism, nor its vision of the historical course of capitalist development" (1985: 4). Although these intellectuals differ in many respects, they appear to agree that the primacy of organized labor should be repudiated because the working class in capitalist countries has failed to live up to its revolutionary expectations, and the model of struggle should now incorporate a multitude of interests emanating from various strata, groups, and social movements. Laclau and Mouffe outlined a new politics for the left based on a project of radical democracy involving new forms of participation. Ellen Meiksins Wood (1986) characterized this position as a "retreat from class" through transcending class interests and building socialism by mobilizing around a plurality of resistance to inequality and oppression.

The new pluralism, as Wood has characterized it, transcends the liberal concern with diverse interests and seeks a democratic community that assimilates differences of gender, culture, and sexuality and celebrates these differences without allowing them to become triggers for domination and oppression. This pluralism "unites diverse human beings, all free and equal, without suppressing their differences or denying their special needs. But the 'politics of identity' reveals its limitations, both theoretical and political, the moment we try to situate class differences within its democratic vision" (Wood, 1995: 258). Wood acknowledged the need for diversity and pluralism but not undifferentiated and unstructured pluralism: "What is needed is a pluralism that does indeed acknowledge diversity and difference, not merely plurality or multiplicity" (263).

Rational Individual Choice

Another tendency, oriented to transcending rigid Marxist formulations, has emerged in the 1990s among intellectuals calling themselves "Analytical Marxists," "Rational Choice Marxists," and "Subjective Marxists." Their ranks include G. A. Cohen, Jon Elster, Adam Przeworski, John Roemer, and Erik Olin Wright. They claim to follow Marxism; emphasize rational choice; approximate positivist approaches to social science; and tend to build on micro foundations, behavioral assumptions, or individual decisions. For example, Elster in *Making Sense of Marx* (1985) argued that the actions of classes are reducible to the actions of individuals, and he attempted to demonstrate that Marx himself was a founder of rational choice theory. In his attention to class, Wright (1985) shifted from his earlier emphasis on structure and contradictory class locations (1978) to a more subjective realm of class analysis. This shift reorients his analysis away from classes, power, and the labor process.

Critics suggest that this rational choice approach has been unaccepting of traditional or structural Marxian conceptions of exploitation and class and is subjective in its social analysis. Class no longer characterizes the process whereby groups of people become differentiated through the labor process but focuses on the development of groups of people into collective units. Ellen Meiksins Wood provided the most comprehensive and exhaustive criticism of analytical Marxism, which she saw as converging with post-Marxism, two approaches that "began as an effort to establish 'rigor' in Marxist theory and . . . ended for many in a general repudiation of Marxism in theory and in practice" (1989: 87).

In summary, the above four approaches sometimes employ but tend to diminish the importance of class in political analyses of individual and group behavior. Although Pareto's theory of elite circulation distinguishes between elites and nonelites, it supplants the term **ruling class** with **governing class**. Mosca emphasized ruling class along with governing class. The position of both thinkers approximates that of Weber rather than Marx. Their concern with a dispersion of interests and power rather than with class has been influential in mainstream political science, especially **interest group** theory. To his credit, Dahl was able to extend this idea to socialist thinking, while at the same time acknowledging but minimizing the importance of class. Dahrendorf carried the dialogue further with his synthesis of Marxist class theory and pluralism, although he was unable to resolve the incompatibility of the two concepts. The post-Marxists have shifted from a Marxist position to a postliberalism, in the case of Bowles and Gintis, who search for conceptual space between Marxism and liberalism and play down class interests, preferring instead to examine individual rights relevant to political and economic life. In the search for a new formulation of socialism and democracy, Laclau and Mouffe also turn from social classes, especially an orthodox view of the bourgeoisie and proletariat in conflict, and instead look to a multitude of interests that stem from various classes, groups, and social movements. Finally, rather than shy away from Marxism but at the same time shifting from the traditional Marxist discourse on class, analytical Marxists emphasize individual and rational choice.

PERSPECTIVES ON CLASS

Juxtaposed to approaches that view society as comprising pluralistic groups or even a plurality of classes or as individuals competing for power or pursuing particular interests, theories of class usually are cast in a structural context and associated with such terms as power structure, **power elite, ruling class,** and other formulations connoting class or stratification. Instrumental and structurally autonomous positions on class appear in these theories. Class also can be envisaged as an overdetermining process.

Power Structure and the Ruling Class

Who rules and the nature of power are issues of significance in political studies. Marx and Engels in the *Manifesto* referred to the modern state as a

sort of committee that manages the affairs of the bourgeoisie. This instrumental view of power and class suggests that the dominant or **ruling class**
is an economic class that rules politically. Variations of this instrumentalist
theme appear in the literature, and they are not necessarily Marxist. For instance, community studies in political science and political sociology traditionally addressed the question of who rules, usually on the basis of
stratification theory or a ladder of strata with an upper class of political
and civic leaders (identifiable by such criteria as income, occupation, and
education) at the top that runs the local community. This upper class often
is characterized as a **power elite** that rules in its own interests and is separated from the lower classes of a community. Among the important studies employing this notion of stratification was the work of Robert and
Helen Lynd in the middle 1920s and again a decade later in their study of
Middletown, or Muncie, Indiana; Floyd Hunter, who in the early 1950s
used panels of persons knowledgeable about community life to identify
decisionmakers in Regional City, or Atlanta, Georgia; and C. Wright Mills
who about the same time examined power clusters in the United States.

In *The Power Elite* (1956) Mills identified an interlocking power elite of
politicians and bureaucrats, high corporate executives, and prominent
military officers. In an effort to deal with some of the critics of Mills, including liberals like Dahl (who contended that the exaggerated influence
of elites could not be measured empirically and therefore analysis of decisionmakers should be based on the more measurable input of interest
groups) and radicals (who felt that Mills should relate leaders to socioeconomic classes), G. William Domhoff in *The Powers That Be: Process of
Ruling Class Domination in America* (1978a) empirically linked members of
the upper class to control of the corporate economy, found that the concept power elite is a bridge between pluralist and radical positions, and
saw power elite as an extension of the concept ruling class. Domhoff concentrated on "networks" of institutions and groups, arguing that his notion of ruling class should be understood in a Marxist context and not as
liberal instrumentalism as some left critics had alleged, although he acknowledged that his approach tended to be static and one dimensional
with a focus on a single class rather than portraying a dynamic relationship of several classes in conflict.

Instrumentalist and Structural Frameworks

In an analysis that moved away from the mere positioning of powerful
people in an economic power structure, Ralph Miliband in *The State in
Capitalist Society* (1969) contributed a Marxist theory of state and class under capitalism. **Instrumentalism** is evident where the capitalist ruling class
wields economic power and uses the state as its instrument of domination

over society. Miliband identified an owning class and a working class, along with two elements of a "middle class," one composed of professional people and the other of businesspersons and farmers in small and medium-size enterprises.

In elaborating a Marxist theory of social classes, Nicos Poulantzas in *Political Power and Social Classes* (1973) developed the thesis that the structures of society (thus **structuralism)** rather than influential people generally determine policy outcomes. Antonio Gramsci (1957) had emphasized **hegemony,** or dominance of some social group or class in power, to explain the success or failure of the ruling class in politics. Once a crisis in the hegemony of the ruling class occurs, for example, the masses may become disenchanted and rebellious, possibly provoking a ruling class to seize control of the state by crushing its adversaries. Then Louis Althusser in *For Marx* (1970) distinguished the structuralist formulations in the later writings of Marx from the humanist ideas in his early writings. Althusser, like Gramsci, turned his attention to the **superstructure** of politico-legal and ideological apparatus and envisaged the state as repressive in its shielding of the bourgeoisie and its allies in the class struggle against the proletariat. Thus the whole of the political class struggle revolves around the state.

Poulantzas was able to test his ideas through the crises and fall of dictatorships in Greece, Portugal, and Spain. In his *Crisis of the Dictatorships* (1976), he employed a dichotomy of dominant and popular classes. To analyze the Portuguese experience he shifted from a traditional Marxist-Leninist emphasis on **dual power** and assault on the state by revolutionary workers and popular forces outside the state **apparatus** to the possibility of a bloodless revolution through penetration and occupation of key apparatuses within the state. In his last work, *State, Power, and Socialism* (1978), he argued that struggle within the state apparatuses was necessary to disrupt the balance of forces and bring about a **transition to socialism**. This position may have inspired some left intellectuals in the early 1980s to move beyond structural interpretations, give less attention to the working class, and turn theory in the direction of newly emerging social movements.

Class as Process

In their review of Marx's theory of class, Stephen Resnick and Richard Wolff (1982) emphasized the class process of extracting surplus labor through different forms, ranging from primitive communist, ancient, feudal, and slave to capitalist; they distinguished between fundamental classes (composed of performers and extractors of surplus labor) and subsumed classes (consisting of persons who neither perform nor extract surplus labor but who share in the distribution of extracted surplus labor and carry out certain social functions in society). Their review of examples of subsumed classes in Marx's writings included merchants, moneylenders, and supervisory managers of joint stock companies. They showed how Marx related surplus value to a distinction of productive and unproductive labor. Drawing from Althusser and Marx, Resnick and Wolff employed the term **overdetermination** to suggest that "each process has no existence other than as the site of the converging influences exerted by all the other social processes. . . . the class process is a condition of existence of each and every other social process" (1982: 2).

With overdetermination as the basis of understanding class struggle, Resnick and Wolff argued that Marxist theory begins with the class process and contradictions that produce struggles in the social formation: "We conceive each and every class and non-class process of the social formation to be in a process of contradictory change." In any social formation the fundamental and subsumed class processes "define the different class positions occupied by individuals." Class processes and positions are conceptualized as "the combined effort of all other social processes," so that in this overdetermined way "each class position is constituted to be in tension, movement, and change." Thus struggle or conflict occurs in "a particular moment or conjuncture in which the overdetermined contradictions embedded in social processes have fused to motivate intense collective effort to change the process in question" (1982: 14–15).

In summary, these approaches emphasize a structural conceptualization of class. In one form or another, class is identifiable in political analysis. Class here is understood, first, instrumentally in terms of power and rule, as in the writings of Mills and Domhoff. Marxist categories premised on the relations of production usually in capitalist society can be contrasted with stratification analysis, focused on class determined by income, status, education, and occupation. Sometimes this analysis has proved to be static in its attention to a single class—say, a dominant class—without dynamically looking at a diversity of classes in struggle. The instrumental view of class also derives from a traditional Marxist position, as in the case of Miliband, whose radical views are appealing even to mainstream political science. In contrast, Poulantzas emphasized the possibility of structural **autonomy of the state** in his depiction of dominant and popular classes. His thinking originally was based on the Marxist structuralism of Gramsci and Althusser, but it was to divert analysis away from the working class and toward newly emerging social movements that offered possibilities for societal transformation. Finally, class is analyzed in terms of process in the work of Resnick and Wolff, who use the term overdetermination to avoid reductionist class analysis and account for a wide range of class positions occupied by individuals; class struggle or conflict emanates from this process.

ISSUES OF CLASS AND GROUP ANALYSIS

Among the issues raised in this chapter is the inclination of North American political science not to take seriously questions of class; Europeans tend to incorporate class in political analysis. I have also shown how both Marx and Weber focused on class and how they influenced social science in different ways. Whereas the Weberian attention to status groups and a decentralized bureaucracy has been especially important to the mainstream, the Marxian use of class analysis has been incorporated in alternative approaches. The North American neglect of class has been explained in terms of "exceptionalism," but it also derives from the influence of American political orthodoxy in the form of liberalism, as Louis Hartz characterized it in his criticism of the liberal tradition (*The Liberal Tradition in America*, 1953). David Ricci linked this liberalism to a political culture of middle-class ideals and practices and emphasis on consensus, group interests, representative government, individual freedoms, equality, and so on. Class distinctions were overshadowed by these preferences in American society.

The search for a science of politics was also associated with empiricism, evolutionary theory, and positivism, as political scientists tended to focus on the institutions of government and their origins and development rather than on social classes. Analysis tended to be descriptive, with emphasis on stability rather than the underlying disruptions of class struggle in American society. These trends were reinforced especially after the Second World War when the Cold War obsession with communism awakened political science to the problematic of Marxism and its political ideas, including historical materialism, dialectics, the theory of surplus value, and class analysis. The Marxist approach, often presented as scientific reasoning, thus directly challenged liberal ideas: "The competition of elites, parties, and groups in America is no more than an internal affair of the ruling class. . . . The underlying assumption of the Marxian syllogism here was diametrically opposed to that of mainstream political science" (Ricci, 1984: 171). The response of intellectuals was to suggest the end of ideology and the exhaustion of ideas on the left and right, a position, for example, of Seymour Martin Lipset who argued forty years ago in *Political Man* (1960) that workers had gained political citizenship while conservatives had tolerated the welfare state.

Behavioral social science as a behavioral science used quantitative procedures for testing theory. At a macro level, efforts to conceptualize a grand theory of the political system obscured attention to the state as conceptually related to social classes. Middle-range and structural-functional analysis favored formal and informal political institutions but not class. At a micro level, behaviorism examined class in terms of income and education, but class analysis based on conflict and struggle was generally ignored.

Ideology and class continue as significant for some scholars, however. For example, Clegg, Boreham, and Dow (1985) combined Marx's concerns for processes of class formation with Weber's more empirically developed categories of class structure in a model of class analysis of advanced industrial societies. They argued that property forms have become more impersonal and institutional since the early twentieth century and that ownership and control no longer fuse in individual persons. In another example, Michael Burawoy (1985) reasserted the central role of the working class and the primacy of production, arguing that the industrial proletariat has made significant and self-conscious interventions in history. In defense of the thesis that the process of production decisively shapes working-class struggles, he argued against those who diminish the role of the working class.

Pluralists and power structure instrumentalists alike have encountered conceptual difficulty with their indiscriminate use of loose categories such as **circulating elite, power elite,** upper class, **governing class,** and **ruling class.** Often these terms are used in isolation from other levels of socioeconomic class, resulting in static analysis. Marx often referred to class in a popular sense, envisaging a social class as sharing certain characteristics such as income, so that sometimes he mentioned the industrial class, the ideological classes, and unproductive classes. He differentiated classes, however, in relation to the historical development of the forces of production and the appearance of a surplus product beyond the needs of the workers or direct producers so that the ruling class could be clearly distinguished from the working class in terms of relations of production. Class thus is comprehensible in light of a society's dominant mode of production, a notion radically different from the Weberian status groups and location of class in the market and relations of circulation. The latter emphasis leads to the common ground of consensus and bargaining, the former emphasis to the conflictual arena of class struggle.

Several problems emanate from the polemic over whether class analysis is limited by structural constraints: whether class categories can incorporate the expanding "middle" stratum; what are the implications for productive and unproductive labor; and what are the prospects of organizing strategies and class alliances for mobilizing different elements, raising class consciousness, and promoting struggle for reformist and revolutionary change.

The issue of the middle class of salaried intermediaries and its role in society has spawned alternative theories of class structure in an effort to transcend the rigid emphasis on only two classes, polarized around labor and capital. Poulantzas, for instance, referred to the evolving middle class as "the new petty bourgeoisie," and Barbara and John Ehrenreich named it "the professional-managerial class." Erik Olin Wright (1978) concentrated on "the new middle class," expounding his idea of contradictory class locations wherein this class contends for power in a class society through collusion with capitalists or alliances with labor. He stressed that classes are defined in relational terms, by social organization of economic relations and by social relations of production rather than exchange. He recognized three traditional classes (capitalist, labor, and the petty bourgeoisie), and he identified other class positions in terms of their contradictory class locations, including under capitalism managers and supervisors, semiautonomous employees, and small employers. He applied this conception to various modes of production through history and suggested that under feudalism the bourgeoisie was in a contradictory location between lords and serfs; under capitalism managers and bureaucrats have been in a contradictory location between bourgeoisie and proletariat; and in state bureaucratic socialism the intelligentsia and experts between bureaucrats and workers (see Figure 4.3).

The question of mobilization strategies leads to an assessment of traditional institutions such as political parties, in particular the role of vanguard parties in revolutionary situations, and more recently to the new social movements of women, ethnic minorities, ecologists, and pacifists. Consequently, academics and practitioners have divided, some continuing to emphasize the role of the working class and other class elements that conjuncturally may coalesce to bring about transformation; some combining analysis of class with the social movements and elaborating theories of race and class, feminism and class, and ecology and class; and others turning away from the working class and political parties and limiting their attention to the social movements in search of post-Marxist explanations. Marxist political scientists like Miliband believe that divisions in society based on gender, race, ethnicity, nationality, and religion are often related to and influenced by class location. Post-Marxists like Laclau and Mouffe have looked for diverse interests in the new social movements as they moved beyond Marxism to broaden its appeal and charac-

FIGURE 4.3   Classes and Modes of Production

Mode of Production	Major Classes	Contradictory Location
Feudalism	Lords and Serfs	Bourgeoisie
Capitalism	Bourgeoisie & Proletariat	Managers & Bureaucrats
State Socialism	Bureaucrats & Workers	Intelligentsia & Experts

terize socialism as a form of participatory democracy. They see the working class as only one of a number of possible agents involved in social transformation. They argue that society is capable of organizing in an infinite number of ways. Politics and ideology are separated from any social basis, and in its place discourse determines all action. André Gorz (1980) questioned assumptions about the role of the working class in the formation of socialist society and gave attention to groups based on gender, race, age, and community. These authors relate to democratic practices under capitalism, with a central question being whether capitalist democracy allows space for the organization of workers to pursue their own class interests. A further question involves the relationship of class to formal, indirect, and representative forms of democracy in contrast to the informal, direct participatory forms of democracy.

Countering the prevailing dissatisfaction with class, Scott G. McNall, Rhonda E. Levine, and Rick Fantasia (1991) argued that a class analysis remains fundamental in scholarly study of social and historical processes. The Marxist model is distinctive because of its attention to class conflict and exploitation. Furthermore, the division between Weberian and Marxian perspectives has faded with the focus on problems of proletarianization, the role of culture in preserving class boundaries, and the independent position of bureaucracies in shaping the middle classes.

In this historical overview, I have examined past and present contributions to theories of class and group in an effort to balance the influence of mainstream political science, especially in the United States, with alternative views, particularly from Europe. Familiarity with rich conceptual and analytical sources everywhere is essential for understanding the history of class analysis. In political science, for example, the debates between the British Marxist Ralph Miliband and the Greek Marxist Nicos Poulantzas refocused attention to state and class during the 1960s.

It is also clear that class theory in political science is strongly related to theoretical trends, debates, and conceptualizations in other social sciences. For example, the political sociologists Peter Evans and Theda Skocpol during the middle 1980s convinced mainstream political scientists that the concept of state should be brought back into the discipline. A focus on the state can lead to class analysis, as I explained in Chapter 3. In Chapter 7, I show how the history of the concept of democracy in the United States was explicitly tied to the underlying class structure of society, at least as late as the New Deal, but thereafter "the image of a class-divided society began to fade from American political rhetoric as interpretations of shifted from an analysis of relations of production to patterns of consumption.

In his writings on France in the middle of the nineteenth century, Marx provided an extraordinary class analysis of a political situation. His examination of the finance aristocracy, industrial bourgeoisie, petty bourgeoisie, peasantry, lumpen proletariat, industrial proletariat, bourgeois monarchy, and big bourgeoisie in France not only yielded a host of class terms but combined with a close look at political institutions and political parties, led to such notions as the exceptional state and relative state autonomy, among others, which have guided much contemporary political analysis.

5

THE CULTURAL DIMENSION

INDIVIDUAL AND COLLECTIVE PREFERENCES

A concern with culture dates to nineteenth-century studies in anthropology. Culture generally involves knowledge, beliefs, customs, and habits of people. The anthropologist Franz Boas referred to culture as assimilating individual reactions as affected by the habits of the group in which one lives. Culture is conservative in its persistence as these traits are carried on from generation to generation, so that culture might tend to reinforce old patterns or resist change detrimental or threatening, say, to indigenous communities.

Differing perspectives affect various understandings of culture, however. For example, in what generally may be thought of as a prevailing mainstream interpretation, Max Weber referred to culture as somewhat autonomous, shaped by individual orientations or rational self-interest. Alternatively, Karl Marx explained culture in terms of its dependence on the political, social, and economic setting of the society at large. Both thinkers interpreted culture on general and particular levels. Weber viewed culture as composed of beliefs and symbols around ideal types of traditional, charismatic, and rational authority; thus individual actions, shaped by custom, would orient to beliefs that support and maintain the collective society at large. Through rationalization of authority, secularization of society evolves, and rules of procedure become routine. In contrast, Marx envisaged the beliefs and symbols of culture as a **false consciousness** reflecting the superstructure or the ideological and political underpinnings of capitalist society. Culture thus tends to shield the interests of the ruling capitalist class. Although culture tends to evolve and change through time, radical changes are likely only through historical changes in the material base, through a transformation in the mode of production, and in class relations. If culture derives from the material practices of society and, more particularly, from the consequences of the relationship of the workers to their production, then the capitalists may be free to exploit labor and the workers must sell their labor, thus alienating themselves from the product of their work.

MAINSTREAM POLITICAL
CULTURE AND SOCIALIZATION

In comparative inquiry, culture has been related to politics in several ways. First, the link to a national character was a means of identifying national traits associated with various countries, but this usually led to unsatisfactory stereotyping at a general level while obscuring particular qualities. This dissatisfaction prompted a reformulation, especially in mainstream political science, and a preference for portraying nations as political cultures, perhaps best exemplified in the five-nation study by Gabriel Almond and Sidney Verba published as *The Civic Culture* (1963). The premises of their political culture were identifiable, first, by civic virtue and responsibility, sharing of values with others, trust and confidence in one's fellow being, and freedom from anxiety; second, by participatory and pluralistic democracy based on the toleration of individual freedoms and consensus among the government; third, by order through rational bureaucracy; and, fourth, by stability through modernization. These premises suggest the possibility of analyzing political culture at both general macro and specific micro levels.

In their macro empirical investigation, Almond and Verba surveyed attitudes in five countries. Their conceptualization differed from a rather simplistic typology that Almond had suggested earlier in which the Anglo-American system was seen as homogeneous and secular, that of continental Europe as fragmented, that of the less developed systems as mixed, and that of the totalitarian system as synthetic. Almond and Verba's interviews focused on the knowledge and beliefs people have of their political system, its leaders, and operation. Thus political culture at this general level serves to characterize nations or national political systems. This depiction incorporated the degree to which secularization was in effect, implying the give-and-take interactions affecting culture and its parochial (unaware), subject (apolitical), and participant (involved) orientations to politics. In the evolution to a higher participatory society, Almond and Verba recognized historical traditions dating back to ancient Greek philosophers, whose theories of stable democracy are relevant to recent history. They argued that political culture is not a theory but contributes to the shaping of theory and to an understanding of the psychological or subjective dimension of politics.

At the micro level political culture serves to examine individual preferences, and thus the study of communication, especially in the mass media, helps to understand how political attitudes and opinion are shaped. Communication also relates closely to socialization and how individual perspectives are formed through experiences in the family, school, and job. Studies of political socialization focused on formal aspects of civic training during the 1920s and early 1930s, on personality and politics during the Second World War and the decade thereafter, and on the political formation of children and adolescents since the 1960s. This later theme stimulated a plethora of studies, including those on the learning process whereby new members of society, such as infants, interact and acquire social behavior. In this kind of study individual socialization equates with all social learning, although some social scientists would narrow the process to individual learning based on behavior that a group approves, and others would identify socialization as the process whereby a child internalizes parental norms. Although the concept generally is used in relation to children, it also is applicable to adults. Thus socialization might be simply the inculcation of skills, motives, and attitudes for the performance of roles in society.

The main criticisms of macro political culture theory revolve around reductionism, bias, and explanatory value, as catalogued in the following list:

Idealized as capitalist-technological political secularization
Inadequate, ambiguous, unproven, or false in assumption
Reductionist, culturebound, nonexplanatory, and descriptive
Particularistic rather than holistic, speculative
Static, passive, and conditioned rather than active and spontaneous
Ideological and biased

Critics suggest that most social science is culturebound and that most generalizations are valid only within particular cultural situations. The tendency to look at culture with Western preconceptions of modernity clearly is culturally biased. Furthermore, the simple typologies of Almond and Verba are largely descriptive rather than analytical, do not employ any theoretical construct, and therefore tend to be nonexplanatory and nonpredictive. Another problem is the common biased belief that the ideal political culture is found in the attributes of a democratic environment, a rational bureaucratic development, and a popular sovereignty usually associated with advanced industrial society.

The more narrowly based political socialization studies have been criticized as conservative because they focus on continuities rather than discontinuities among agencies during different periods of an individual's life. For example, attention to parents may show that they impart only what they have learned, and thus major changes in society and culture may be ignored. Another problem has been an emphasis on childhood and adolescence rather than adult learning. Socialization theory has tended to be speculative, tentative, and imprecise. The mainstream research has focused almost exclusively on attitudes in stable, democratic societies and the experience of the United States and Western Europe.

The critical observer might also probe into the ideological implications of culture and socialization. Education, in particular, might be understood to be crucial to state-sponsored socialization. In the United States, for instance, values and norms of liberal democratic pluralism might be imbued in the system so that culture and socialization become not independent of but dependent on the state or system itself. This pervasive diffusion of ideology could contribute to the passivity and false consciousness of the world in which individuals live. Individuals, for example, might be socialized to view needs or problems as unimportant.

ALTERNATIVE PERSPECTIVES ON CULTURE

The Brazilian philosopher Paulo Freire developed a method to motivate illiterate adults to read and write. He emphasized a basic language of words around the problems that needed to be transcended—hunger, slums, lack of health care, and so on. In his *Pedagogy of the Oppressed* (1970) he referred to the dialectic between determinism and freedom and how consciousness and action lead to change. Once people reflect deeply on a problem, they move from uncommitted awareness to action. He emphasized the revolutionary implications of culture in the sense of denouncing oppressive society or demanding a just society. In this sense the transformation of the individual confronts the pervasive influence of mainstream education as it is shaped by the capitalist state. The same may be true for some socialist states, but usually where a profound revolutionary experience has shaped the socialist outlook there are efforts to raise consciousness.

Such a perspective prompts an exploration of the alternatives. Initially it may be useful to consider the possibility that academic studies of socialization may lean toward stability rather than change. Scholars who limit their variables to easily measurable values may fall in this camp. Scholars whose worldview may be shaped by their class position, for instance, may describe working-class children as incompetent because they had not been socialized in the ways of children of higher classes.

Alienation and Humanism

Both capitalist and socialist societies may make use of political socialization, and the formation of consciousness and false consciousness among the masses may serve the interests of both established and revolutionary societies. Our concern, however, is with how individuals act in history. In his early writings, especially in *Economic and Philosophic Manuscripts* (1844), Marx was concerned with the alienation of the individual, especially in the workplace. He suggested that material forces shape one's consciousness. György Lukács called this **false consciousness.** Antonio Gramsci referred to a hegemony or a bloc of bourgeois forces, the dominance of which was forged through distortions or delusions about politics imposed on people.

The Marxist view of the individual follows two lines of thinking. A vulgar Marxist interpretation suggests that the material base unilaterally determines the ideological understanding and passivity of the individual. An alternative view, Marxist humanism, argues that such a view is profoundly not Marxist. Erich Fromm and Herbert Marcuse, for instance, suggested that the individual is shaped not only by the material conditions of history but also by social activity in the present and future. People do not exist in passivity, subject to their material relations, but may become active in transforming their situation.

Yet another approach that gives attention to the individual is found in rational choice theory. It evolved through conservative thinking but also has incorporated Marxism. Work by conservative thinkers such as James Buchanan, Anthony Downs, Mancur Olsen, William Riker, and Gordon Tullock in the late 1950s and 1960s focused on normative theory, assuming that all individuals are rational in their decisions. For example, the market is shaped by rational individuals who pursue their own self-interests. These models incorporated a notion of methodological individualism in which benefits and costs are considered before taking action. Mainstream comparative political scientists like Gabriel Almond also drew on the metaphor of the invisible hand and the market in the thought of Adam Smith as a means of expressing the ideal of democratic politics and the competitive struggle for power in their descriptions of democratic politics.

The Marxist extension of these propositions evolved in progressive intellectuals such as Jon Elster and Adam Przeworski, who emphasized rational decisionmaking and equilibrium models similar to the preference of neoclassical economics. In his *Capitalism and Social Democracy* (1985) Przeworski analyzed the failure of social democracy while emphasizing the lack of choice as an evolutionary structurally determined phenomenon. He argued that in such situations choice is structurally determined by parameters outside the realm of individual choice.

These thinkers suggest the possibility of a political culture in which individual choice is the norm and social classes and class struggle do not determine the outcomes. Their analysis appeals to mainstream social science because of its quantitative analysis, statistical application, and mathematical formal models. Although they insist that their approach is Marxist, these writers find legitimacy in their approximation to positivist theory. Critics contend, however, that the rational choice approach is subjective, dogmatic, and unaccepting of traditional or structural Marxism and its conceptions of exploitation and class.

Social Movements and Collectivity

Traditionally socialization of the individual occurs through family, job, school, or community groups, among other experiences. Political preferences are inculcated and acquired through the mass media and through involvement in group activity or political parties. Political scientists and political sociologists emphasize the socializing influences of interest groups in coalescing individuals and pressuring for preferences around economic, political, or social issues. Political parties involved in mobilizing voters around campaigns may exert influence as well, although in the United States these parties are not as highly disciplined and effectively organized as, say, in Great Britain. The rise of the "new" social movements thus is a relatively recent phenomenon.

Initially, the **new social movements** became conspicuous in the rapidly changing events affecting dictatorships in southern Europe and in the Southern Cone of Latin America. Two essential sources help us to understand its early roots. The term seems to have originated with Manuel Castells (1973), who depicted case studies involving resistance to urban projects, ecological protest, and squatter movements. This urban agitation appeared not to be based on traditional conflicts between labor and capital such as strikes, and social scientists began to see a proliferation of social conflicts not based on class and class struggle but on a new politics emanating from new forms of participation. This signified a shift from the old view of societal change emanating from traditional institutions to a new view of possible change through the social movements themselves and their autonomy and spontaneity.

About the same time Nicos Poulantzas (1976) analyzed these changes in southern Europe. He was especially attracted to the situation in Portugal, where after the coup of April 25, 1974, and the collapse of authoritarian rule, hundreds of new social movements emerged alongside many political parties. The specter of mass involvement and participatory democracy pushed events in a revolutionary socialist direction. After observing the rapidly forming neighborhood groups, peasant organizations, labor unions, and leftist parties, Poulantzas came to believe in the possibility of radical change occurring within the traditional structures and institutions of the state and society at large rather than transforming the institutional fabric through a deep confrontational revolutionary movement for which the conquest of power was dependent on control of arms. Political transitions in Greece and Spain as well as in Argentina, Brazil, and Uruguay were also accompanied by broad movements in search of solutions for various constituencies and motivated by the prospects of participatory and democratic outcomes.

What then are the new social movements? They are often spontaneously organized around a political project for change. Through effective leadership they may successfully confront prevailing powerful interests and struggle against domination, exploitation, and subjugation. They promote democracy and participation. They tend to be more temporal than political parties and usually orient to specific interests. Such movements may mobilize, for instance, around women's rights and recognition, concern with spreading peace and preventing war, protest over environmental damage, mobilizing poor people to assume responsibility for neighborhood issues, and so on.

The new social movements differ from the old movements of labor unions, working-class parties, and proletarian organizations, some of which were inspired by Marxism and many of which have been integrated into established bureaucratic networks. The new movements, in contrast, appear to be innovative and capable of operating outside established government circles or traditional institutional settings. The new movements associate with opposition to established rule; struggle against sectarianism or rigidly conceived political positioning around issues; seek new cultural links; serve as intermediaries between empowered planners and producers and disempowered citizens and consumers; and idealize their activities in programs of postcolonial, postproletarian, and postindustrial theory and practical politics.

Intellectuals have incorporated the new social movements into their understandings as a way of avoiding determinist assumptions such as that societal change depends on the consciousness and actions of a working class or that society must be understood only through the reductionist tendencies of class analysis. One political scientist observed that the new movements "articulate the ideologies and class interests of a contradictory and complex social bloc: informational 'new middle class' workers; anti-industrial resistance groups, local hi-tech entrepreneurs, anti-life world colonization movements, and traditional culture defense groups" (Luke, 1989: 149).

Focus on the new social movements has stimulated interest in cultural studies and their potential for undermining hegemony in the academic disciplines and promoting interdisciplinary study, the transcending of rigidly conceived class analysis by examining the problems of the middle class and the position of women, and the importance of race and ethnicity in coping with societal problems. Other significant topics include the role of peace movements in mitigating violence and war around the world, the way in which the environmental movement has been co-opted by industrial capital, and how ecofeminist theory and politics evolved out of the radical feminist movement.

Popular interest in issues about sex and gender influenced the formation of a new social movement commonly called the new women's movement. Issues of gender include the sexual division of labor based on male and female roles in the workforce and society and the relations between the sexes. Feminism is important in the movement, although not all women who consider themselves politically active are feminists, and the differing emphasis on women, feminism, and gender is evident in journals such as *Feminist Studies, Women's Studies, Signs, Sex Roles, Psychology of Women Quarterly,* and *Gender and Society.*

Interest in the new social movements extended to Latin America and areas outside the United States and Europe. The principal concern has been with emancipation, or a plurality of emancipations—for the environment, for human rights, and for liberation from oppression and subjection. Essential would be the struggle with the power to dominate and to transcend the mentality of colonization and neocolonization in a search for a new context of identity and a "postcolonialism." Most of the movements emerged spontaneously with the demise of dictatorships during the 1980s and the desire to find justice over acts of torture and repression, to ensure freedom of expression, and to engender democracy.

Although the attention to the new social movements stimulated new thinking and creative approaches to the study of culture, such studies may also be limited by a focus on single issues such as feminist rights, ecological devastation, or neighborhood plight without adequately linking analysis to the constraints and impacts of capitalist or socialist systems. A narrow approach might undermine possibilities of broad alliances of forces to confront, say, capitalist investment, unaccompanied by concern for its impact on peoples or bureaucratic intransigence under some forms of socialism. In the face of the unyielding power of private firms or overarching hegemony under state rule, social movements may dissipate or fade away. Furthermore, even under representative democracies, political parties may ultimately prevail through co-optation or marginalization of the new social movements.

Intellectual Shifts

If prevailing cultural patterns tend to conserve and limit transformation and if even the new social movements have not lived up to their promise of promoting rapid structural changes, then what possibilities might there be for finding satisfactory individual and collective outcomes? Long ago the sociologist Daniel Bell argued that cultural contradictions arise from the historical self-discipline and work motivation as requisites in the sphere of capitalist production. Max Weber characterized this behavior under capitalism as associated with the spirit of the Protestant "ethic." The evolving cultural patterns lead to discrepancies, gaps in knowledge, wealth, and class, and it is obvious that individual work drive and self-discipline have not evolved in a free and unified universal world culture and that instead individual preferences and self-interests undermine any collective resolution. The consequence, according to Fred Halliday (1989), is a proliferation of "particularisms," especially "pervasive racism and chauvinism," in the advanced capitalist countries; a prevalence of "nationalistic frenzy and hatred" that undermines the internationalism, fraternity, and equality of the socialist world; and "indigenous conflicts and ideological regressions" throughout the Third World (234). The conflicts emanating from these situations have cultural roots, linked in part to what Edward Said (1993) emphasized as the special cultural centrality of British, French, and U.S. imperial experience: "that imperialism invented the novel, that modernism substituted art for empire, that postmodernism is a reactionary denial that any of this ever happened" (384).

The roots of this problem are twofold: first, in global capitalism or imperialism in all its manifestations and the relationship between dominant and dominated countries; and second, in the discrepancy between state and civil society, with the state apparatuses regulating and affecting people and the civil society, which long has been portrayed as something special in American life. Michael Schudson (1998) suggested that contemporary citizens are remarkably well off. His optimistic analysis appeared when the Cold War was at an end and the economy booming at the conclusion of a decade in which legislation dismantled welfare measures and affirmative action programs while permitting a widening income gap between rich and poor.

Thus the persistent allegiances to traditional ideas and to prevailing cultural patterns shape ideas and thought. Two generations of progressive U.S. intellectuals may have been affected by these tendencies. On the one hand, the New York intellectuals of the 1930s and 1940s turned against their own ideals, renounced their leftism, withdrew from Marxism and socialism, and retreated from political activism during the Cold War. This intellectual transformation was carefully documented in a series of important books, including Alexander Bloom's *Prodigal Sons* (1986), Terry A. Cooney's *The Rise of the New York Intellectuals* (1986), and Alan M. Wald's *The New York Intellectuals* (1987). On the other hand, the New Left similarly declined after 1968; its collapse has been amply described in a number of retrospective accounts, including Gregory Nevala Calvert's *Democracy from the Heart* (1991), Todd Gitlin's *Sixties: Years of*

Hope, Days of Rage (1987), Maurice Isserman's *If I Had a Hammer* (1987), George Katsiaficas's *The Imagination of the New Left* (1987), and James Miller's *Democracy in the Streets* (1987). The historian Perry Anderson (1990) analyzed a parallel transformation of notable English progressives, with attention to ideological differences among socialist intellectuals and changing culture in Britain.

How to explain these ideological shifts? For one thing, the pervasive influences of capitalism in most societies appear to undermine efforts to find satisfactory individual and collective outcomes. For another, the fragmentation of modern culture undermines commitments to integrating culture with beneficial human activity.

One path out of this dilemma might be cultural resistance. In his *Struggle for Mozambique* (1969) Eduardo Mondlane, the leader of the independence struggle in Mozambique, described various forms of indigenous resistance to the commercial and cultural penetration of the Portuguese colonizers in East Africa. The revolutionary leader of the liberation struggle in Guinea-Bissau, Amílcar Cabral, in his *Unity and Struggle* (1979) showed how the armed revolutionary struggle emanates from culture based on history and the successes of resistance and struggle. The new song movement of Latin America combined dynamic music with revolutionary lyrics aimed at eradicating imperial cultural influences in the brief interlude of a socialist government under Salvador Allende in Chile from 1970 to 1973, and it was evident in the revolutionary struggles in El Salvador and Nicaragua during the 1980s.

These examples illustrate how people deal with domination and power over their lives. The question was taken up by James Scott in *Weapons of the Weak* (1986), with attention to how peasants engage in everyday forms of resistance (sabotage, arson, defiance, and so on) that lead to collective protest. He illustrated with examples to suggest that economically subordinate groups may resort to everyday resistance to power and dominance. Given their structurally disadvantageous positions in society, their defiance may challenge the dominant classes or ruling governments through coordinated direct efforts (strikes, demonstrations, land seizures, riots, rebellions, and so on) to change or reform conditions.

Fredric Jameson alluded to the fragility of this resistance, however, and questioned the perception that modernism is vanishing in a world of ever-dominant capitalism. He affirmed that even cultural resistance can succumb to the capitalist system: "Not only punctual and local countercultural forms of cultural resistance and guerrilla warfare but also even overt political interventions . . . are somehow secretly disarmed and reabsorbed by a system of which they themselves might be considered a part, since they can achieve no distance from it" (1991: 49).

Culture and Socialist Experiences

The treatment of culture in Marxist analysis relates to the level of the superstructure, the ideology, the legal system, and agencies in the state and the political arena, not to the mode of production, forces of production, or social relations of production that prevail at the material base or infrastructure of society. Culture usually reflects the preferences and drives of capitalist society, and therefore is seen as a negative influence and often ignored in Marxist understandings. Culture, however, is found in every society, and it is important to understand its implications for socialist experiences as well as to compare culture under both capitalism and socialism.

Three models of social organization and ideological and cultural formation help in this comparison, according to Samir Amin (1977b). First is the North American example, rooted in the capitalist formation and ideology of Europe with its tradition of "mechanistic materialism" that assumes science and technology will diffuse into every aspect of social life and transform social relations for a more harmonious society. The problem here, according to Amin, is that "bourgeois" science has been unable to transcend the level of primitive materialism because it conditions the reproduction of alienation and allows capital to exploit labor. Second is the former Soviet model, which shares with the North American model the notion that consumption, technology, and labor derive from the development of the productive forces; but socialism distinguishes itself through its relationship to the public ownership whereas capitalism relates to private ownership of the means of production. Third is the Chinese model, which in contrast did not initially anticipate that socialism could take over capitalism's patterns of consumption and labor. Each of these models represents a different cultural sphere and economic orientation. Applying such terms as materialism and idealism to class struggle furthers a comparison of these models, since class struggle shapes the relations of production, makes possible the development of productive forces, and alters the relationship of the base to the superstructure. In other words, under socialism rather than capitalism a conscious, nonalienated, and classless society may eventually appear.

Given these relationships, culture might imply a struggle against bourgeois (capitalist) ideology, art, and philosophy. Lenin understood culture as class culture, created in the image of the ruling capitalist class. In capitalism, he argued, the bourgeoisie uses culture to increase its wealth and to intensify the exploitation of those who work. In imperialism, bourgeois culture undergoes decay, and the cultural level of the population declines. In socialism, culture is directed toward the satisfaction of the needs of the popular masses. Thus Lenin saw culture as generated, on the one hand, in a democratic and socialist culture, of the mass of working and exploited people and, on the other, in the ruling culture of the bourgeoisie. Lenin developed his conception of class culture in the early years of the Russian Revolution; his theme was elaborated by Charles Bettelheim (1976). Stalin modified Lenin's conception by giving attention to the national traditions and the many nationalities in the Soviet Union. He developed a theory of nations that attacked reformist nationalism, for instance, with its tendency to substitute national for revolutionary aims. He set forth a theory of national minorities, identifying an ethnic group as a national minority if it did not possess the characteristics of a nation.

This brief mention of the theories of Lenin and Stalin may further an understanding of various perspectives on national culture, from the melting-pot notion whereby immigrants lose their original nationality identification and become ethnic minorities in the new nation to the idea that the conditions of national assimilation are giving way to an increased imperialist exploitation and oppression of workers in a colony. James Blaut (1977) used the case of Puerto Rico to illustrate this latter situation, drawing his analysis from the differing theories of Lenin and Stalin. He showed how Stalin's theory of national minorities did not pertain to colonies, which Lenin incorporated into his theory of imperialism. He favored Lenin's approach because the theory of imperialism includes all nations under contemporary capitalism, whereas the theory of national minorities was useful for describing an early period of rising capitalism in Europe.

The shaping of a socialist culture depends on changes in education and ideology. The cases of the Soviet Union, China, and Cuba may be instructive in this regard. Studies of early Russian childhood experience reveal various approaches (Clawson, 1973). Among early perspectives in the revolution were the views that children should be separated from the conservative prerevolutionary milieu of the average family; that the system of child rearing and education prior to the revolution should be retained; and that there should be freedom for individual youth to develop according to personal motivations. During the early years of the revolution (1917–1921), a period characterized as "decentralized experimentation," Lenin and the Soviet leadership hesitated to intervene in education. From 1921 to 1932 education centered on liberating the individual child and lessening competition between individuals. Thereafter, from 1932 to 1936, experimentation was abolished and a traditional approach of formal curriculum, exams, grades, and disciplines was implemented. From 1936 to 1964 there was official recognition of the family experience for the child. Thereafter Soviet education specialists recognized the ineffectiveness of deliberate political socialization during early childhood and stressed the role of the family as the primary socialization agent. After that there was no substantial change in Soviet policy toward family and education, but some writers in the Soviet Union and Eastern Europe turned their attention to the individual and the meaning of life in a collective socialist society. In the *Economic and Philosophical Manuscripts* (1944), Marx focused on this question by exploring the implications of the alienated worker under capitalism. This early work was influential among intellectuals such as Adam Schaff of Poland, who in his *Marxism and the Human Individual* (1970) argued that Marxism is radical humanism, autonomous in the sense that the individual creates his or her own development and struggles in revolutionary ways against the dehumanization of life.

This concern with the individual and the struggle for a radical humanism, especially in the revolutionary experiences of China and Cuba, gave rise to the theory of the new person. When the Chinese revolutionaries came to power in 1949 under Mao Zedong, although the leadership initially was influenced by the Stalinist orthodoxy and the Soviet model of heavy industrialization, the vast majority of the population lived in the countryside, and the goal of Chinese socialism was to raise the material level of the population. But it also aimed to promote the development of human beings on an egalitarian basis. An important Maoist thesis placed value on breaking down specialization, dismantling bureaucracies, and undermining centralizing and divisive tendencies. The economist John Gurley described this as culminating in the emergence of the new person shaped by

> The proletarian world view, which Maoists believe must replace that of the bourgeoisie, stresses that only through struggle can progress be made; [that] selflessness and unity of purpose will release a huge reservoir of enthusiasm, energy, and creativeness; that active participation by the "masses" in decision-making will provide them with the knowledge to channel their energy most productively; and that elimination of specialization will not only increase workers' and peasants' willingness to work hard for the various goals of society but will also increase their ability to do this by adding to their knowledge and awareness of the world around them (1971: 19).

The revolutionary successes and failures mitigated against these lofty ideals. Once in power, the Chinese revolution evolved from overturning the old feudal order through a phase of some thirty years of political consolidation and hard work. A period of reforms and the building of a socialist market economy during the 1990s was accompanied by unevenness and distinction among high party cadres of ministers and other important officials, middle-cadre leaders, and low-level militants. The class nature of Chinese society increasingly was discernible in bureaucrats, new capitalists, affluent agrarian middle-size and big capitalist farmers, the mass of subsistence peasant farmers, workers, and small merchants, together with an emerging petty bourgeoisie of small venders in urban areas. These differences were playing out through an extraordinary development process. Whether it evolved toward capitalism or socialism depended on the commitment of a divided leadership in the Communist party, and although many observers characterized it as capitalist oriented, it was too early to dismiss the socialist implications of what was happening in China. Despite the repressive crackdown on the June 1989 demonstrations and obvious problems caused by the disruptive and rapidly changing economy, what occurred in China stood in stark contrast both to the dismal failure of capitalism to solve the problems of poor nations everywhere and to socialist failures not only in Eastern Europe and the former Soviet Union but in the Third World.

Substantial changes were also occurring in Cuba, where the revolution triumphed in 1959 under the leadership of Fidel Castro and Che Guevara. Guevara (1967) emphasized individual sacrifice in a collective society: "It is rather that the individual feels greater fulfillment, that he has a greater inner wealth and many more responsibilities. In our country the individual knows that the glorious period in which it has fallen to him to live is one of sacrifice" (42). His vision incorporated sacrifice overcoming feelings of individualism and emphasis on solidarity among the people. The political being must be socially responsible, devoid of selfishness and egotism. The new person must work for the benefit of the collectivity and struggle against injustice and the exploitation of person by person and the division of society into classes.

Early in the revolution alienation diminished with the emphasis on changing patterns of consumption. All persons who so desired were given opportunity to work. At the same time basic necessities were provided to ensure at least a minimally sufficient material standard of living. Emphasis on moral rather than material incentives accompanied the changing consumption. Workers would contribute to the development of the revolution rather than to their own personal gain. The work ethic would be to serve society not the individual.

These ideals of the new person were assimilated into efforts to reshape Cuban political culture. A massive campaign by students and workers resolved the problem of adult illiteracy in 1961. Education encouraged workers to aspire to a conscious commitment to the revolution and to mix education in the schools with work on farms. Cuba sought to become one encompassing school, with individuals trained in the necessary skills and conscious awareness relevant to becoming new persons (Fagen, 1969).

Cuba demonstrated remarkable progress in education, as attested in a study by Sheryl Lutjens (1996), a specialist on Cuban education and bureaucracy, who showed that despite some decentralization through various participatory opportunities, centralization remains problematic in the seeking of socialist democracy. After losing its former trading partners in the breakup of the former Soviet Union and Eastern Europe, Cuba relied on innovative and creative ways, including an opening to outside capital and its contradictions. Thus Cuba's evolving political culture has been shaped by a mixture of moralism and idealism, loyalty and commitment, and the assimilating of traditional values and revolutionary ideals. The Cuban scholars Rafael Hernández and Haroldo Dilla (1992) referred to "a new civility" and to "a participatory political culture" shaped by historical experience, with more than three decades of revolution and involvement by an ideologically diverse citizenship striving for change despite a continuing U.S. embargo and radically altered relations with Russia and Eastern Europe.

PROSPECTS FOR CULTURE THEORY

Mainstream theories of political culture remain influential. Indeed in recent years there has been renewed interest among political scientists and political economists, with the term continuing to be used rather loosely in describing the cultural implications of politics in nations around the world. The problem is that the underlying mainstream emphasis on ideal rather than real situations emanates from the Anglo-American experience and such notions as civic virtue, pluralism, liberal democracy, rational bureaucratic practices, and stability. The ambitious effort to identify comparative cultural patterns in the civic cultural studies yielded descriptive data about political life that were relatively well understood. The specific attention to communications and socialization studies was mostly wrapped in case situations, usually focused on childhood and adolescent learning in stable and representative democratic societies. Mainstream contributions thus are limited, both in promise and results.

Alternative theory and approaches confirm the relevance of studying culture and politics and have been mostly effective in exposing the biases and weaknesses of mainstream contributions. Particular attention to the ties of culture to capitalism and the way in which alienation, consumption patterns, and work incentives affect the majority of people has yielded interesting analysis. The new social movements served to challenge traditional institutions. Likewise, the idea of the new person under socialism is both provocative and challenging in its idealized form, although in fact there has been no real and meaningful experience verifying its possibility. Figure 5.1 identifies these trends and contrasts the major ideas in cultural studies at the macro or micro levels in mainstream and alternative approaches. The reader is encouraged to explore the literature in more depth, both to comprehend the cultural constraints of capitalist society and to elaborate a theory of how culture can be a means for confronting alienation or achieving selflessness, commitment, and creativity in the society at large.

FIGURE 5.1   Cultural Preferences

	Individual (Micro)	Collective (Macro)
Mainstream Perspectives (Anglo-American Model)		

(Capitalist)	Socialization through,
	   family, job, school
		Civic Culture
		   based on individual
		   and group interest

(Weberian)	Values of:
	   civic virtue
	   liberal pluralism
	   rational self-interest
	   materialism
		Values of:
		   capitalist base and
		   ruling class
		   bourgeois world-
		   view

	Outcomes of:
	   alienation
	   false consciousness
		Outcomes of:
		   parochial, subject,
		   and participatory

Alternative Perspectives		
(Socialist)	Rational-choice Marxism	New social movements
(Marxist)	Morally based	Classless society
	Humanist	Proletarian worldview
Worldview		
	Resistant to outside culture New person as selfless	

6

THE ECONOMIC DIMENSION

CAPITALIST AND SOCIALIST DEVELOPMENT

This chapter conceptualizes development and identifies fundamental characteristics of both capitalist and socialist development. It sketches major historical understandings of how development has affected peoples through time, initially in the era before capitalism; during the rise of merchant capital; and on to industrialization, the impact of imperialism and colonialism, the consequences of backwardness and underdevelopment, and moments of resistance and revolutionary experiences. It also traces various theoretical directions so that students of development may begin to sort out lines of thinking in the array of developmental ideas, strategies, and policies evident especially since the Second World War.

CONCEPTUALIZING DEVELOPMENT

A general definition of **development** might begin with the proposition that in any particular society the basic needs of all people should be resolved. In a broad sense this might imply such human needs as survival, belongingness, and leisure. The proposition, however, implies a more fundamental level. Evidently it is problematic whether capitalist societies can meet such basic needs as health, food, shelter, education, and employment.

At the level of politics, the formal representative character of many capitalist societies and some socialist societies usually is viewed as a step toward development. Yet in capitalist societies large numbers of people often absent themselves from the electoral process, political participation is minimal, and grassroots political involvement may be dwarfed by electoral campaigns influenced by moneyed interests and big capital. Although socialist societies generally have been able to deal with basic human needs through the socialization of most means of production and planned distribution of resources, they generally have failed to establish either effective representative or participatory democracies. Yet development oriented toward the welfare of all classes, groups, and individuals along with democratic means are essential in the face of international trade policies, capital movements, and flows of labor.

Capitalist and socialist systems relate to this proposition about human development in different ways. **Primitive accumulation** is a starting point in capitalism, where the producers or laborers are separated from the means of production. **Accumulation** under capitalism underlies the economic base, generating a deep-rooted division of labor, social class distinctions, and income gaps between rich and poor. Accumulation may occur under both competitive and **monopoly capitalism**, with the market as a determinant for the production of commodities. Accumulation also takes place in socialism, where the state and state workers usually coordinate the economy through central planning. Experience shows that socialist systems have generally provided for the basic human needs of their peoples, for example food and shelter, health, education, and welfare, and social democratic regimes in industrialized European countries also have looked out for the needs of a large portion of their populations. The problem remains how to combine these forms of economic and social development with the opening of space for citizens to participate in political and economic matters affecting their livelihood. A combination of representative and participatory forms could be employed, but also there is a need to deal with bureaucracy and the hegemonic role of the state. For example, bureaucracies need not be organized along hierarchical lines, and participatory forms can be integrated with administrative activities. Furthermore, central planning can be controlled by institutionalized democratic structures, and popularly elected governments could oversee planning.

The fashionable term these days is **sustainable development**. It partially relates to providing for basic human needs, but its meaning is diffuse and vague. In either capitalist or socialist economies sustainable development implies the enhancement of the quality of life of contemporary peoples without degrading nature and the ecosystem and impairing the welfare of future generations. Development must be designed for the human being to satisfy basic needs while protecting the environment on a global scale. At the same time there must be recognition that capitalist development usually leads to an increase in the numbers of poor and vulnerable people while degrading the environment.

Mainstream perspectives tend to suffer from a weak theoretical framework, including an incomplete perception of poverty and environmental degradation and a misunderstanding of the role of economic growth and participation. Sustainable development must not depend solely on economic growth as the means to eliminating poverty. Structural, technological, and cultural causes of poverty must be weighed in assessing the compatibility of resources and ecological and environmental protection and sustainability. The reports of the World Commission on Environment and Development and the Worldwatch Institute's annual state of the world reports reflect these concerns. Economic development must not lead to depletion of natural resources and environmental degradation. The struggle to overcome poverty and inequalities must be combined with protection of the earth, a problem for both industrial and less developed countries.

Individual countries must assert their particular preferences in a world that may be characterized in confusing and different ways. Since the late eighteenth century that world has been known as "imperialist," in line with theories and interpretations about dominant core nations and their devastating impact on peripheral areas of the world. More recent understandings see the world as "globalized," and "interdependent," globalized being a fashionable characterization of contemporary world capital alongside the distorted impression that somehow unequal relationships among nations are being mitigated, and interdependent referring to an emerging balance in relations between strong and weak nations and the mistaken assumption that dependency is withering away.

This discussion suggests that development is economic and political as well as social. Figure 6.1 compares and contrasts economic, social, and political dimensions of development according to a preference for capitalism or socialism. The orientations of these two systems are generally known, but their identification here may be helpful for recognizing that

FIGURE 6.1   Dimensions of Development

Dimensions	Capitalism	Socialism
Economic	Monopoly capital and state through capitalist market	State planning and state bureaucrats through socialist market
Social Needs	Basic services through welfare reforms in advanced industrial societies	Basic human needs and egalitarianism
Political	Bourgeois representative formal and indirect democracy	Participatory, informal, and direct democracy

particular objectives and desires tend to shape a developmental process with varying orientations.

THE HISTORICAL EVOLUTION OF CAPITALIST AND SOCIALIST DEVELOPMENT

In primitive classless societies people participated collectively in decisions affecting life in the community and the outside world. People struggled to survive the forces of nature and their generally poor living conditions. One of the first divisions of labor occurred in ancient times with the appearance of towns and professional artisans who engaged in the production of commodities that they exchanged freely and more or less equally in the market for products they immediately needed. Another division of labor took place with the introduction of money and the appearance of the usurer or merchant specializing in international commerce. Mercantilism was an elementary form of capitalism; it was characterized by social relations in which the owners of capital appropriated the surplus value produced by workers. Merchant capital was especially conspicuous in Western Europe during the fourteenth to the sixteenth centuries. Modern capitalism was characterized by a clear separation of producers from their means of production and subsistence, the formation of a class—the bourgeoisie—that owns and controls those means of production, and the appearance of a class—the proletariat—that owns only its labor and must sell this to the owners of the means of production in order to survive.

Until the late nineteenth century, capitalism was usually characterized by "free" competition, but about that time technology spawned new industries and capitalists began to form cartels, trusts, and holding companies. A concentration of **finance capital** (bank capital that penetrates and dominates industry) resulted in a decline of **competitive capitalism** and the growth of monopolies. Lenin characterized this period as imperialism, or the highest stage of capitalism. The era of imperialism was driven by the large industrial monopolies and the export of capital from the advanced nations to less developed regions of the world. This era comprised a "classical" phase, from the late nineteenth century to the end of the Second World War, and a "late" phase thereafter. Whereas the monopoly was prominent in the classical phase, the multinational firm was conspicuous in the late phase.

Socialism implies collective, rather than private, ownership of the major means of production and appropriation of the social surplus product (the production of workers beyond their requirements for subsistence). In the transition period from capitalism to socialism, remnants of capitalism are evident: Labor power continues to be sold for wages, some surplus product is appropriated as individual privileges, and a money economy prevails. The new economy may also be managed by bureaucratic elements uncommitted to the principle of political and economic participation by all the people, and private rather than public interest may be a motivating force. The shift from a capitalist mode of production toward a collective mode is apparent only with the overcoming of these tendencies. The struggle for socialism aims to replace the capitalist state with the workers' state and to substitute proletarian (worker) democracy for bourgeois (capitalist) democracy. The provision for the basic needs of all the people, usually under a planned economy with widespread popular participation in decisionmaking, becomes a priority, along with such goals as the elimination of a commodity and money economy, inequality, classes, the state, and alienated labor and their replacement with the creative use of work and leisure. The achievement of these goals would lead to communism, a higher stage of socialism.

This path to socialism and communism involves changes in the state. The state evolved historically as functions once performed by all the people in primitive, classless societies were assumed by separate groups of people, for instance, police and soldiers, judges, and hereditary rulers who took over ordinary citizens' tasks of arming and protecting themselves, judging their equals, and delegating responsibilities to others for particular activities. These groups exploited and profited from the work of the people over whom they ruled. Marx and Engels in *Manifesto of the Communist Party* implied that the state is the instrument of the ruling classes, and Lenin in *State and Revolution* argued that the police and standing army were instruments of state power against which the people should struggle until the state disappeared altogether.

Imperialism and Colonialism

Imperialism derives from the Latin word *imperator*, which connoted autocratic power and centralized government. In ancient history the notion of empire dates to the Egyptians, Greeks, and Romans and later to the Arabs. Roman imperialism reinforced the traditional local ruling hierarchies as their power extended across Europe. Modern imperialism generated a new basis of power among subject populations; for example, it was associated with sympathizers of the Napoleonic empire, and after 1848 the term was used pejoratively to describe the pretensions of Napoleon Bonaparte. During the 1870s it was employed as a characterization of the practices of expanding British colonialism, and by the end of the century it was commonplace in descriptions of the dominance of one nation over another.

A traditional, or "old," meaning of imperialism was tied to mercantile capitalism and the early phase of industrial capitalism, from 1650 to 1770, characterized by European countries exploiting the resources of peripheral areas, such as gold and silver in the Americas. It also was associated with the era of slave labor and the search for commodities that would benefit England, Spain, and the leading European powers. It was important from the 1770s to 1870s, when England sought new markets in Africa and Asia after losing most of its American colonies.

The traditional explanation of the Western experience of empire, **colonialism**, and mercantilism can be illustrated in more detail. From about 1500 to 1800 Spain dominated with its control of precious metals in South America; to a lesser extent Portugal exerted control through its major commercial contacts in Africa, Asia, and Brazil and its trade in spices, slaves, and ivory. Portuguese hegemony declined during the late sixteenth and early seventeenth centuries when Portugal was unified with Spain under Spanish control. As Spain and Portugal lost control over maritime traffic, the Dutch, then the English, and ultimately the French expanded their influence and slaves moved from Africa to the Americas, sugar from the Americas to Europe, and manufactured goods from Europe to Africa. European influence expanded throughout the eighteenth century and, especially in Asia and in Africa, during the nineteenth century. About the year 1800 the mercantile period was distinguishable from the emerging classical epoch of capital development as Great Britain emerged as the dominant colonial power, with India as the crucial link in its empire. The industrial revolution served as the underpinning of a new era in which mechanized production and the abolition of poverty appeared as possibilities.

This "old" meaning of imperialism was supplanted by an understanding of the "new" imperialism, usually referring to the intense rivalry of the advanced European nations. The era of the new imperialism, known also as the industrial transformation, was associated with the industrial revolution and, in particular, with the rise of European manufacturing along with demand for raw materials from the periphery and the need to find markets abroad to alleviate a surplus of production at home. Great Britain led the way in this era with its dominance over world markets and its access to raw materials through its vast network of colonies, enhanced in the late nineteenth century by the scramble for territory in Africa after the Berlin Conference of 1885. As a consequence of British imperialism, along with U.S. expansion at the end of the nineteenth century, the world was conditioned by a division of labor between primary producing underdeveloped states and industrialized states, export capital from Europe, and the dominance of the large firm as an accumulator of capital.

Backwardness and Underdevelopment

Most of the developmental literature emanating from Western Europe and the industrial nations has emphasized the prospects for industrializa-

tion and modernization of the forces of production in a universal drive toward advanced forms of capitalism. After the Second World War it became apparent that the anticipated progress had not materialized in the
newly emerging nations of Africa, Asia, and Latin America. Both traditional historians and progressive theoreticians insisted that this failure
was generally attributable to feudalism or semifeudalism, conditions implanted after the conquest of outlying areas and their colonization during
the sixteenth and seventeenth centuries. At the time of the discovery of
the Americas, for example, Spain and Portugal were emerging from the
feudalism of the Middle Ages, and the institutions implanted in Latin
America were similar to those in the homeland. Furthermore, capitalism
had not yet diffused into these areas and allowed them to modernize as
most of Western Europe had done. Many critics identify this perspective
as Eurocentric and biased toward the Western experience of industrialized nations.

After the Second World War intellectuals in the outlying areas of Africa,
Asia, and Latin America challenged some of the prevailing assumptions.
The imperial networks established by Great Britain, France, Holland,
Portugal, and Spain had begun to collapse, and as colonies gained inde-
pendence the less developed new and old nations of Africa, Asia, and
Latin America became politically identifiable as the Third World.

Sentiment against the imperialism of the industrial nations produced
new theoretical formulations. Argentine and Brazilian scholars were especially important in elaborating an alternative view to modernization,
and brief mention of their contributions provides a context for understanding **underdevelopment** and **dependency**. Perhaps the best known
was the Argentine economist Raúl Prebisch, who was involved in the formation of the Economic Commission for Latin America (ECLA) and initially served as its director. ECLA offered a view that divided the world
into two parts, a center of industrialized countries and a periphery of
underdeveloped countries. It advocated an autonomous capitalism
premised on tariff protection against high-cost imports and the building
of an infrastructure of resources and promotion of industrialization in the
outlying countries. These ideas leaned toward a strong state role in the
promotion of development and the implementation of what became
known as import substitution industrialization (ISI). Although the legacy
carries on in the 1990s, ISI has faded away and ECLA has adapted its outlook to accommodate the widespread neoliberal tendency to trim the
state and privatize the public sector.

Another direction evolved through the analysis of the Argentine law
professor Silvio Frondizi and the historian Sérgio Bagú, who set forth
early ideas fundamental to an emerging understanding of underdevelopment and dependency. Frondizi emphasized the contradictions between

two imperialisms: British commercial imperialism and U.S. industrial imperialism. Both he and Bagú, along with the Brazilian historian Caio Prado Júnior, examined the negative influences of capitalism during the colonial period. They provided early understanding of what became known as the **new dependency,** brought about by multinational industrial capital, the latest of several historical phases (the others being **colonial dependency** and **financial-industrial dependency**) identified by the Brazilian political economist Theotônio dos Santos. Finally, the economist Celso Furtado explained how capitalism brought prosperity and then depression to the Brazilian Northeast, in a case study of how capital can exploit resources and bring about underdevelopment and immiseration.

These perspectives were shared by the economists Paul Baran and André Gunder Frank, Europeans whose thought became influential in the Third World. In *The Political Economy of Growth* (1957), Baran conceptualized the term **backwardness** and demonstrated the dependent relationship of the underdeveloped parts of the world. Influenced by Baran and aware of Latin American sentiments about these questions, Frank hypothesized in his *Capitalism and Underdevelopment in Latin America* (1967) that capitalism in the dominant "metropoles," or core countries, had promoted the underdevelopment of the outlying dependent "satellites," or less developed countries.

Resistance and Revolutionary Experiences

In his classic *Primitive Rebels* (1959), the historian Eric Hobsbawm identified a variety of cases of primitive or archaic forms of social agitation in Europe, including social banditry, rural secret societies, peasant revolutionary and millenarian movements, religious sects, and early labor and revolutionary organizations. His rudimentary classification of these movements and identification of activity previously thought of as anomic, spontaneous, and insignificant in history stimulated attention to questions of protest and resistance. In a pioneering effort to turn back and reassess such movements, my colleagues and I in *Protest and Resistance in Angola and Brazil* (1972) delved into particular case studies in the Portuguese-speaking world. In these studies, **protest** was manifested in a variety of ways: as complaint; objection; disapproval; or display of unwillingness to accept an idea, course of action, or social condition. Protest involved the active desire for change, perhaps the consequence of environmental devastation, exposure to material conditions giving rise to anticipation of a better life, or frustrations when expectations are not satisfied. Protest may be a response to institutional failure to accommodate immediate demands or to suppression, exploitation, or rejection. **Resistance** is intimately related to protest on an individual or collective level. It may be the reaction of a segment of a population to certain environmental (for example, pollution), economic (poverty), or social (exploitation) conditions, and it may evolve into an organized mobilization aimed at mitigating those conditions. Under **colonialism**, indigenous populations manifested resistance to outside intervention in the form of conquest, control of trade, extraction of resources, or abduction of people as slaves. Sometimes resistance was manifested through voluntary religious organizations, for example, syncretist movements that fused indigenous and colonial religions into a faith with political overtones. Resistance usually implied defense of indigenous traditions, and sometimes it evolved into an embryonic stage of nationalism.

Protest and resistance relate to physical and human conditions. For example, prolonged drought or floods may provoke a popular response to those in power. Peasants in Northeast Brazil may invade warehouses of foodstuffs to overcome hunger and misery, but their actions may also lead to political consequences such as the ousting of inattentive authorities. People who understand they have no participatory role in decisions that shape their lives may share feelings of exploitation and oppression and eventually rebel against established authority. The possibility of conflict thus evolves around fundamental disagreements over values in society, whether between economic and social classes, religious sects, ethnic groups, ideologies, or even geographical regions.

Often examples of protest and resistance are ignored and treated by others as a series of episodes unrelated to history. Historians frequently minimize such episodes or identify them as marginal or unimportant phenomena, probably because they differ from more commonly known social movements. The people comprising these movements may be illiterate or known only to their friends; they may appear as inarticulate or unable to express their aspirations about the world they have only known as long dominated by a system of rulers, soldiers, police, tax collectors, and the like, all of whom they distrust and despise. Sometimes they are unable to satisfy their basic needs through protest and resistance and resort to revolutionary methods.

Revolution thus may evolve through a protest movement or moment in time. The so-called Republic of Palmares, founded by runaway black slaves in the interior of Brazil in the seventeenth century, was both a reaction to their exploitation and an effort to find autonomy. It changed their conditions and allowed them to establish a lifestyle probably similar to that in their homeland Africa, but ultimately it succumbed to the will of the dominant society. Members of the Canudos movement of the mystic Antonio the Counselor similarly sought refuge in the Brazilian hinterland but succumbed to the force of authority after several years of resistance and struggle in the 1890s. The anarchist, communist, and socialist movements that emerged in republican Spain all sought revolutionary alternatives but ultimately fell to the fascist forces under General Franco during the civil war of the late 1930s. The popular movement under the Chilean president Salvador Allende that came to power through elections in 1970 eventually was crushed by the right-wing military.

These movements all failed for various reasons. A deeply successful revolution likely emanates from a movement and leadership with a vision of future society tied up in a selfless pursuit of confronting social and economic problems, allowing widespread participatory practice in politics, and meeting the basic needs of all people. Such elements appeared in the early Bolshevik experience during and immediately after the Russian Revolution. They were evident in the concept of the new man in the early years of the Chinese revolutionary success under Mao Zedong and under Che Guevara during the Cuban insurrection and the successful coming to power of the revolutionaries in 1959. They appeared in the vision of Amílcar Cabral, a contemporary of Mao and Guevara who established himself as a significant revolutionary thinker and whose thought and organization served to mobilize a successful revolutionary struggle against Portuguese colonial rule in Africa.

THEORETICAL DIRECTIONS

The evolution and spread of capitalism worldwide has shaped the growing disparity between the advancing industrial nations at the core of the international capitalist system and the undeveloped and underdeveloped backward nations at the periphery. Explanations of this disparity have absorbed the attention of many thinkers from Marx to the present day, but identification and brief discussion of various currents in the literature on development and underdevelopment may be helpful. The following discussion, therefore, first examines traditional and classical sources of imperialist theory, from Marx to Hobson, Hilferding, Lenin, Luxemburg, Bukharin, and Schumpeter. Second, the discussion builds on imperialism theory as a foundation for understanding different theoretical directions in the literature on underdevelopment and development that emerged generally after 1945 in an era characterized variously as late capitalism, the new dependency, and dependent capitalist development.

Theories of Imperialism

Marx elaborated a theory of capitalism and its development, but it is unclear whether he was concerned with a theory of imperialism, since he did not use the term; nor did later Marxist writers base their understandings of imperialism on Marx's writings on colonies (Brewer, 1990: 25).

Marx and Engels in *Manifesto of the Communist Party* (1848) came close to a conception of imperialism in their reference to the need of the bourgeoisie to search for a constantly expanding international market: "It must nestle everywhere, settle everywhere, establish connections everywhere . . . In place of the old local and national seclusion and self-sufficiency, we have intercourse in every direction, universal inter-dependence of nations" (Marx and Engels, 1848/1958, 1: 37).

Ideas of imperialism became commonplace with the breakup of Africa into colonies toward the end of the nineteenth century. In their criticisms of imperialism, the major thinkers viewed it in political and economic terms. Two camps emerged in the debates on the political economy of imperialism. On the one hand, V. I. Lenin, influenced by the English liberal J. A. Hobson and sharing with Rudolf Hilferding and Nikolai Bukharin what has become characterized as a classical Marxist understanding of imperialism, emphasized the merger of industrial and bank capital into finance capital, the expansion of capital exports, and the increase in military production and militarism. Largely inspired by the European experience, these classical Marxists believed that a socialist revolution would eventually resolve the contradictions. They concentrated on the advanced rather than backward countries, and they tended to revise the understandings of Marx. The other camp emphasized political aspects such as conflict and rivalry that were to diminish in the face of the growing impact of capitalism around the world. Hobson, Karl Kautsky, and Joseph Schumpeter envisaged that an ever-developing capitalism eventually would transcend the drive of imperialism and bring peace to the world. Figure 6.2 provides a sketch of these differences, and the ensuing discussion delves briefly into the principal ideas of these thinkers.

In his major book, *Imperialism* (1902/1965), Hobson dated British imperialism to the period 1870–1885 with the partition of African lands and the acquisition of vast territory. He briefly examined German, U.S., French, Italian, Portuguese, Spanish, Belgian, and Russian imperial designs. He characterized the new imperialism as distinct from the situation in the sparsely peopled lands of temperate zones where white colonists carried with them the civilization of the mother country. He probed into commercial imperialism and argued for the expansion of the home market, believing that the loss of foreign markets would be less significant than expected. In developing this thesis of **underconsumption,** or oversaving, Hobson wished to discredit some of the then-current theories of why a nation-state such as Great Britain should pursue imperialist policies. He employed aggregate economic and demographic statistics to demonstrate that imperialism was economically inefficient. He argued that there was no economic justification for the high costs associated with sealing off a conquered region from other imperialist interventions.

FIGURE 6.2   Theories of Imperialism

Theorist	Theory Emphasis	Strengths	Weaknesses
Hobson	Domestic under-consumption	Focused on financiers	Descriptive, lacking analysis
Hilferding	Finance capital	Thorough analysis of joint stock companies, major marxist contribution to a theory of imperialism	Dated analyis, perhaps exaggerated emphasis on role of banks
Luxemburg	Capital accumulation and penetration in primitive societies	Anticipated negative impact of capitalism on noncapitalist nations	Undue attention to under-consumption rather than profit, Bukharin labels her "voluntarist"
Bukharin	Monopolies of banks and corporations in advanced stages of capitalism	Combined analysis of internationaliza-tion of capitalist relations of production with formations of blocs of finance capital	Stressed the contradictions of capitalist modernization process rather than its imperfect and uneven development
Lenin	Imperialism as monopoly and highest stage of capitalism	Clearly articulated conception	Eclectic, polemical, and political emphasis
Kautsky	Peaceful resolution by capitalist class	Advocated theory of ultra-imperialism	Optimism on progressive nature of capitalism
Schumpeter	Withering away of imperialism	Provided a historical context to show imperialism based on interests of ruling classes	Misguided emphasis on political imperialism as well as the demise of imperialism

Rudolf Hilferding concentrated on the centers of **finance capital** in the advanced industrial countries, but he also examined their impact on less developed areas of the world. He understood that capitalist expansion, based on the export of capital, was accompanied by force. As capital spreads into precapitalist societies, it destroys the old social relations. He believed that the penetration of capital into the less developed nations could be beneficial, especially in the early stage of building infrastructure, but if this capital was directed to the extraction of raw materials for export to the industrialized world there could be a drain of profit abroad, resulting in economic and political dependence. In *Finance Capital* (1910) he elaborated on the collusion of industrial and financial capital in a new form of capital mobilized through banks and extended to large enterprises in exchange for shares of stock. He identified three stages in the history of capitalism: an incipient phase of usurer capital, a classical phase of industrial capital, and a phase of finance capital. Monopoly capital and a shift from competitive to cartel industries characterized this last phase. The pursuit of imperialism is inevitable, he argued, as finance capital seeks to exploit outlying areas.

Rosa Luxemburg, a Polish Marxist whose later years were devoted to German socialism, elaborated a theory of imperialism in an effort to explain continuous capital accumulation. A central concern was the examination of capital penetration into primitive economies. She identified three phases of capital accumulation: first, the clash of capital with the natural economy in areas where there are primitive peasant communities and a common ownership of land or a feudal system; second, the capitalist struggles with a commodity economy; and third, the rise of imperialism. Luxemburg understood imperialism as the conversion of surplus into capital and its spread throughout the world economy, and she was interested in situations where accumulation is arrested and capitalism tends to collapse. In *The Accumulation of Capital* (1913), Luxemburg drew on Marx for an analysis of imperialism and capital accumulation. In this and other works she provided us with a rich discussion of the relation between the state and capital and between militarism and racism, providing a deeper analysis than that brought out earlier by Hobson. She also focused on finance capital. Most important, she examined the manner in which capitalism is thrust on noncapitalist nations and anticipated by decades the need for modern students of development to look at imperial relations. Rather than focus on advanced forms of industrialization, her analysis turned to those societies that were not being incorporated in the capitalist mode of production.

In 1915 Bukharin wrote the bulk of his *Imperialism and World Economy*, for which Lenin wrote a preface apparently a few months before writing his own treatise of imperialism. Bukharin's writing on the subject was not particularly original, but it succeeded in coherently presenting theory with evidence. He closely followed the argument of Hilferding, in particular elaborating on the organization of capital on a national level where the overcoming of competition would be simpler than on a world scale. Finally, Bukharin envisaged imperialism as an advanced stage of capitalism in the world economy. He argued that the world economy comprises a system of production and exchange relations on a world scale. Exchange relations were a primitive form, whereas trusts and cartels represented the highest form of capitalist organization at the international level. Uneven development reflected differences in the productive forces of various countries, but a rapid development of the productive forces of world capitalism had accounted for the expansion of the world economy since the end of the nineteenth century. This expansion accompanied new economic formations, particularly capitalist monopoly organizations such as trusts and cartels and the banks that finance them. Banking capital would transform into industrial capital to become finance capital, and capitalist monopolies would transcend national boundaries, resulting in a consolidation of developed powers at the center and undeveloped countries in the periphery. National capitalism, Bukharin believed, seeks expansion into three spheres of the world economy: markets for the sale of commodities, markets for raw materials, and capital investment. The result is capitalist expansion and imperialism.

Lenin acknowledged his debt to Hobson, whom he characterized as a bourgeois social reformer. He also drew on Hilferding's understanding that imperialism in the form of finance capital is a late and highly developed form of capitalism. He argued that under the new capitalism the export of capital by monopolies becomes a major characteristic of imperialism, associated with uneven development and the accumulation of a surplus of capital in the advanced nations under the control of a financial oligarchy of bankers who increasingly invest their money in industry and transform themselves into industrial capitalists.

Lenin's pamphlet *Imperialism: The Highest Stage of Capitalism* (1917) derives mainly from other writers, especially Hilferding and Bukharin, and although it is theoretically not original for the most part, it has nevertheless been central to intellectual thought on imperialism. Lenin's intent was political rather than scholarly, and the work was designed to provide a basis, even a call, for political action. As a political statement, it clearly identifies a series of trends or tendencies in the development of capitalism and its spread throughout the world. Lenin also desired to counter the polemics of Kautsky, especially the theory of **ultra-imperialism** and the notion that the capitalist nations eventually would rationally and peacefully align and divide up the underdeveloped world. In the pamphlet

Lenin briefly identified five characteristics of monopoly capital: the formation of a high stage of capitalism based on a concentration of production and capital; the creation of finance capital and a financial oligarchy, formed through the merging of bank capital and industrial capital; the export of capital rather than commodities; the formation of international monopoly capitals that control the world order; and the division of the world among the capitalist powers. The effect of the export of capital, in Lenin's view, was to slow development in capital-exporting countries and accentuate it in capital-importing countries. But Lenin was unclear whether the capitalist economy was constituted by the nation-state or the entire capitalist world. He left open the question of what entity divides the world into economic spheres but suggested that it was the national groups of finance capital.

Lenin's position was similar to, but more complex than, that of Bukharin. Lenin agreed with Bukharin in three areas: War is rooted in modern capitalism; capitalism in achieving its highest stage of monopoly thereby generates a revolutionary situation that will culminate in socialism; and the opportunism of the Second International was no accident but stemmed from the very nature of imperialism itself. Lenin probably saw Bukharin's view of capitalism as exaggerated. Not until 1916 did he accept the proposition that state capitalism was appropriate in characterizing the metropoles.

In juxtaposition to these thinkers were those who believed that capitalism signified a potential new order of peace and compromise. Joseph Schumpeter in *Imperialism* (1919) argued that imperialism would ultimately be undermined by democracy and competition. He was highly critical of what he considered to be the economically deterministic conclusion of Marxists, who viewed imperialism as a given stage of capitalist development.

Karl Kautsky was associated with many of Lenin's views until disagreements and debates divided the two men after 1914. Key issues of imperialism revolved around the contradiction in the German experience of political expansionism, military power, and the evolution of capitalism. Kautsky suggested as early as 1884 that the colonies were necessary for capitalist expansion. In his *Class Struggle* (1892), he affirmed that the evolution of markets was tied to territorial expansion and that European colonial policy would lead either to war or to a union of European states (a notion he later defined as ultra-imperialism). Kautsky envisioned capital as being transformed into a universal world trust. This ultra-imperialism, in the view of Bukharin and others, was theoretically possible but not relevant to the practical world in undermining national states or groups. Kautsky understood **merchant capital** to be monopolistic and militaristic, whereas he believed industrial capital tended toward peace and order and opposed colonialism. This view was altered at the turn of the century in his writing on commercial policy and social democracy, in which he anticipated both Hilferding and Lenin by focusing on the struggle for markets as European nations overproduced and by noting a trend toward the formation of cartels, tariff protectionism, and military expansion.

The Legacy of Imperialism in Developmental Theory

The idea of a sequence of stages in the process of development is inherent in the evolutionary theory of the nineteenth century. In his work on imperialism and especially the state, Lenin alluded to stages in the process of capitalist development, and his concept of monopoly as the highest imperialist stage of capitalist history was influential for later work, some of which deserves brief discussion.

Similar to the classical theories of imperialism, which variously emphasized underconsumptionism (Hobson), finance capital (Hilferding), and monopoly capital (Bukharin and Lenin), analyses by postwar theorists, for example Baran and Sweezy in their *Monopoly Capital* (1966), also focused on the advanced character of capitalism, especially in its monopoly form, and its impact on colonial and less developed areas. Gabriel Palma (1978) carefully examined Lenin's thought for the roots of a theory of **underdevelopment**. These writers showed the negative consequences of the imperialist advance, yet some on the left, for example, Bill Warren (1980), have attempted to demonstrate that imperialism tends to destroy precapitalist social formations and pave the way for capitalist development of the forces of production everywhere.

Imperialism theory carries directly into several currents in the developmental literature:

Subimperialism
Internationalization of capital
Postimperialism

Dependent capitalism is usually characterized as being unable to reproduce itself through the process of accumulation. But in some dependent countries where an authoritarian military takes charge, the economy can be reorganized so as to oppress the working class and allow for a project of subimperialism. The regime facilitates foreign investment and technology and increases domestic industrial capacity, but must seek new markets, necessitating expansion into neighboring countries. The dependent country thus becomes an intermediary between imperialist countries and other less developed countries that are vulnerable to exploitation. Ruy Mauro Marini (1978) called this situation **subimperialism** and saw it as comprising two elements: "a medium organic composition on the world scale of national productive apparatus, and . . . the exercise of a relatively autonomous expansionist policy" (34–35). Marini observed that "sub-imperialism is an historical phenomenon, and . . . its study demands a careful examination of its process of development" (36). It contributes to the concentration of industrial capital and U.S. hegemony over a world system of production. Critics suggest that this perspective is economically determinist and limited so that only a revolutionary and not a reformist course would be necessary to overcome the ensuing exploitation.

The theory of **internationalization of capital,** as elaborated by Christian Palloix (1977), permits an analysis of the movement of capital and class struggle on an international level, particularly the foreign investments and capital accumulation by capitalist enterprises of the center that operate in the developing countries and the rapid growth in the internationalization of other forms of capital such as private and public export credits, bank loans, and commodity exports. Palloix drew on volumes 2 and 3 of Marx's *Capital* in setting forth an analysis of capital and labor, the mode of accumulation, and the social relations of production as the basis of a Marxist appraisal of the world economy. His concentration on the shift of circuits of capital from a national to international level allowed analysis of the recent historical experience of multinationals in "underdeveloped" nations, especially in the late 1960s. He argued that the international mode of accumulation links more countries to a worldwide division of labor and diminishes possibilities for autonomous development, thus leading to an intensification of the contradictions in capitalism and an increase in class struggle. The analysis thus leads to the differentiation of the working class on an international level and the interlinking of national and international economies. With the appearance of new forms of internationalization of capital, for example, the rise of oil prices in 1973 and the ensuing economic crisis in Europe and most of the world, capital could be directed from the center to the periphery in the search for new investments and markets, permitting the possibility of national capital accumulation in some countries even as others continued to suffer from blocked development or dependency. Under such conditions autonomous development might occur in the periphery, resulting in new forms of production and reproduction, including manufacturing rather than the traditional reliance on raw materials, and in increasing technology and exports.

The influence of classical imperialism also is evident in the notion of a **postimperialism,** in the view of David Becker and Richard Sklar (1987), who have argued that global institutions tend to promote the integration of diverse national interests on a new international basis by offering access to capital resources and technologies. This postimperialism is reflected in "the mutuality of interest between politically autonomous countries at different stages of economic development. . . . their interests are not fundamentally antagonistic and do not entail automatically the intensified domination of the less developed countries by the more developed" (6). Becker and Sklar posit the formation of a new transnational class composed of two segments: privileged nationals constituting a managerial bourgeoisie and foreign nationals who manage the businesses and transnational organizations. This coalescing of dominant class elements across national boundaries suggests the rise of an international oligarchy. A theory of postimperialism serves as an alternative to a determinist Leninist understanding of imperialism and to dependency orthodoxy. Given the dominance of international capital in Third World situations, however, it is unlikely that a managerial **national bourgeoisie** will emerge as hegemonic.

Innovative Theories of Capitalist and Socialist Development

It is clear from the preceding discussion that the traditional theories of imperialism directly influenced subsequent theory and that a recycling of concepts and ideas is evident in some of the developmental literature of recent times. Much of the developmental writing only implicitly relates to earlier theory and debates, however. One means of unraveling the multitude of ideas about development might be to relate it to either capitalist or socialist outcomes (Chilcote, 1984). The advocacy of reformist capitalism initially was associated with a strong state through policies oriented to building infrastructure in each less developed nation and implementing protectionist policies and **import substitution**. Ensuing thinking, however, envisaged the state as combining reforms with foreign and domestic capital that would overcome backwardness and promote capitalism in its belated forms. Socialist aspirations were often linked to theoretical positions on backwardness, underdevelopment, and dependency, with policy and action oriented to ways to confront imperialist capital, either through peaceful or revolutionary means. The discussion and Figure 6.3 delineate these distinctions and identify and characterize the principal modes of thinking, which I have elaborated elsewhere (Chilcote, 1992). An assessment of these trends reveals their strengths and weaknesses and suggests how thinking has evolved over the second half of the twentieth century.

Reformist, Nationalist, and Capitalist Theories

The concern about imperialism, especially in the Third World, provoked a nationalistic turn inward and a reaction against outside influence and

FIGURE 6.3   Innovative Theories of Capitalist and Socialist Development

Reformist, Nationalist, and Capitalist	Revolutionary and Socialist
Inward Development (Prebisch, Sunkel, Furtado)	Capitalist Development of Underdevelopment (Frank)
Internal Colonialism (González Casanova)	
Associated Dependent Capitalist Development (Cardoso)	New Dependency (Santos)
	Unequal Exchange (Emmanuel)
World Systems (Wallerstein)	Unequal Development (Amin)
	Late Capitalism (Mandel)

penetration. Although the new thinking reiterated the diffusionist belief in the possibility of positive capitalist development, it also recognized limitations along with the Western biases toward modernization premised on the past European and North American experiences. As a manifestation of sovereignty or identity with historical and cultural symbols intrinsic to a domestic experience, nationalism thus combined with sentiments against imperialism into a worldview that backward countries might be able to transform themselves through an expanding capitalism that develops autonomously.

Ensuring autonomous development was the concern of Raúl Prebisch and the development economists around the Economic Commission for Latin America (ECLA). They modified their neoclassical economic understandings in an effort to cope with and overcome backwardness in Latin America. They also favored a strong state that could create barriers to unwanted foreign capital and trade in the form of subsidies, tariff protection, or import substitution. Rather than socialize the means of production, their state would coordinate private and public enterprise in overcoming obstacles generated from outside.

Internal colonialism signifies a relationship similar to the colonial ties between nations but involving dominant and marginal groups within a single society. For example, according to the Mexican political sociologist Pablo González Casanova (1969), internal colonialism was represented by the monopoly of the ruling metropolis in Mexico City over the marginal outlying Indian communities. The underdevelopment and deformation of the marginal society was the consequence of its exploitation by and dependence on the developing metropolis. During the early 1970s, this view was applied by social scientists in the United States to minority groupings and impoverished ghettos of African Americans and barrios of Latinos, and it was extended to an analysis of internal colonialism in the Soviet

Union. This approach was eventually abandoned, however, in the face of criticism that it served only to influence liberal interpretations and polemics of minority groups and ignored an analysis of class struggle.

During his 1994 presidential campaign, the renowned social scientist and later president of Brazil, Fernando Henrique Cardoso, proclaimed that all his past thinking was irrelevant to what he would do during his term in office. In fact, his theory of associated dependent capitalist development proved to be a guiding base for his policies. Brazil was a dependent nation long oriented to serving the needs of both international and domestic capital. Its industrialization and capital accumulation could be promoted through state mediation of international and domestic capital with limits on state intervention and the privatizing of much state enterprise. Unlike those who viewed capitalism as leading to stagnation and underdevelopment in the periphery, Cardoso argued that the penetration of the periphery by industrial-financial capital accelerates the production of surplus value and intensifies the productive forces. He identified new patterns of capitalist accumulation and suggested the compatibility, in certain situations, of capitalist development and monopoly penetration as advanced sectors are linked to the international market, and he envisaged ties of national bourgeoisies to advanced nations.

World systems theory, as discussed in Chapter 3, derived from the methodology of the French historian Fernand Braudel and was elaborated by Immanuel Wallerstein, who set forth the essential concepts for the study of the world capitalist system. Wallerstein distinguished between two types of world systems: world empires in the form of the great civilizations, such as those of China, Egypt, and Rome; and world economies dominated by nation-states and their colonial networks, exemplified by Great Britain and France. Wallerstein (1974) focused on the European experience and identified three essential elements of the world system: a core area in northwestern Europe with highly skilled labor in agricultural production; a periphery in Eastern Europe and the Western Hemisphere where agricultural exports, slavery, and coerced cash crop labor predominated; and a semiperiphery in Mediterranean Europe. Core, semiperiphery, and periphery thus represented three paths of national development in sixteenth-century Europe. Within these three categories, Wallerstein examined a single market, state structures that distort the capitalist market, and the appropriation of surplus labor—all aspects that lead to class struggle within nations and across national boundaries. His perspective has been criticized for its emphasis on trade rather than class analysis.

Despite obvious differences among these various theories and theorists, some generalizations are possible. First, they espouse the position that Third World countries might be able to grow through an expanding and autonomous capitalism. Capitalism and autonomous development constituted the vision of Prebisch, whereas González Casanova and Cardoso recognized the limitations of capitalist development influenced by imperialism but viewed capitalism as progressive, and later Cardoso pushed for the integration of Brazilian capitalist development in the global economy. Prebisch early on turned his attention from the advanced capitalist nations and insisted on dividing the world into a center and periphery, a structural approach generally adopted in developmental perspectives. Most theory assumed a central role for the state in national planning, was concerned with backwardness and lack of development, and focused on market and trade. Implicit in some of these approaches was their advocacy of capitalism as necessary en route to socialism, although this ideal of socialism was obscured by changes in the late 1980s and the influence of neoliberalism during the 1990s.

Revolutionary and Socialist Theories

Juxtaposed to the reformist traditions, a parallel mode of thought was established on a scholarly basis for a revolutionary response to backwardness, exploitation, and underdevelopment. For the most part the ideas were generated by prominent left writers, many of them in Latin America, who criticized imperialism and combined their concern about external influences with analysis of internal structural conditions in their respective countries. They tended to identify the national bourgeoisie or domestic capitalist class with imperialism and to express pessimism over the prospects for a bourgeois-democratic revolution. Implicitly their analysis suggested that significant change could be realized only through a revolutionary socialist course.

Elaborating on the provocative analysis of Paul Baran, André Gunder Frank set forth his thesis on the capitalist **development of underdevelopment**. Frank (1967) argued that the metropoles at the center tend to develop, and the satellites at the periphery to underdevelop. Satellites develop only when their ties to the metropoles are weakest, for example, during depression or world war. Furthermore, areas that now appear to be feudal and backward were once in fact not isolated and precapitalist but able to provide primary products and a source of capital to the world metropolis until they were abandoned and fell into decline. Initially Frank's work was broadly influential, but later it was criticized on the grounds that its historical analysis lacked depth and failed to emphasize a class analysis.

Whereas Frank emphasized underdevelopment, the Brazilian political economist Theotônio dos Santos (1970) refined the idea of the new dependency: "By dependence we mean a situation in which the economy of certain countries is conditioned by the development and expansion of another economy to which the former is subjected" (231). Using this widely accepted conception of dependency, he focused on the situation in countries that suffer from the expansion of dominant countries. His theory incorporated the expansion of imperialist centers and their domination over the world economy, but he also looked at the laws of internal development in countries impacted by that expansion.

Conceptualization of unequal development tends to divide the world into developed and underdeveloped societies, some of which are capitalist and others socialist, but all integrated into an internationally commercial and financial capitalist network. Samir Amin (1977a) reformulated a theory of imperialism by focusing on unequal development and the social formations of **peripheral capitalism**. He also examined autocentric accumulation, international trade patterns, and monetary flows in the capitalist mode of production and concluded that dependency is related to the need of central capitalism for cheap labor in the periphery. Unevenness of development, he believed, is the consequence of **unequal exchange** on a world scale, evident with the impoverishment of the masses and the integration of a wealthy minority into the world system. Although Amin is recognized for his effort to update and reconstruct Lenin's theory of imperialism and Luxemburg's theory of capitalist accumulation, he also has been criticized for inattention to the state and impreciseness in dealing with relations of production.

The theory of unequal exchange portrays capitalist production relations as penetrating a world economy made up of units that are distinguished by differences in specialization in the international division of labor and by unequal wage levels. Basing his theory on a close reading of Marx's *Capital* and the application of what he called "the imperialism of trade" to the exploitation of poor nations and peoples, Arghiri Emmanuel (1972) was able to explain why wealthy nations become wealthier and poor nations poorer. He has been criticized for emphasizing exchange rather than forces and relations of production and for obscuring the exploitation of working peoples in his analysis.

In his overview of capitalism after the Second World War, Ernest Mandel (1975) set forth the thesis of **late capitalism,** an effort to apply the laws of the capitalist mode of production to the postwar period of boom and decline. Late capitalism is a consequence of an integrated international system, which necessitates the transfer of surplus from underdeveloped regions to industrialized regions, thereby delaying the development of the former. Some less developed countries have tried to minimize this tendency by nationalizing international capital (for example, Mexican petroleum in 1938 and Chilean copper during the early 1970s). The notion of late capitalism is similar to ideas around the new dependency perspective, which also attributed lack of development to the rise of multinational corporations and new forms of capitalism after 1945.

POLICY APPROACHES TOWARD DEVELOPMENT

Over the past generation policymakers have searched for development through various approaches that emanated from the past experiences of success and failure among nations everywhere. The prominent approaches revolve around diffusionist development, self-reliant and autonomous development, state and export-oriented development, and sustainable development (see Figure 6.4).

Diffusionist Development

Diffusionist development implies the possibility of transferring capital and technology from the advanced capitalist centers to the outlying periphery as a means of promoting development. Such development is implicit in the "invisible hand" notion of Adam Smith and other economists who believed that eventually all the world would develop under capitalism. It also is associated with neoliberal notions of prosperity for all under a presumably laissez-faire economy and a diminished state and government. Diffusionism has also been linked with modernization in various forms, for example, the political aspects of democracy, particularly formal representative democracy, in advanced capitalist nations as espoused by North American political science.

During the 1950s and 1960s modernization was also linked to nationalism, a European idea that originated with attention to such cultural tradi-

FIGURE 6.4   Development Approaches and Policies

Approach	Theoretical Basis
Diffusionist Development	Neo-Classical Economic Theory
	Neoliberal Theory
	Modernization Theory
	Post-Modernization Theory
Autonomous and Self-Reliant Development	Inward Directed Development
	Export-Oriented Development
	Underdevelopment Theory
	Dependency Theory
	Associated Dependent Development
	Sustainable Development

tions as symbols of national experience, institutional solidarity, sovereignty of the state, and a creed of loyalty and common feeling or will associated with the consciousness of the nation in the minds of the people. Modernization appears to have evolved from nineteenth-century theories of evolution and the belief that the Western world would civilize other less developed areas by spreading Western values, capital, and technology. The U.S. economic historian Walt W. Rostow, in *The Stages of Economic Growth* (1960), and the political scientist A. F. K. Organski, in *The Stages of Political Development* (1965), outlined stages through which modernization evolves. The political scientists David Apter and Samuel Huntington elaborated on modernization, the former distinguishing development and modernization in *The Politics of Modernization* (1965), the latter placing emphasis on the need to maintain stability in the face of the rapid social and economic changes that accompany modernization in *Political Order in Changing Societies* (1968). Huntington was especially influential because of his in-depth attention to institutions.

Throughout the 1960s comparativists sought a model of political development, culminating in *Crises and Sequences in Political Development* (1971), edited by Leonard Binder, but this effort to revitalize modernization theory was immediately attacked by Charles Tilly in *The Formation of National States in Western Europe* (1975). Tilly dismissed the sequence and stage theories and the crisis model of the comparativists and argued that the dependency idea was more useful conceptually and theoretically, particularly in its attention to exploitation, its recognition of an international structure of power that impacts on poor countries, and its understanding that the emergence of the class structure of particular states depends on the international organization of production and distribution. In a reassessment of these ideas Paul Cammack (1997) summed up the work of the theorists of political development as having turned "attention away from the developing world entirely, or addressed it under a special dispensation, granted by themselves, which allowed them to suspend their own norms of rational inquiry in order to maintain the useful fiction that 'non-Western politics' was itself irrational" (201).

During the late 1950s some conservative and liberal mainstream writers suggested the possibility of transcending the turmoil and exploitation wrought by capitalism. Daniel Bell in *The End of Ideology* (1962) affirmed that the old ideologies such as liberalism and socialism were fading in the face of advancing society, and later in writing on postindustrial society he projected moving beyond capitalism. This theme was picked up in the 1980s by Alvin Toffler in his *Third Wave* (1981), which envisaged the future in terms of individual and small group activities in the age of computers. This view envisioned an improvement of living standards; a closing of gaps between classes through mass education, mass production, and mass consumption; and a diminishing of ethnic, linguistic, regional, and religious loyalties along with a marginalization of total ideologies.

In variants of this thought, Amitai Etzioni wrote of "the post-modern era," George Lichtheim of "the post-bourgeois society," Herman Kahn of "post-economic society," Murray Bookchin of "the post-scarcity society," and Kenneth Boulding of the "post-civilized society" (all quoted in Frankel, 1987). In his attention to postmodernism, Ronald Inglehart extended his empirical investigation to a search for "post-bourgeois" man. Although left theorists have assimilated such views, a critical perspective would suggest that postmodernism obscures progressive thinking concerned with criticism of the bourgeois order, the dilemmas of capitalism and socialism, and class struggle. The postmodernists generally avoid analysis of the exploitative relations between capital and labor. Furthermore, their emphasis on politics and ideology as autonomous from economics undermines attention to political economy. Debate on the nature of the capitalist mode of production no longer appears as important. Consequently classes and class struggle are displaced by an emphasis on political pluralism, political organizations, and interest groups.

Autonomous and Self-Reliant Development

Autonomous and self-reliant development may be applicable to both reformist and capitalist as well as revolutionary and socialist experiences. The ensuing discussion examines six types.

Inward-directed development implies autonomous, self-reliant, or domestic capitalist development through the imposition of tariff barriers, building of an infrastructure for the local economy, and import substitution to stimulate production. Essentially this view seeks ways in which less developed nations can adjust to international conditions through government intervention as a means of offsetting the impact of the hegemonic centers. Although it reveals differences between capitalism in the advanced industrial center and capitalism in the backward periphery, its reformist solutions to underdevelopment usually are insufficient to overcome the dominance of international capital.

Extraction and exports of raw materials by foreign enterprises historically characterized the exploitation of many countries in the Third World. Especially in Latin America the dependence on and the extraction of a single commodity, such as bananas in Central America, coffee in Brazil, or oil in Venezuela, was associated with "enclave" economies. Since about the 1960s, many developing countries adapted to world markets as a means of improving the material existence of people in general and of promoting industry premised on low-cost labor for export. Particularly conspicuous in this process initially was the capitalist experience of the "tigers" of East Asia, including Hong Kong, Singapore, South Korea, and Taiwan, although other nations such as China adapted their socialist experience and reforms under a Communist party to the opening of markets to the international capitalist world. This form of development usually has occurred under dictatorships or highly centralized bureaucratic authoritarian regimes and exclusionary states in which popular forms of participation are limited or do not exist.

The argument that capitalism promotes underdevelopment as capital and technology diffuse from the advanced capitalist to the backward nations runs through an important literature emanating especially from Paul Baran (1960) who delineated a "morphology" of backwardness and formulated a basis for understanding the negative repercussions of capitalism. André Gunder Frank (1967) elaborated on this idea, arguing that national capitalism and the national bourgeoisie, unlike their counterparts in Great Britain and the United States, could not promote development in Latin America. He argued that the contradictions of capitalism led to the expropriation of **economic surplus**, which generated development in the metropolitan centers and underdevelopment in the peripheral satellites. This theme has been applied in regional studies such as Frank's *Capitalism and Underdevelopment in Latin America* (1967), Walter Rodney's *How Europe Underdeveloped Africa* (1972), Malcolm Caldwell's *The Wealth of Some Nations* (1977), and Manning Marable's *How Capitalism Underdeveloped Black America* (1983).

Three forms of dependency appear in history: **colonial dependency**, evident under colonialism in trade monopolies over land, mines, labor; **financial-industrial dependency,** accompanied by imperialism and the expansion of big capital at the end of the nineteenth century; and the **new dependency,** characterized by the capital of multinational corporations in industry oriented to the internal markets of underdeveloped nations after the Second World War. Dos Santos (1970) described this new form as conditioned by the relationship of dominant to dependent countries so that the expansion of the dominant country could have a positive or negative impact on the development of the dependent one. The dependency perspective was attacked for its failure to root its conceptualization in the method of Marx, class analysis, and relations of production.

Associated dependent capitalist development is a situation in the periphery in which the domestic bourgeoisie ties itself to capitalism, associates itself with international capital, and through the mediation of the state stimulates capitalist accumulation. According to Cardoso (1973), the accumulation and expansion of local capital thus depend on the dynamic of international capital. Socialist critics argue that this view promotes capitalist exploitation. Cardoso referred to "situations," rather than a theory of dependency and argued that perspectives of dependency must take into account forces of change and relate them to a global perspective. After summarizing Lenin's theory of imperialism, Cardoso emphasized a relationship between dependency and imperialism but concluded that the thinking of Lenin was dated and in need of revision so as to deal with a new phase of imperialism, capital expansion, and accumulation since the Second World War. Criticism of these ideas included the observation that the association of dependency with capitalist accumulation was simply a manifestation of bourgeois nationalism. The theory was further blurred by conceptual ambiguity, especially in regard to class analysis; the disproportionate emphasis on dominant rather than exploited classes; and a hope that the domestic or national bourgeoisie might bring about a developmental solution.

Sustainable development may occur with a capitalist or socialist economy that enhances the quality of life of contemporary people without impairing the welfare of future generations. Development must be designed for the human being to satisfy basic needs while protecting the environment on a global scale. At the same time there must be recognition that capitalist development may also increase the numbers of poor and vulnerable people while degrading the environment. Thus individual countries must assert their particular preferences within a globalized and interdependent world. Economic development must not lead to depletion of natural resources and environmental degradation. The struggle to overcome poverty and inequalities must be combined with protection of the earth, a problem both for industrial and less developed countries.

Strategies and Issues of Capitalist and Socialist Development

Some of the issues and strategies for dealing with development are outlined in Figure 6.5.

Figure 6.5 presents alternative directions in which societies may choose a path to development. Space does not permit elaborate discussion of these alternatives, but the reader could use them to focus on issues and dilemmas of development. A capitalist path is likely to emphasize growth over providing for the needs of people, although the welfare schemes of advanced societies to some extent have dealt with issues such as housing, food security, education, and health care; most socialist societies have directly attempted to deal with those and other concerns as they affect people everywhere. Other issues, such as private or public ownership, impact both capitalism and socialism, although capitalist societies tend to reinforce the notion of private ownership; the ownership role of the state becomes a crucial issue in both capitalism and socialism. Socialist societies usually implement planned economies, but these may be centralized or decentralized, and recently there has been interest in encouraging a

FIGURE 6.5   Strategies and Issues of Capitalist and Socialist
Development

Strategies	*Issues*
Capitalism Versus Socialism	Growth or Human Needs
	Private or Public Ownership of Means of Production
	Market or Planned Economy
	Capitalist Path or Non-Capitalist Path
	One Path or Multilinear Paths
	Physical Investment (Plant and Equipment) or Human Capital Investment
	Evolution versus Revolution
	Growth or Distribution of Resources
	Reforms or Radical Restructuring
Endogenous Versus Exogenous Orientation	Self-Reliance or Interdependence
Market or Planning	Industrial or Agricultural
	Industrial or Environmental Protection
	Development or Non-Development
Aid Versus Trade	Import Substitution or Export Promotion

socialist market economy; successful capitalist societies employ central
planning at the state level in conjunction with domestic and foreign capital. No society has successfully skipped capitalism altogether en route to
socialism, but socialist objectives do not usually call for a commitment to
the development of the capitalist forces of production prior to the drive to
socialism. Such issues as evolutionary or revolutionary development or
reformist or radical restructuring have already been alluded to in my discussion of approaches and theories. Endogenous or exogenous orientations revolve around strategies of evolving development within a society
rather than turning to outside relationships. In the choice of a marketing
or planning strategy, emphasis on industrial or agricultural activity depends on the availability of resources; the drive toward industrialization
in the face of the degradation of natural resources and the environment;
and decisions as to whether development in the form of growth should be
rapid, slow, or delayed altogether. Aid or trade alternatives depend on
the extent domestic production can be protected from outside penetration
and exports can be promoted to generate foreign exchange earnings
needed for investment in capital goods and other essentials.

WHITHER IMPERIALISM AND
DEVELOPMENT THEORY?

After the Second World War, as the old empires began to break up and many new nations, especially in Africa and Asia, became independent, new modes of thinking appeared. Two principal directions are identifiable. One built on the classical theory of imperialism, adapting it to new conditions, in particular the rise of multinational corporations and the transcending by capital of the boundaries of many nations around the world. The other tendency was a reaction, on the one hand, to neoclassical and mainstream developmental economists who argued that the problems of the Third World would be solved by the diffusion of capital and technology from the advanced nations to the backward nations and, on the other, to theorists of imperialism who emphasized external factors as the explanation for the retarded conditions of the new and old nations in the periphery that conscientiously sought a means of autonomous development without outside influence. Both directions drew on classical theory of imperialism; together they provided the historical context in which questions about development have been discussed in the present chapter.

These questions have included how developmental theory may or may not have resolved the failure of classical and contemporary interpretations of imperialism to focus on the internal conditions of countries in the Third World and to find ways to overcome imperialism and lack of development. This search has looked at the legacy of imperialism in developmental theory. It has delved into the implications of development within capitalism or socialism. It briefly elaborated on general trends that imply possible policy paths toward development, including both diffusionist development and autonomous and self-reliant development. Finally, it identified strategies and issues affecting these outcomes.

This inquiry has also addressed the essential question of whether at the end of the twentieth century the Third World has a theory of development in the face of imperialism and international capital. The answer may be both affirmative and negative, depending on particular situations and conditions as well as one's own perspective. During the 1970s and into the 1980s theories of dependency and underdevelopment took the center of debate in the field of development. Significantly, progressive intellectuals, looking for ideas to interpret and lead their societies into the modern world of capitalism and socialism, debated, identified theoretical weaknesses and strengths, and moved on to alternative understandings as dependency and underdevelopment theory gained popularity and influence in mainstream social science. As these ideas began to fade, some mainstream scholars began to ask whatever happened to the old ideas.

Robert Packenham's (1992) belated response to this mainstream influence reflected his preoccupation with how Marxism had penetrated much of the thinking, a curious characterization given that most Marxists had abandoned it and that they rarely had attributed it to Marx and the classical Marxist thinkers of imperialism. It is useful to ask whether these theories were rendered impotent with the end of the Cold War and the apparent stability and peace in the world today. Clearly changes in the world of socialism and the end of the Cold War further obscured some of the old questions. In the face of the "new international order" and "globalism" many of the theories of underdevelopment and dependency were no longer fashionable.

As developmental specialists searched in vain for new ideas, concepts, and theories, it also became clear that they were confronting an impasse. Some developmentalists began to recycle or reformulate the once-discredited modernization theory of a half century earlier. Other mainstream and progressive developmentalists continued to use dependency theory, offering retrospective assessments of earlier work. And some specialists, such as Peter B. Evans and John D. Stephens (1988), saw a paradigmatic shift in comparative political economy toward comparative and historical comparisons, with emphasis on states and markets, development and democracy, and accumulation and distribution. A couple of examples illustrate this shift. First, Evans, Rueschemeyer, and Stephens (1985) identified tensions between international markets and state strategies and the ways in which hegemonic power shapes commodity and capital markets at the international and local levels. Second, in his analysis of state-society relations in the Third World, Joel Midgal (1988) focused on weak states such as Egypt, India, Israel, Mexico, and Sierra Leone in rejecting modernization theory and modifying world system and dependency theory so as not to emphasize exclusively the role of metropolitan or core countries. He found fault with empiricists who claimed to rely on evidence alone and not on preconceived mental constructs and felt that most of the literature was overly focused on state-centered analysis while uncritically neglecting power at the top.

A persistent theme in this book has been the ties of contemporary thinking to the past, with an underlying recycling or repetition of old ideas and debates. For instance, the dependency idea can be understood as a reflection of **competitive capitalism** and its idealistic projection of an outcome based on the utopian socialism of the late nineteenth century. Furthermore, themes about imperialism at the turn of the twentieth century were somewhat similar to those on dependency and underdevelopment after the Second World War. Distinguishable were progressive European disenchantment over imperialism in the earlier period and progressive Third World resistance to imperialism in the later period, together with an effort to turn inward to an understanding of why development was not taking place. In both situations resentment was directed against the imperialist advanced capitalist core of nations.

When attention turned to underdevelopment and the failure of capitalism or to late capitalism in the peripheral areas, unity in theory was evident in moments of outside aggression or economic penetration and collaborating authoritarian states in the periphery. Transcending the dictatorships and ushering in formal democracy usually implied more subtle forms of cooperation with the imperialist powers, concessions and compromises, and confusion over theory and policy. Most of the literature tended to focus on conditions of backwardness, inequality, exploitation, and underdevelopment in early studies and to challenge traditional interpretations.

Theory benefited from innovative questioning of late capitalism and delving into explanations for underdevelopment. We learned a great deal about surplus and backwardness, capitalist development of underdevelopment, the new dependency, and subimperialism. Critical attention to capital accumulation, international capital, and the hegemony of the international capitalist system opened up possible different paths to capitalism and socialism and led to empirical studies based on a theory of capitalism in the periphery. No single unified theory evolved, however, as many theoretical trends became discernible, including inward-directed development, associated dependent capitalist development, export-oriented development, and sustainable development.

This review shows how theoretical lines have become blurred and conceptualization fuzzy, with theory frequently abandoned altogether. Long ago Samir Amin affirmed that all the world was essentially capitalist, even in those areas where socialism had taken hold. He questioned whether present-day allusions to a new international order, global markets, and globalization are simply distortions of imperialism and the failure of capitalist development in the periphery. Some of the revisionist literature of the 1990s advanced the notion that the advanced capitalist world may not be totally responsible for the wretchedness and exploitation of the Third World. Today the drive of many countries is toward integration with the capitalist world and abandonment of any path leading to autonomy and sustainability. Fernando Henrique Cardoso, now president of Brazil, has revised his earlier thinking in favor of adherence to internationalism:

> Currently the majority of sociologists and political leaders, especially those from developing countries, identify the integration to, and the participation in, the international system with the solution to their problems rather than with the cause of their difficulties. . . . The new concept is not based on winners and losers, but on the equilibrium of interests based on peaceful negotiations between states (quoted in Grosfoguel, 1996: 132).

Such a response from an intellectual turned politician reflects not only pragmatic involvement in mainstream politics but a broad pattern of accommodation to a politics centered on global reorganization. However well the term "globalization" may reflect the pervasive and expansive world economy, it must not divert from a concern with capitalism and its impact. Whether we examine transnational or multinational corporations, the international political economy, or finance capital, it is important to recognize that the world economy and the global system are inherently capitalist and have been so at least since Marx's time.

7

THE POLITICAL DIMENSION

REPRESENTATIVE AND PARTICIPATORY DEMOCRACY

Democracy is a term relevant to historical epochs of stability and turmoil. During times of stability democracy may justify the legacy and continuity of a political system, and it frequently has been associated with a practice of political bargaining and consensus as well as the preservation of individual freedoms and rights in the society at large. During moments of disruption, democracy may be employed in the struggle to eliminate class discrepancies and overturn injustices, with the goal of economic, social, and political equality. Its meaning appears to date to ancient Greece. A dictionary takes us to the Greek roots of the concept, with *demos* referring to people and *kratia* to authority in the sense of government by the people or government as a supreme power retained by the people and exercised either directly in the form of absolute or pure democracy or indirectly through a system of representation.

This distinction between a pure or direct form and a representative or indirect form of democracy is relevant not only to ancient times but to experiences of the past few centuries when under both capitalism and socialism representative democracy was practiced and the pure form occasionally appeared. This issue is at the root of comparative inquiry. We might ask, for instance, is formal or representative democracy a precondition for participatory and ultimately pure democracy en route to some higher form of society, be it under or beyond capitalism or socialism? Must representative democracy be transcended in the struggle for a participatory democracy? Are these two democracies merely different forms in the path toward a higher democracy? Is formal democracy a necessary but not sufficient condition for the transition to socialism? Is a change in regime or in the apparatuses of the state also a necessary condition for such transitions? If the state has some relation to democracy, then what of civil society? These questions hint at the complexity of realizing any vision of democracy in the contemporary world and at the reasons why democratic theory is so varied and imprecise. No unitary theory of democracy exists, although the representative and formal strains remain prevalent and dominant.

In this chapter I delve into some of these questions, particularly as they pertain to past and present capitalist and socialist experiences. Initially the search for a definition and the distinctions between representative and participatory democracy might take us to the ancient texts on Athenian democracy, to which scholars have devoted much attention.

Athenian democracy serves as an important example, and the recent scholarship on classical political thought is an effort not only to recognize the limits of an idealized conception of Greek theory and practice but to show that the North American inclination to ignore ancient democracy has distorted our comprehension. Our impressions may have been shaped by the suspicions and questionings of Aristotle, Plato, and Thucydides or the interpretations of later advocates of democracy such as James Madison and Alexander Hamilton, who in *The Federalist* character- ized Athenian democracy as nothing other than mob rule.

Sheldon Wolin, comparing the Periclean Athens of the fifth century B.C. and the New England township of the Jacksonian era, noted that Alexis de Tocqueville slighted ancient Athens with his claim that American democracy was more perfect than that of antiquity. The comparison leads modern liberals and even radical democrats to the impression that Athenian democracy was a curiosity rather than an inspiration, an im- practical form of government or even an extremist example of political participation: "It is no exaggeration to say that one of the, if not the, main projects of ancient constitutional theorists, such as Plato (*The Laws*), Aristotle, Polybius, and Cicero, as well as of modern constitutionalists, such as the authors of *The Federalist* and Tocqueville, was to dampen, frus- trate, sublimate, and defeat the demotic passions" (quoted in Grofman, 1993: 476). An alternative view suggests that the complexity and depth of Athenian democracy appear in the form of an assembly and people's courts, the council and popularly elected officials, and a system of checks and balances: "Looking to this scholarship we do not see either direct mass rule or concealed elite dominance; rather, it is a complex system" but "once we recognize the institutional richness of the Athenian system, we ought to be suspicious of overly romanticized notions of Athenian democracy that render it indistinguishable from modern notions of pure participatory democracy" (Grofman, 1993: 471).

In their reliance on democracy, the Athenians developed ideas and practices of civic virtue and political education that enhanced the exercise of democracy and expanded ways for people to assume the responsibilities of power. Wolin (1993) believed that Athenian democracy may actually have involved forms of direct participation.

Protagoras, for instance, offered a defense of democracy that emphasized the universality of virtue. He believed that those who live in a civilized community are exposed to learning processes that inculcate civic virtue through experiences in the family, the school, and political life. Although there were differences and tensions between rulers and ruled under ancient democracy, civic identity and political status were dissociated from socioeconomic status and class inequality. Citizenship under ancient rule meant that political equality could coexist with and even transform socioeconomic inequality, so that "democracy was more substantive than 'formal.'" This ancient Greek relationship did not appear in feudalism, in which political rights were not redistributed, nor was it evident in capitalism, in which "democracy could be confined to a formally separate 'political' sphere while the 'economy' followed rules of its own" (Wood, 1995: 202–203).

This brief encounter with the origins of Athenian democracy helps in further understanding of democracy in its representative as well as participatory forms.

REPRESENTATIVE DEMOCRACY

In working toward a synthesis of the generally acceptable understandings of representative democracy, we begin with typologies, partially derived from the thinking of Dankwart Rustow (1970) and David Held (1987) and incorporating more recent ideas, as delineated in Figure 7.1.

Elitist Representative Democracy

In *Democracy Theory* (1965, revised 1987), Giovanni Sartori offers a starting point in developing a generally accepted understanding of representative democracy. He defended a mainstream theory of democracy, in particular, the notion that restraint of arbitrary state power through the rule of law is the essence of civilization under modern social situations. Sartori distinguished between elitist and participatory forms of democracy by expressing enthusiasm for the former and criticism for the latter. Although he presented a theoretical synthesis and his text represents a useful academic contribution, the framing of his discussion in known representative democracies of the capitalist world has obvious limitations in the search for a comprehensive conceptualization of democracy.

FIGURE 7.1   Forms of Representative Democracy

Type	Orientation
Elitist Representative Democracy	Rule of law as a restraint on arbitrary state power
Stable Democracy	Sufficient per capita income, high literacy, urban residency
Political Culture Democracy	Parochial and participatory representation
Reconciliation of Conflict	Class interests, bargaining, resolution
Democratic Institutional Decisions	Competitive elections
Political Democracy	Pluralism, freedom of expression, and political preference
Democracy, Accountability, and Capitalist Accumulation	Constitutional practices, elite economic, and social pluralism
Stage Democracy	Primitive to maturing egalitarian social relations

Stable Democracy

Inquiry into an early effort at synthesizing various conceptions of democracy could also be useful. Among the three explanations identified by Dankwart Rustow (1970) was stable democracy, particularly in the experience of the United States, associated with economic and social criteria such as per capita income, literacy, and urban residence as identified in *Political Man* (1960) by Seymour Martin Lipset. More recently, Lipset (1996) associated the uniqueness of such qualities as liberty, populism, and laissez-faireism as qualities rendering continuity to democracy in the United States.

Political Culture and Democracy

Based on the criteria and data that Gabriel Almond and Sidney Verba presented in *The Civic Culture* (1966), it is possible to identify a democracy linked to **political culture** and certain beliefs or attitudes among citizens in civil society such as civic virtue and responsibility, sharing of values with others, trust and confidence in others, freedom from anxiety, toleration of individual freedoms, and consensus, rational order, and stability. Their criteria distinguished among parochial attitudes among people who are relatively unaware of politics, subject attitudes where people tend to follow those who rule, and participatory activity among people who are aware and knowledgeable and able and willing to be involved in shaping political and economic decisions that affect their lives. The ideal form of civic culture consists of individuals and orientations sharing this latter inclination.

Reconciliation of Conflict

In situations of conflict, especially class differences in value and interest, democracy is linked with reconciliation, bargaining, and resolution as idealized in *The New Belief in the Common Man* (1942) by Carl Friedrich and depicted in *Class and Class Conflict in Industrial Society* (1959) by Ralf Dahrendorf. In this approach there is an assumption that dispute, ideological differences, and tensions can be worked out in advanced capitalist societies. Thus a rational order in decisionmaking can evolve through both individuals and groups.

Institutional Decisionmaking and Democracy

In a search for a "middle-range" definition of democracy, Terry Karl based her conception around institutions that allow all adults to exercise their voting rights as citizens and to choose their leading decisionmakers in competitive, fair, and regularly scheduled elections that are held in the context of the rule of law, guarantees for political freedom, and limited military prerogatives. Recognizing the ambiguities of democracy, Philippe Schmitter and Terry Lynn Karl (1991) observed, "For better or worse, we are 'stuck' with democracy as the catchword of contemporary political discourse. It is a word that resonates in people's minds and springs from their lips as they struggle for freedom and a better way of life; it is the word whose meaning we must discern if it is to be of any use in guiding political analysis and practice" (75). They defined political democracy as a system of governance "in which rulers are held accountable for their actions in the public realm by citizens, acting indirectly through the competition and cooperation of their elected representatives" (76). Contemporary democracy thus is based on a variety of competitive processes and channels for the expression of interests and values: "associational as well as partisan, functional as well as territorial, collective as well as individual. All are integral to its practice" (78).

Political Democracy and Pluralism

A set of minimum conditions for modern political democracy such as pluralism, freedom of expression, and political preference shape the conception of Robert Dahl in his *A Preface to Democratic Theory* (1956). Among the themes that have been elaborated in this approach are constitutionally vested control in elected officials over government decisions about policy, fair and frequent elections of public officials, adult suffrage and access to running for office, freedom of citizens to express political preferences, availability of alternative sources of information, and freedom to form independent parties and interest groups.

Democracy, Accountability, and Capitalist Accumulation

Such criteria as constitutional norms and economic and social pluralism approximate the essential components of democracy as identified by Richard Sklar (1987). The involvement of the citizenry may be viewed with suspicion by powerful political and economic interests so that the principal problem, he argued, is the prevalent belief that mass political participation is detrimental to capital accumulation. What is needed is attention to the accountability that underlies developmental democracy and fosters pluralism in political and economic life: "The norm of accountability appears to be the most widely practiced of democratic principles; it is by far more prevalent in the world than freedom of association to compete for governmental office, or popular participation in authoritative decision making" (1987: 714). This link of political and economic considerations and the relationship of capitalist accumulation to democracy has been of concern to both Evelyne Huber Stephens (1989) and John Stephens (1993). Historically associating democratic tendencies with industrialization or with situations where elite contestation emerged, such as in times of agricultural export expansion, both concluded that democracy is possible when pressure emanates from subordinated classes and economic elites perceive a threat to their interests.

Stage Democracy

The conception of stage democracy suggests evolution from primitive to maturing egalitarian social relations, specifically a series of developing historical stages, reminiscent of Daniel Levine's (1988: 383) reference to democratization, first in a temporal sense in which democracy is created and maintained through an early stage involving the initial decay of an old regime and implementation of a new system; and second, to the nurturing and evolving of egalitarian social relations.

These mainstream understandings, with emphasis on the U.S. practice of democracy, are widely accepted in academia today, but they are not without criticism. Ellen Meiksins Wood's allusion to the participatory inclinations of Athenian democracy serves as backdrop to her exposure and indictment of the origins and evolution of the now-dominant U.S. form of representative democracy. She attributed this form to the tradition of "popular sovereignty" that constituted the public realm between monarchy and public in which the demos was represented not by the people but by the privileged aristocracy of landlords. In her view this resulted in a "check on monarchy and state centralization," whereas "the 'political nation' which grew out of the community of feudal lords retained its exclusiveness and the political subordination of producing classes" (1995: 205). In England this exclusive political nation was represented in parliament, whereas the American experience was shaped by the Federalists, whose "task was to produce an ideology, and specifically a redefinition of democracy, which would disguise the ambiguities in their oligarchic project" (214). Wood goes on to show how this conception of democracy evolved into its liberal form "based on pre-modern, pre-capitalist forms of power" and dependent on "the emergence of capitalist social property relations" that allowed for "an economic sphere with its own power relations not dependent on juridical or political privilege" (234). In other words, under liberal, representative, or formal democracy, the sphere of domination under capitalism and private property was relatively untouched by political power, the consequence of a flawed liberalism that was "not equipped to cope with the realities of power in a capitalist society, and even less to encompass a more inclusive kind of democracy than now exists" (237).

PARTICIPATORY DEMOCRACY

Forms of representation usually are associated with capitalism and most understandings of democracy, but participatory forms also have appeared under socialism. The sense here is that ideology may be important in assessing the depth and potential of democracy. Ideological perspectives do not necessarily determine political outcomes on the question of participation, however. Since the late 1980s, for example, a series of meetings by left intellectuals and practitioners in Latin America revealed their willingness to move from revolution and armed struggle into liberal or bourgeois political settings, participate in electoral strategies, encourage pluralism, and seek reforms in the direction of radical change. Some of this congruence is due to shifting allegiances in a rapidly changing world dominated by expansive and dominant international capitalism. Some of it may simply be the exhaustion of revolutionary fervor in the face of international pressure to repress revolution and maintain stability, such as the counterrevolutionary movements supported by the United States in El Salvador, Guatemala, and Nicaragua.

This is not to suggest that ideological tensions and class conflict are altogether mitigated. Indeed direct democratic participation may well be enhanced as capitalist interests favor the rich and ignore the poor. This may lead to pressures from below, such as efforts among the poor and marginalized to work through voluntary organizations or international bodies, self-reliance among the poor, self-liberation, collective actions, and worker management. The following section looks at some of these possibilities in an effort to contend with the problematic of participatory democracy (see also Figure 7.2).

Mass Political Involvement

Illustrative of the successful mobilization of moral protest against the inhumanity of segregation in the United States, the civil rights movement and its leadership evolved organizationally and attracted wide support but were unable to unify broadly in a common cause and instead splintered into a plethora of movements. Beyond civil rights, local organizations have focused on basic issues through political education alongside action programs, such as the organizations set up by Saul Alinsky in industrial urban areas. A third level of organizing evolved in citizen initiatives, with a shift from particular to broader concepts that provide potential for democratic politics. In California, for instance, many successful initiatives on protection of the environment and the coastline along with campaign reform and other measures illustrated the possibilities of direct citizen decisionmaking. Yet at the same time, big capital, exercising its in-

FIGURE 7.2   Participatory Approaches

Mass Political Involvement	Town Meeting
	Civil Rights Marches
	Citizen Initiatives
	Popular Protests
	Local Self-Autonomy
New Social Movements	Feminist and Gender Organizations
	Ecology Movements
	Peace Groups
	Neighborhood Associations
	Landless Peasant Movements
Economic Decentralization	Market Socialism
	Self-Management
	Workers Management
	Post Liberalism

fluence through the mass media and scare tactics, often has undermined this process. Another approach involved popular protest in college towns such as Berkeley, California, and Madison, Wisconsin, beginning during the 1950s and 1960s with the emergence of the New Left and its politics of searching for change through radical and democratic means. The Students for a Democratic Society (SDS), especially under the influence of Tom Hayden, stressed participatory democracy. The members' passion for direct action, community, and self-action was expressed in the "Port Huron Statement." Years later Hayden and his then-wife Jane Fonda undertook a grassroots effort to mobilize progressive movements around these issues and to influence the political process at the local level in California. Such activities rely on local initiative through the "self-development" of people and principles of self-reliance, participation, cooperation, and raising consciousness.

New Social Movements and Identity Politics

The **new social movements** represent an alternative to traditional participation in politics. The tumultuous events of 1968 were driven by some of the early new social movements, which were unique in that they were not always working-class led or based. Whatever their importance historically, they were temporal and did not rise to prominence in a reformulated political economy. Disillusionment over the ineffectiveness and decline of the labor movement, however, prompted attention to the politics of identity.

Identity politics have been involved in the emerging new social movements of recent decades. The sociologist Stanley Aronowitz (1994) acknowledged that their influence over participatory political life has been limited. He focused on two ideological factions. The first, with economic justice as its goal, is found in the wing of the "redistributive" left and included trade unions; the civil rights movement; single issue groups in housing, education, welfare, and social security; liberal democrats; and socialist parties. The second comprises the new social movements of feminism, black nationalism, and ecological concerns. This rise of identity politics, Aronowitz argued, coincided with the decline and fall of the socialist left in the 1980s. As a unifying concept for the disparate social movements, radical democracy drew its inspiration from the French Revolution of 1789 and the Paris Commune of 1871 and based its principles, first, around insistence on direct popular participation in crucial decisions affecting economic, political, and social life and institutions; second, on democratic management in state ownership of enterprises and changes in work time and size of enterprises and social institutions; and, third, on plural universalism whereby the power to make decisions rests with those affected by them. Aronowitz saw radical democracy as "a universal . . . that is hostile to the tendency of modern states to centralize authority . . . entails limiting the power of representatives by genuine self-management of leading institutions to their control by a bureaucratic/political class . . . refuses the imperative of hierarchy and privilege based upon economic power" (64–65). He summed up the radical strategy as addressing "the politics of family, school, and neighborhood from the perspective of individual and collective freedom—not from the viewpoint of control and reproduction of processes of individual and generational development" (70).

The contradictory nature of these movements, however, must be examined more closely. Two examples may help. First, another advocate of participatory democracy, Carole Pateman (1991), exposed the past practices in the male-dominated discipline of political science, showing how both origins and practices opposed equality on racial and gender terms. Even theorists associated with the revival of interest in participatory democracy, she argued, tend to avoid the feminist literature. Anne Phillips (1991) demonstrated that theoretical writings about liberal, republican, and participatory democracy in general have neglected the feminist side. Second, in a critical examination of left differences in socialism and ecology, Ted Benton (1989) showed how influential traditions of the left have created tensions in these two movements. He elaborated a socialist critique of ecological politics as well as the main premises of Green hostility to socialism.

Economic Decentralization

Progressive intellectuals not satisfied with the rigid economistic formulas of communist theoreticians and practitioners after the Second World War have searched for alternatives in Marxism. One perspective, market socialism, caught their attention during the decade of the eighties. Its major proponent, Alex Nove, in *The Economics of Feasible Socialism* (1983) outlined a model of how socialism could be responsive to the market and solve problems of inefficient distribution, rigid pricing, and involvement of large numbers of people in the economy. Market socialism undoubtedly appealed to the nondogmatic left, especially in Europe, but the ideas of Nove appear to have served as an option for a left that has encountered difficulty in rejecting the involvement of the state in the economy while facing the ideological hegemony of the new right and neoliberalism nearly everywhere. In the absence of any serious alternative, this model appealed to many intellectuals, but it was vaguely expressed and not based on any particular experience. Experimentation with the market by formerly socialist economies in Eastern Europe appeared to be leading those countries into an increasing inability to cope with the problems associated with foreign capital, including debt, lack of autonomy and planning, and an inability to provide basic services structured under the previous socialist governments. Questionable too was the logic that regulation could fairly treat all enterprises the same when, in fact, in local situations the market is coercive, nontransformable, and alienating to the extent that market socialism can not function well.

Throughout history there have been occasional moments of spontaneity in which workers organized and elaborated schemes of self-management. In Portugal during 1974 and 1975 some owners fled their factories and their workers occupied the premises and organized factory management committees. Although international capital was uncooperative regarding sales, credits, and raw materials, the enterprises continued to function for a brief period.

Recognizing the potential role of social forces outside the sphere of production, such as youth, minorities, and women, Cornelius Castoriadis (1988–1993) worked out a system of direct democracy through self-managed councils of workers:

> To achieve the widest, the most meaningful direct democracy will require that all the economic, political, and other structures of society be based on local groups that are concrete collectivities, organic social units. Direct democracy certainly requires the physical presence of citizens in a given place, when decisions have to be made. But this is not enough. It also requires that these citizens form an organic community (1988–1993, 2:98-99).

Criticized as impractical and misdirected and lacking in a coherent strategy, this approach fails to engage the state with the goal of democratically transforming it.

Disillusioned with the prospects for democracy under liberalism or socialism, some intellectuals have searched for an alternative middle path. Chantal Mouffe (1992) argued against the limitations of individualism and envisaged an articulation between liberalism and socialism. Her principal concern was formulating ideas on how citizen and community fit a radical and plural form of democracy, that is, how to defend the greatest possible pluralism without destroying the framework of the democratic political community.

On the economic side, a search for democratic practices underlies the emphasis of Samuel Bowles and Herbert Gintis in *Democracy and Capitalism* (1986). They advocated a "heterogeneity of power," or power derived from a variety of sources, in suggesting that democratic societies in Europe and North America are not driven by class struggle or economic tensions but instead by contradictions between and among different structures of power. They believed that personal rights eventually would triumph over property rights, reaching into the economy and all aspects of social life to produce a really radical, or what they proclaimed as a postliberal, democracy. Their optimism emanated from the radical potential of the dominant liberal discourse of liberal democratic societies and their belief that the left should use this language of liberalism in the popular struggles in which it is involved and abandon the socialist rhetoric. Their thesis is delineated in a series of propositions about the relationships of domination that characterize capitalist society: that class domination or exploitation need not be any more important than race, gender, or other forms of oppression; that the class relationship between capital and labor is largely political; that class conflicts do exist in the workplace; that liberal democratic capitalism is a system of contradictory rules; that liberalism provides the language for progressive movements in advanced capitalist countries; and that the effectiveness of revolution as a means to resolving societal inequities is exaggerated.

In an incisive criticism of Bowles and Gintis and their project to extend democratic rights from state to civil society, Michael Burawoy (1989) faulted them for overestimating the power of liberal discourse and not explaining how the struggle for postliberal democracy will take place. In raising a similar concern, Jeff Goodwin (1990) questioned radical socialists who have abandoned much of the old socialism and look for democracy as a solution. He identified a loose theoretical unity among them in their neglect of nonclass and noneconomic forms of domination, their belief that class struggle alone will not bring about human liberation and that broad popular alliances must serve this purpose, their conviction that socialism represents only one aspect or moment in the path toward a free society, and their premise that those seeking human liberation should abandon socialism and look for a different and more comprehensive democratic ideology or discourse. He noted that their account of struggle between personal and property rights is problematic and not clearly differentiated from the class analysis they wished to dissociate from. He objected to their assumption that democracy and freedom are the exclusive concerns of liberalism and not concerns of Marxism or socialism. He showed instead that the extension of democratic rights to the economy is precisely what socialism is all about and furthermore that Marxism can be used to exploit the ambiguities and contradictions of the liberal discourse.

Throughout the twentieth century, experimentation in participatory democracy occasionally appeared in revolutionary and liberating settings. These may have been brief, localized, and without influence elsewhere, but they were instructive and exemplified the possibilities of participation on a mass scale.

The seizure of power by revolutionary and progressive forces in Portugal on April 25, 1974, was the beginning of a struggle throughout southern Europe to overturn authoritarian rule and usher in a democracy. Similar regimes also fell in Greece and Spain. The revolutionaries of the radical left pushed for a more informal and direct participatory system associated with revolutionary ideals. Although formal and parliamentary democracy quickly established itself and reformist social democratic and socialist parties emerged to wield power in the ensuing decades, the period from 1974 to 1976 reflected all sorts of participatory experiences, including leftist revolutionary political parties and social movements oriented around gender and **feminism**, peace, ecology, and other issues in the search for involvement outside parliamentary and formal representative institutions; grassroots neighborhood and civic organizations that operated outside established channels; and renegade peasant and labor groups that typically ignored nationally organized labor unions.

The failure of a revolutionary outcome in most of these situations signified a shift in the ideological parameters of democratic struggle, away from the twentieth-century political tendencies associated with socialist revolutionary experiences in Russia and China and toward a mainstream representative and formal democracy premised on parliaments and political parties. The brutal military intervention in the Chilean Unidad Popular experiment during the 1970s brought a disillusioning end to an evolving "peaceful" way to provide for the needs of people and promote socialist development through a legitimate and democratically elected government under Salvador Allende. During the decade of the eighties, military regimes in Argentina, Brazil, Chile, and Uruguay succumbed to democratic forces organized around labor movements and popular social movements, but inevitably they too evolved toward formal political systems. Toward the end of the decade the bureaucratic and stagnant socialist regimes in Eastern Europe and the Soviet Union also crumbled, with a mix of forces attempting to fill the political vacuum in the search for a means to shift economic preferences from socialist to capitalist outcomes.

A purer revolutionary thrust appeared where deep revolution took hold in some parts of the world, for example, the triumph of the Cuban revolution in 1959 and the victory of the Sandinista revolution in Nicaragua in 1979. The former experimented with both orthodox and alternative approaches to socialism but oriented its experience with development of the economy and efforts to provide the people with ways to meet their basic needs, whereas the latter tried to deal with basic needs and, in the face of a devastated economy, sought to build a pluralistic political system that ultimately brought its defeat through elections. Armed struggles elsewhere, conspicuously in El Salvador, but also in Guatemala, were negotiated and reconciled into outcomes that restored formal and representative democracy in the form of parliaments, political parties, and electoral practices. The emergence of an indigenous movement in

Chiapas, Mexico, challenged the dominant ruling party and opened up
the possibility of political autonomy in that region and elsewhere in the
country.

Autonomy is increasingly difficult, perhaps nearly impossible, in the
face of international capitalism and policies aimed at integrating the
world under the United States and other dominant nations. In each situation, however, an experience can be found and studied as a lesson in how
broadly based democracy might function effectively. No single model is
apparent, and each situation can only be judged in the light of its specific
conditions and possibilities. Each offers hope that a synthesis of the various moments of opening to alternative experiences might yield a new
course toward a reformulation of democracy that would truly involve
popular participation in decisions about the economy and political life
and ensure provision for basic human needs for all.

ISSUES OF DEMOCRACY IN
CAPITALISM AND SOCIALISM

Both the theoretical literature and historical experiences about democracy
relate to both capitalism and socialism. In *Capitalism, Socialism, and
Democracy* (1942), Joseph Schumpeter comprehensively examined issues
of democracy in capitalism and socialism, but his work did not sway influential proponents of capitalism to look seriously at democracy in socialism. For example, the political scientist Gabriel Almond (1991) used
Schumpeter's work to justify his defense of democracy under capitalism
and to denigrate its prospects under socialism: "The relation between
capitalism and democracy dominates the political theory of the last two
centuries. . . . capitalism is positively linked with democracy, shares its
values and culture, and facilitates its development. This case has been
made in historical, logical, and statistical terms" (468). As we shall see,
however, the contradictions of capitalist development may interfere with
the implantation of formal and representative democracy. The Brazilian
political scientist Francisco Weffort (1992), for instance, has insisted that
many of the new representative democracies, especially those appearing
during the 1980s, have faced "profound and prolonged economic crisis
that resulted in social exclusion and massive poverty." Indeed, democracy in many of these countries will likely break down because they "are
building democracy on top of a minefield of social apartheid" (1992: 20).
Thus democracy may serve the interests of capitalist development and
thereby enrich the few, but only at the expense of the masses of impoverished and immiserated people, especially in the less developed nations.

During the 1990s the neoliberal drive to scale down the state and reform or eliminate welfare services has involved painful social costs with-

out participation from below among people unable to overcome hunger, unemployment, and illness. Thus it is useful to critically assess how democracy has been associated with capitalism and socialism and, in particular, the issues emanating from these relationships (see Figure 7.3).

Democracy and Capitalism

The political scientist Samuel Huntington (1991) argued that the world is now engaged in its third wave of democratization. The first wave, during the one hundred years from the 1820s to the 1920s, brought democracy to some thirty nations; the second, after the defeat of fascism in the Second World War, increased the number to thirty-six nations; and with the third wave, which began with the Portuguese coup of April 1974, the number grew to more than sixty. Each wave confronted a backlash of reaction to authoritarianism and was associated with the struggle for political and civil rights, fair elections, the right to form political associations, freedom of the press, and elections open to all. Representative and formal democracy eventually shaped these emerging experiences at a time when capitalist development was becoming prevalent almost everywhere.

Today the democratic nature of the capitalist state is at issue. Conceptually democracy has radically changed throughout the twentieth century. Early on in the United States, democracy was generally conceived in terms of class, with the people constituting a mass of political

FIGURE 7.3 Issues of Democracy in Capitalism and Socialism

System	Issues
Capitalism	Capitalism favors bourgeoisie, not working class
	Rational or irrational treatment of interests
	State as hegemonic or responsive to popular interests
	Monopoly of power under the dominant class or plutocracy and pluralism of classes and groups
	Conflict or harmony in ordering democracy
Socialism	Pluralism as a basis to counter capitalist hegemony
	Reforms may or may not limit state power and provide democratic accountability
	State as instrument of ruling class or mediator of public interests
	Possible mix of representative and participatory forms in the transition process
	Actually existing socialism versus a new socialism

consumers (the productive class) in opposition to the aristocrats (the wealthy unproductive class). About the time of the New Deal, this underlying class conception of society evolved into a compromise between classes so that democracy and plutocracy might live in harmony, and the class divisions and conflicts of society became less conspicuous in subsequent interpretations (Hanson, 1989).

Advocates of the capitalist state carry this proposition further and believe that the modern state is uniquely responsive to popular demands and interests and therefore is democratic. There is no struggle between the capitalist ruling class (bourgeoisie) and the working class (proletariat) over issues of power. Indeed, their respective interests may overlap or merge, and various lines of political involvement and interests may prevail along with a diverse and pluralistic politics, based on consensus and checks and balances in a complex and highly differentiated society dispersed among many groups, institutions, and organizations.

Thus many observers see the capitalist state as uniquely democratic in form. Almond and many of his peers believed that constitutions, the rule of law, and elections are forms of representation that reflect the will and participation of people, thereby transcending situations in which a monopoly of power is held by the economically dominant class. In *Pluralist Democracy in the United States* (1967), Robert Dahl described the democratic order as involving a wide dispersion of power and authority among government officials and private individuals and groups. The structure of power is segmented, not organized into a clear hierarchical pattern. Characteristic of this democratic order are opportunities for freedom of thought, consensus and dissension, and participation in politics; the peaceful management of conflict and constraints on violence; and a widespread confidence and loyalty to a constitutional and democratic polity. In reality, however, we find that formal democracy is limited by structural constraints, the nature of the political party system and its agenda of issues, and the indirect control of capital over the state.

In the name of a formal freedom and equality in the marketplace as well as of a plurality of political power, capitalism mobilizes a politics of hegemony to ensure stability in the formal practice of democratic government. Bob Jessop (1990) captured the essence of this: "Hegemony involves political, intellectual and moral leadership rather than the forcible imposition of the interests of the dominant class on dominated classes." This leadership becomes hegemonic through a national popular project that expresses national interests through a set of policies or goals as being in the national interests, and in order to sustain itself it "requires systematic consideration of the demands and interests of various individuals and social groups, compromise on secondary issues to maintain support and alliances, and the continuing mobilization of support" (181).

Many socialists assume that a pluralist politics is not possible in capitalist societies, in contradistinction to the belief of mainstream thinking that links pluralism with the professed democratic character of advanced capitalist societies. Jessop has taken a different tack in his affirmation that pluralism indeed has its "roots in capitalist social relations and provides the basis of the distinctive forms of capitalist politics." This fact should not lead socialists to oppose pluralism: "Rather we are committed to developing a counter-hegemonic project which will progressively polarize the majority of these pluralist forces around support for socialist democracy and progressively neutralize support for capitalist hegemonic projects" (1990: 184). Indeed, Robert Dahl long ago in the initial issue of *Comparative Politics* (1978) shifted from the Anglo-American model as the basis of pluralism to a view that pluralism and socialism were compatible and backed up his point with reference to several European cases. Jessop also dealt with the liberal assumption that the modern capitalist state serves the public interest and is not necessarily an instrument of class rule at home and abroad. According to this view, the state mediates competing interests and represents the public and national interests rather than any particular segment of society. The state does not directly act in the interests of capital. Jessop made clear that the long-term interests of capital, however, are not without contradictions, especially in the face of crises and various paths of capitalist accumulation.

The question of liberal democracy, its relationship to capitalism, and its prospects of evolving from authoritarian regimes and dictatorships was widely analyzed during the 1970s and 1980s. Comparisons between changes in southern Europe and South America, for example, were common. Basic premises of liberal democracy frequently were extended to the Third World but also rebutted by social scientists in the area, such as the Egyptian scholar Samir Amin and many of his contemporaries. The idea in liberal democracy, for example, that the market represents economic rationality could be countered by the proposition that social relations determine the market and that there is no rationality in capitalism.

Also questioned were the notions that democracy parallels capitalism, that without capitalism there can be no democracy, and that a wide open door to the world and free trade is the key to development. Amin countered that there is little evidence that peripheral areas have been able to overcome many problems of underdevelopment and that the masses of people have received minimal benefits.

Many beliefs about democracy emanate from perceptions and understandings about the U.S. system of capitalist democracy. Joshua Cohen and Joel Rogers (1983) argued that democracy does not constitute a harmonious union between capitalism and democracy but rather is a temporary alliance in an "unstable structure of inner antagonisms, each striving to forsake the other" (49). In this system workers have formal and procedural but not substantive political rights, and therefore workers are in a weak position to affect national policy or to organize. Capitalist democracy directs the exercise of political rights toward the satisfaction of certain interests (51). Cohen and Rogers asked why people accept such a system and concluded, "Capitalist democracy is capable of satisfying the standards of rational calculation encouraged by its structure" (52). Capitalist democracies create the conditions of rationality within the system and tolerate only short-term struggles that can be absorbed by the capitalist structure. It is thus irrational for any individual worker to struggle to overthrow capitalism: "The achievement of short-term material satisfaction often makes it irrational to engage in more radical struggle, since that struggle is by definition directed against those institutions which provide one's current gain" (57).

These criticisms of U.S. society extend to the limitations and futilities of some minorities. In a provocative opinion piece, Lani Guinier (1994) advocated the need to refocus on the problems affecting marginalized groups in the United States. The key would be to reform the legislative decisionmaking process by providing "mechanisms to ensure that disadvantaged and stigmatized minority groups also have a fair chance to have their policy preferences satisfied" (*Los Angeles Times*, May 27, 1993). She characterized liberal or capitalist representative democracy as tyranny of the majority and argued such systems favor incumbents, discourage voter participation, and limit competition and choice.

Democracy and Socialism

Democracy usually is associated with Western forms of government, especially parliamentary activity and political parties, yet it also was a concern in classical Marxist literature, and it is relevant to socialism everywhere, as Frank Cunningham (1987) showed with a discussion of the limits of democracy in socialist societies dominated by bureaucratic and authoritarian rule.

Early on in his writings, especially in "On The Jewish Question" (1843), Marx suggested that the differences between representative and participatory democracy may not be substantial, since the state possesses power to shape and determine what rights exist and how citizens may exercise them. Antonio Gramsci and more recently Nicos Poulantzas emphasized that law and violence are inherent in the modern capitalist state. Both looked to authoritarian and fascist forms of the capitalist state. In *Selections from the Prison Notebooks* (1971), Gramsci emphasized the law as instrumental in shaping customs and attitudes among citizens. In his last book, *State, Power, and Socialism* (1978), Poulantzas emphasized the role of the state, through issuing rules and passing laws, in shaping a milieu of coercion and controls. The state permeates all social life, and Poulantzas believed that rather than resolving this dilemma through an assault by forces outside the state, changes might be effected through the institutions of representative democracy alongside direct popular democracy in the transition to socialism.

A mixture of representative and participatory forms appears in the thought of Marx and Engels. Marx was interested in the popular character of the Paris Commune of 1871 and its governmental system: The armed populace replaced the standing army, political power of the police was diminished, public service was carried out at workers' wages, and all public servants were elected and subject to recall. Marx's reflections on the commune raised the issue of democracy in the transition to socialism, for he believed that ultimately the inherent contradictions of capitalism would lead to a higher form. Toward the end of his life, in the 1880s, an era of parliaments, political parties, and universal suffrage in Europe, Marx envisaged participation in the capitalist state as one form of class struggle, but he did not elaborate any theory of socialist democracy. Later Engels wrote on German social democracy, understanding electoral politics as a useful means of educating, organizing, and mobilizing workers for change by securing meaningful reforms. Carl Boggs (1995) summed up: "The ideal of socialism meant public ownership of the means of production, abolition of inequality and exploitation, breakdown of the old social divisions—and democracy. It is hard to doubt the democratic sensibilities and intentions of classical Marxism: if capitalism signified oligarchy and domination by its very logic, then socialism was inherently democratic" (31–32). Aronowitz (1990) went a step further to suggest that the criticism of bourgeois democracy by Marx and Engels did not neglect the possibility that the working class could make use of the liberal state and its civil liberties "for the purpose of organizing to overturn and replace it." Indeed a socialist conception of democracy, as Marx envisaged it, "consists in a 'free association' of individuals each of whom is expected to participate fully in the decisions affecting the collective" (256–257).

But no clear strategies for the democratic socialist transformation were elaborated. A majoritarian revolution could eventually transform society, but "the absence of a political theory of the transitional process was one of the most striking features of early Marxism, with profound consequences for twentieth century socialist politics" (Boggs, 1995: 33). After Marx the search for a political strategy was accompanied by debates and factional schisms around four tendencies (Boggs, 1995: 36–37): the orthodox or centrist Marxism of Karl Kautsky and Austro-Marxist thinkers; the reformist-evolutionary line of Edward Bernstein; the vanguardist-insurrectionary tendency of Lenin; and the radical left thrust of Rosa Luxemburg. Kautsky,

a leading thinker in the German social democratic movement, advocated a
strategy of a (bourgeois) parliamentary road to socialism through which
the capitalist economy would gradually be overturned. Bernstein believed
in a relatively smooth evolutionary transition to socialism, devoid of crisis
and precipitous events and carried out through the parliamentary institutions of liberal democracy. Lenin proposed a revolutionary assault on the
capitalist state, arguing that reforms and transformation could not take
place within the existing state. This notion of dual power would lead to direct democracy, as envisaged in his *State and Revolution*, yet he also advocated a vanguard party and hegemony under firm political and economic
discipline. Luxemburg felt that the imminent crisis of capitalism undermined any transformation within the bourgeois state, that the parliamentary road would not lead to resolution of this problem, and further that authoritarianism under the vanguard party would undermine democracy in
the long run. Unlike Kautsky, Bernstein, and Lenin, "Luxemburg was the
first important Marxist theorist to pose the question of socialist democracy" (Boggs, 1995: 50). Eventually she and others worked out an institutional alternative to a party-centered socialism in the form of a federal system of local councils through which popular control could emanate from
the workplace and community.

The recent rise and fall of authoritarian, bureaucratic, and state socialist
regimes in Eastern Europe and the Soviet Union has produced some new
thinking, reassessment, and criticism of the prospects of democracy under socialism. Michael Löwy (1991) argued that Western characterizations
of communist states and descriptions of "really existing socialism" were
false and misleading. Little private capital existed in these societies, and
thus they could claim not to be capitalist. Indeed their principal failing
was a lack of democracy and the exclusion of the majority of people, primarily workers, from political power. Löwy affirmed that a moribund
bureaucracy, rather than communism, was dying, and that the radical
movements advocating socialist and democratic alternatives had been de-
feated. Although there was not much hope for optimism in the short run,
he believed, socialist democracy in which people decide and make economic choices and policy would be a possible road to the future. Even
though the left is in a deep state of ideological confusion and disarray,
Marxism serves to remove obstacles to the free development of the productive forces, and it functions through praxis and the dialectical materialist method as a means of criticizing all ideas and practices.

What are the implications of these understandings? The structural
changes and new directions appear to comprise two fundamental struggles: one against the bureaucratic authoritarian socialist state, the other
the more traditional resistance to the neocapitalist and neocolonial state
and capitalist monopolies. At the state level the bourgeoisie was made up
of state officials, middle classes, and a petty bourgeoisie, but this class

was divided among supporters of authoritarian socialism, democratic socialism, and the restoration of capitalism. The split was caused, on the one hand, by corrupt bureaucrats who held power and special privileges and defended restoration of the market economy to benefit themselves (typical of bureaucrats in Russia and China) and, on other hand, by democratic socialists aligned with honest officials.

How to respond to these changes in the socialist world? The search for democracy might be worked out through reconsideration of traditional conceptions of socialism, for example, the assumption that gradual reforms serve to mitigate the problems and limits of the modern state. The inadequacies and problems of the system may be manifested through democratic accountability or pressures from popular sectors. Excesses can be dealt with by placing limits on the scope of government and educating the public at large. Jessop (1990) argued that the struggle for democracy is not the same as the struggle against capitalism and that socialists, to win hegemony, must fight enemies of democracy on the left and the right as well as "draw attention to the increasing atrophy of parliamentary institutions and civil liberties in the advanced capitalist states themselves together with a growing ideological antipathy to democracy" (1990: 187). He argued for an alternative view in the struggle to modify social relations so that socialists can explain why democratic forms of government are possible but limited under capitalism. Socialists must work within the existing system to expose its limitations while winning short-term concessions, develop an alternative hegemonic project that links these short-term interests to democracy, and transform the separation between economic and political life by introducing "a coordinated system of industrial self-government and democratic economic planning and to reorganize the state itself through the extension of democratic accountability" (1990: 189).

This argument suggests that orthodox interpretations of Marx are of limited value. The relationship of capital to society has fundamentally changed since Marx's time. Thus global capitalism has rendered largely irrelevant Marx's conception of the early industrial character of nineteenth-century societies. In the face of a higher level of complexity, the alternative would be to seek the formation and solidarity of democratic ideals through discourse and the realization of the conscious democracy found in some of Marx's writings and evident in brief moments of historical experimentation.

MODELS OF EMPOWERMENT AND TRANSFORMATION

The discussion thus far suggests that democracy can be associated with both mainstream and alternative models. Four illustrations from the literature that reflect these directions and may be helpful in comparative analysis are identified in Figure 7.4.

FIGURE 7.4   Models of Empowerment and Transformation

Proponent	Model
Rustow	Pluralism and Consensus
Aronowitz	New Historic Bloc of Autonomous Groups
Boggs	Radical Democratic Transformation with Collective-Coop Forms
Albert and Hahnel	Consumer-Worker Consensus

One early delineation of a model of democracy assumed national unity as a background condition for the vast majority of citizens in the political community they belong to. It idealized democracy in its representative form as drawn from comparative research undertaken by Dankwart Rustow (1970). It incorporated a preparatory phase of prolonged and inconclusive political struggle, related to periods of intense economic development and the commensurate rise of new social classes in conflict with traditional classes to establish a dynamic process of democratization—in short, a phase of polarization rather than pluralism and consensus. In the ensuing phase the top political leadership of the country makes a conscious decision to shift from oligarchy or some authoritarian form to democracy. This decision in favor of democracy emanates from the mix of many forces, such as the splintering of ruling groups and parties, and is likely to involve compromise, universal suffrage, and awareness of changes by professional politicians and the citizenry. Finally, the phase of habituation represents the implementation of policies to fulfill the promises of the decision phase. Ways are found to resolve conflicts within human groups. Conciliation and accommodation appear in the political process, which also directs itself toward economic and social issues. Politicians and citizens learn from the resolution of some issues to put their confidence in the new rules; competitive recruitment and democratic practices become commonplace; and political parties link politicians with the mass electorate. In sum, the model suggests a sequence from national unity, through struggle, compromise, and habituation, to democracy. For Rustow, it has particular historical relevance in advanced capitalist countries, but it should be clear that this is an idealization of a process that may characterize particular situations at particular moments, and it can be used to measure the experience of nations against their success and failure in involving people in solving real problems. Yet there are few pure experiences, and none of any substantial duration, that have successfully involved masses of people in participatory ways to resolve problems.

In setting forth an approach for adapting Marxism to the ideals of democracy, Stanley Aronowitz (1990) argued for a democracy "constituted only by understanding citizenship as self-management in economic, social, and cultural aspects," a principle he posited as inherent in Marx and his thought. Aronowitz believed that a new historic bloc of forces could emerge from "a micropolitics of autonomous oppositional movements." He saw this bloc evolving from a new set of premises around the question of autonomy of labor unions, with new forces of liberation involved in building a relationship between society and movements concerned with gender, environment, race, and other issues: "There would be no question of the hegemony of the working class, as traditionally constituted, over the historic bloc, nor of the claim of Marxism to represent more than its own historic perspective" (167). Indeed, the new historic bloc must counter the hegemony of the bour geois bloc in its drive toward socialist transformation. Marxism would remain significant in its insistence on the importance of a theory of human emancipation, a theory that does not, however, dogmatically hold to a particular doctrine. These ideas are drawn from Antonio Gramsci's theory of ideological hegemony, advanced as a central explanation for the persistence of a ruling bourgeoisie: "Gramsci inverted the Hegelian concept of civil society, and Marx's appropriation of it as the economic infrastructure, by positing the so-called superstructures—particularly ideology and its apparatuses—as the major condition for bourgeois hegemony" (Aronowitz, 1990: 168).

Having all but abandoned the socialist project of moving industrial society toward the Marxian vision of an egalitarian, democratic order, with the abolition of classes, workers' self-management, and socialization of public life, Carl Boggs (1995) argued for a transformative agenda in the industrialized countries designed around "a radical-democratic extension of collective and cooperative forms in all spheres of life" (180). The agenda must seek new practices, meanings, and identities. Ultimately it must undermine the legitimacy of the structures of domination, coalesce multiple alternatives, and search for a fuller understanding of mass consciousness and collective will. The old agenda of historical materialism and hierarchical party-centered models must be abandoned, according to Boggs. The practical roots of an alternative can be found in experiences such as the 1956 Hungarian revolution or the May 1968 upheavals in France against the old forms of capitalist, bureaucratic, and cultural domination. Boggs urged an entirely new approach to development "consonant with human needs, self-management, and ecological balance, tied to a system of socialized ownership, planning, and investment" and incorporating a process of collective empowerment and recovery of citizenship that "stands at odds with the main organized currents of the socialist tradition" (1995: 220).

A final illustration, based on a model developed by Michael Albert and Robin Hahnel (1991a) turns away from traditional approaches around representative capitalist democracy and socialist democracy to a participatory scheme in the direction of a modified socialism. Albert and Hahnel's vision is based on three elements. First is the elimination of hierarchy in work relationships so that "conceptual" workers would not dominate "manual" workers. This is accomplished through "balanced job complexes" to combine opposed roles and to diffuse separate categories. Second is the attainment of "material equity" through promotion of consumption in relation to a combination of need and effort, allowing each individual to share in a material, social, and emotional involvement in cooperation and solidarity with the aim of the greatest good for all. Third is "proportionate participation" of all workers and consumers in "an informed negotiation" in which all of them collectively determine "what is produced, with what methods, and how it is distributed, all in light of one another's circumstances and with a say proportionate to their involvement in each decision's implications" (summarized in Z *Magazine*, July-August 1997: 62). This ensures self-management and participation. Albert and Hahnel described their model in terms of participatory economics, in which each unit, however large, has to make its decisions while maintaining material and social equality throughout the economy. This would allow consumers to exercise power over their own consumption as well as over workers as they are affected by the products and the side effects of production, even as workers exercise power not only over their own labor but also over consumption in relation to having to produce what others consume. This approach envisages a new culture oriented to the community at large.

All these examples envision democracy in some ideal form. All of them are premised on the participation of people in the affairs of their society. Rustow's vision is simply an idealization of what democracy was supposed to be a generation ago, when it was assumed that the development of a representative democracy was part of a unilinear process coinciding with the modernization of society minimally through capitalism and perhaps eventually through socialism. It is fair to assume that this model persists in the mind of many North American scholars even today, although the consolidation of capitalism and its pervasive global impact on societies everywhere have undermined the attainment of the idealized form. In contrast, in a period of decreasing interest in Marxism, Aronowitz combined positive ideas in the thought of Marx with the idea of self-management and the possible formation of a new bloc of forces to

counter the hegemony of the dominant bourgeoisie. The alternatives outlined by Boggs and by Albert and Hahnel seek middle ground between
these approaches, with the former perspective embracing a radical democratic transformation of society and the latter seeking to skirt the traditional approaches of representative capitalist and socialist democracies.

It is to be hoped these alternative formulations along with the various
theories, frameworks, and ideas about democracy presented in this chapter will motivate the reader to delve deeply into case studies, evaluate the
successes and failures of past and present experiences, and formulate an
approach that might be useful in analyzing the complexity of the contemporary world.

PART THREE

Conclusion

8

THE UNENDING SEARCH
FOR A PARADIGM IN
POLITICAL ECONOMY

This book illustrates various lines of thinking as related to the major theories and issues of contemporary social science, their impact on comparative inquiry in political science, and the endeavors of scholars working in political economy. The problematic of a paradigm in shaping and conditioning political economy is considered. Attention to capitalist accumulation makes possible the examination of political as well as economic issues. Political scientists focus on issues related to the political superstructure, and economists look at the base, specifically questions about precapitalist and capitalist formations and mode of production. Accumulation, superstructure, and base are depicted in Figure 8.1 in relation to comparative and international dimensions of political economy. In the social sciences scholars tend to identify economics with theories of imperialism and underdevelopment (development) and political science with theories of state and class. These distinctions are not necessarily mutually exclusive, and the respective disciplines should pay attention to all three concepts.

Accumulation generally is associated with capitalism. Primitive communal production, in which labor collectively participates in and owns the means of production and there is no exploitation of classes, disappeared long ago. Slavery, in which the owner of the means of production owns the worker and accumulation of wealth falls into the hands of a few, also has been largely overcome. Competitive capitalism grew out of feudalism, in which the feudal lord owned the means of production but did not fully own the worker. Alongside feudal ownership there was some private property in the hands of peasants and artisans, whose ownership

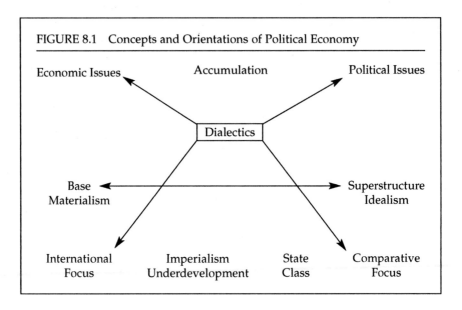

FIGURE 8.1   Concepts and Orientations of Political Economy

was based on personal labor. Marx described how capitalist ownership disrupted those relations of production as large mills and factories replaced handicraft shops and large firms with machinery took the place of the old feudal estates and peasant farms. Marx and his contemporaries were concerned with the general theories of the motion of capital. Marx examined commodities and capital; the transformation of money into capital, labor power, and surplus value, and the process of capitalist production as a whole. In the last sections of the first volume of *Capital,* he looked at primitive accumulation and the accumulation of capital. He described the process by which money and commodities transform into capital and the owners of money and the means of production confront workers.

Whether influenced by Marx, Ricardo, or Smith, political economy thus fundamentally addresses the broad historical sweep of capitalism, especially during the twentieth century. This book has emphasized the Marxist contribution and radical political economy. Marx laid the foundations for such study in *Grundrisse* (1857–1858) and *Capital;* and works such as Paul Sweezy's *The Theory of Capitalist Development* (1942) and Ernest Mandel's *Marxist Economic Theory* (1968) summarized and interpreted Marx's findings, emphasizing in particular the economic ramifications.

Mandel (1975) focused on the evolving capitalist mode of production and distinguished competitive (1780–1880) and imperialist (1880–1940) from "late" capitalism, which evolved after the Second World War. He attempted to integrate theory and history in the tradition of Marx, dialectically moving from abstract to concrete and concrete to abstract, from the parts to the whole and from the whole to the parts, from essence to appearance and from appearance to essence, from totality to contradiction and contradiction to totality, from object to subject and subject to object. Although his work failed to give us a modern version of *Capital*, it represented a serious effort to fill a gap in political economy.

Other works in political economy combine theory with history. Samir Amin (1974) affirmed that accumulation or expanded **reproduction of capital** is essential to the capitalist mode of production. His analysis incorporated capitalist modes in combination with precapitalist modes of production, and he argued that capitalist and socialist world markets are not distinguishable, for there is only one, the world capitalist market, in which socialist countries marginally participate. He also conceived of contemporary capitalism as an international system, not a mix of national capitalisms. Perry Anderson (1974, 1975) delved into questions relevant to feudalism and capitalism as Europe emerged from the Middle Ages. Immanuel Wallerstein (1974) dated the modern world system from the sixteenth century but saw four periods in its evolution: origins (1450–1640), mercantile consolidation (1640–1815), industrial expansion (1815–1917), and the contemporary capitalist world (after 1917).

These four writers—Mandel, Amin, Anderson, and Wallerstein—among others, rekindled an interest in the history of political economy. However imperfect their work may be, it orients us toward old and new questions that have been neglected by much of the current work in economics and political science. These writers drew heavily on a foundation of Marxist thought and located their analysis in the origins and evolution of the capitalist system of accumulation. They also transcended the problems of partial analysis that occur when underdevelopment is examined in isolation from development, for in fact the two are unified and integrated in the process of capitalist accumulation.

Both political science and economics have devoted attention to development and underdevelopment and thus to the process of accumulation. Development economics is a major field in economics, and political scientists also address questions of accumulation through studies relating politics and policies to development processes and underdevelopment. Both disciplines focus on international and comparative political economy. The sketch of concepts above distinguishes international from comparative political economy in this manner. Earlier chapters identified the theoretical directions around these concepts, but a brief summary may help the reader in understanding crucial differences.

Inquiry in international political economy might trace imperialism from the Greek and Roman empires to its mercantile "old" form in the sixteenth and seventeenth centuries to its monopolistic "new" form in the nineteenth and twentieth centuries. Two perspectives of the new imperialism have prevailed. One, the Marxist or radical view, argued that imperialism was a reflection of an expanding capitalism, necessitated by the contradictions of the capitalist mode of production. Representative of this view would be the thought of Rosa Luxemburg, Nikolai Bukharin, V. I. Lenin, Paul Baran and Paul Sweezy, and Harry Magdoff. Luxemburg elaborated a theory that explained continuous capital accumulation and examined the penetration of capital into primitive economies. Bukharin drew from Rudolf Hilferding's notion of finance capital and described imperialism as an advanced form of capitalism. Lenin understood imperialism to be the highest stage of capitalism and focused on the concentration of production in large industrial monopolies as well as the large banks. Baran and Sweezy suggested that a theory of imperialism exposes the development of social and economic conditions in capitalist countries and leads to analysis of the unequal relations between advanced and backward nations. Magdoff looked at the expanding U.S. "empire" and the patterns of foreign policy, aid, and trade. The other, non-Marxist, or liberal, view argued that the inequities of the capitalist system could be readily adjusted. The thought of J. A. Hobson and Joseph Schumpeter and to a lesser extent Karl Kautsky contributed to this view. Hobson identified underconsumption as the principal cause of imperialism; Shumpeter argued that imperialism was a precapitalist phenomenon that would gradually disappear in a rational and progressive era of capitalism; and Kautsky, a leading Marxist of his time, whose view leaned toward liberalism, felt that the class conflicts of capitalism would diminish through peaceful processes.

As with theories of imperialism, Marxist and non-Marxist perspectives are evident in the attention of comparative political economy to the role of the state. The construction of a Marxist theory of the state necessitates initially an understanding of the thought of Hegel, Marx, Engels, and Lenin. Marx systematically criticized Hegel's doctrine of the state, accepting that a fundamental contradiction exists between the state and the civil society of citizens but insisting that forms of the state be separated from an ideal or abstract conception and instead be rooted in the material conditions of life. Whereas in ancient Greece and during medieval times in Europe there was a sense of unity between the people and the state and between private and public interests, under capitalism, Marx argued, there is a separation of state from civil society, and an estrangement develops between public and private life. In addition, the civil society fragments into private interests competing against one another as the state legitimizes the pursuit of particular interests through private property, and private property promotes inequality and disunity among the people.

Engels summed up Marx's early writings on the state and showed the significance of economic considerations. Lenin drew on the theory of the state elaborated by Marx and Engels. He insisted that the state does not reconcile the class conflict but ensures the oppression of one class by another.

Three traditions revolved around these early perspectives and contributed to a theory of the state: **instrumentalism,** in which the state is the instrument of the ruling or dominant class, a position advanced by Ralph Miliband; **structuralism,** in which the state organizes and unifies the interests of the bourgeoisie, even when that class is unable to dominate the state, a view found in Nicos Poulantzas; and a critical perspective, represented in Herbert Marcuse and others of the Frankfurt school, that exposes the mystification of the state in terms of ideology and false consciousness.

In contrast, the mainstream view of the state might find its origins in the formal-legal studies of James Bryce and Woodrow Wilson, among others in the early twentieth century. The prevailing conception sees the state as a political marketplace through which filter the demands and interests of competing groups and individuals. Several views are noteworthy: one in which neutral state agencies mediate conflict that emanates from party and group competition; another according to which agencies of the state function as bases of political power and competition among these agencies for funding determines their relationship to the parties and interest groups; and finally, a theory of institutions that fills gaps in theories of property rights, the state, and ideology. In arguing for this theory, Douglas C. North (1981) exposed the assumptions and weaknesses of neoclassical theory by demonstrating that in the neoclassical model there are no organizations or institutions except the market and that change occurs through changes in relative prices in an impersonal market (8–9).

These themes of political economy have stimulated comparative inquiry in case studies in both advanced and less developed nations. The reader may wish to explore some of the scholarly efforts to build comparisons through theory and historical experience. A dozen or so examples lead us in this direction. In an examination of how capitalist development in Latin America accompanied the rise of a labor movement, Ruth and David Collier (1991) employed a historical method of examining similarities and contrasts among eight countries of Latin America. Theoretical and case studies of revolutionary situations in the Third World, with particular attention to the prospects for socialist transition and development, constitute the important contribution of Richard R. Fagen, Carmen Diana Deere, and José Luis Corragio (1986). Departing from a discussion of the agrarian question in Europe and the Third World, David Goodman and Michael Redclift in (1982) explored the capitalist transition and underdevelopment in Brazil and Mexico. Comparative historical and political analysis of the rise of the West and its development, departing from the perspectives of Marx, Smith, Hume, and Weber, served as the basis of contention with prevailing Marxist interpretations in the work of John A. Hall (1985). Paul Kennedy (1987) compared the Hapsburg empire, Great Britain, and the United States; Giovanni Arrighi (1994) contrasted the rise and decline of powerful states since the thirteenth century; Michael Mann (1986) delved into networks and the structure and history of European states; and Dieter Senghaas (1985) assessed the historical experience in the light of various theories of development. Arend Lijphart (1984) used a data base to compare the majoritarian and consensus models of democracy in twenty-one European countries. Barrington Moore Jr. (1966) searched for the revolutionary origins of England, France, the United States, China, India, and Japan, a theme also in Theda Skocpol's (1979) examination of the causes of social revolutions and the outcomes in China, France, and Russia.

*　*　*

This book suggests the possibility of an established paradigm or mainstream understanding of particular issues and questions as well as an alternative possibility. The distinctions between non-Marxist and Marxist perspectives, however, lead to the question whether a Marxist paradigm has been established. Michael Harrington (1976) responded in the affirmative: "Even though it shares insights with, and has influenced, the various social sciences, it is distinctive and cohesive both as a method and in the results it facilitates. It poses the right questions about the contemporary world, it suggests some profound ways of seeking out the answers; and it is therefore relevant to the theory and practice of the twenty-first century" (184). Harrington traced the crusade against Marxism that has been waged by U.S. academic disciplines since the Second World War. The Marxist paradigm, he argued, does integrate the separate analyses of the social science disciplines, but it does not make up a preconceived model of society. It offers important methodological themes; is critical even of its own concepts and terminology; and makes no pretense of being free of values but is aware of biases and ideologies that permeate social science. Its values link to politics favoring the working class rather than the ruling bourgeoisie. It does not prescribe any particular solution for the ills of capitalist society, whether democratic planning by the majority or bureaucratic and exploitative collectivism. Furthermore, it offers a complex theory of social classes; looks for contradictions in society; and distinguishes possibilities, symptoms, and causes in an analysis of crisis and changing technology. Finally, it is not unified and, in fact, there are many Marxisms.

The pursuit of political economy suggests provocative and controversial possibilities. Marx considered traditional political economy as essentially an ideology, and he attempted to transcend ideology by questioning bourgeois political economy in a manner that would eventually allow political economy to wither away, together with the categories it seeks to explain, and permit the evolution of a new science. The new science, according to Ernest Mandel (1968), "will have little in common with past and present economic theory, with bourgeois political economy, or with the Marxist criticism of it" (2: 730).

This observation suggests that ideas of political economy have revolved around the nature of the capitalist society and the prospects for it evolving to some more egalitarian form, whether socialism or some unnamed form transcending capitalism. During the nineteenth century the debates between Marx and his contemporaries focused on the strengths and weaknesses of capitalism. The debates carried on into the twentieth century with attention to colonialism and imperialism and the outreach of capitalism into less advanced regions of the world, and they continue at the end of the century as capitalism consolidates its powerful hold over all the world.

The changes in capitalism and interpretations about it through time relate closely to an array of schools and thinkers of political economy, outlined in Figure 8.2. Many of these influences are mentioned in this text as well. The scheme reflects several dichotomies of thinking: between Western and Eastern Marxism, between Marxists and non-Marxists, and between materialist and humanist Marxists.

The present volume relates closely to, and indeed is drawn from, two other works, which the reader is encouraged to explore more deeply. The first of these, my *Theories of Comparative Politics,* was published in the early 1980s and substantially revised and published in a second edition in 1994. It has been translated and published in Brazil, China, Korea, and Russia. The mission of these books was to identify and assess the prospects for a paradigm in political science and comparative politics in general—but in political economy in particular—and to guide students and academics to question debates that appear to be settled, to challenge established theories and concepts, and to probe new areas of inquiry. These books focus on Marx and Weber as precursor thinkers who influenced ideas around such themes as system and state, culture, development and underdevelopment, and class—themes embraced in the present volume, but the earlier work is more detailed and is exhaustive in its referencing, providing annotations to a comprehensive listing of references.

FIGURE 8.2   Dichotomies of Theories

System in Equilibrium Group Interests	State as Hegemonic Class Struggle
Individual Preferences	Collective Preferences
Capitalist Development	Socialist Development
Representative Democracy	Participatory Democracy

The sequel, *Theories of Comparative Political Economy* (forthcoming), elaborates on themes emanating from the conclusions of the early work as well as other concerns that are fundamental to theory and inquiry in comparative political economy. The present generation of political scientists wrestles with the question of what is political and what is political science. The economists debate the prospects of development under equilibrium or inegalitarian conditions. Many acknowledge the contributions of Marx to these questions, yet most tend to steer clear of Marxism, preferring instead to distinguish politics from economics and to avoid issues of state, power, class, and class struggle. It is to be hoped that such issues will be meaningfully addressed through attention to political economy.

The present volume simplifies the detail and sketches out the general patterns in a manner intended to encourage the reader to explore the themes more deeply. Once the lines of debate are revealed, issues become controversial and critical thinking ensues. The themes of the main body of the book are dialectically juxtaposed, as outlined in Figure 8.2.

In affirming the importance of political economy for social science, and especially for economics and political science, it may be said that the ultimate objective of political economy may instead be its own demise. Marx contended and interacted with the ideas of the great political economists of his time, including Smith and Ricardo, but for Marx political economy was simply ideological. The search for a radical political economy involves the questioning of mainstream political economy and capitalism itself. Out of that process should emerge a new science that "will have little in common with past and present economic theory, with bourgeois political economics, or with the Marxist criticism of it. Marxist economists can claim the honor of being the first category of men of learning to work consciously toward the abolition of their own profession" (Mandel, 1968: 2: 730).

GLOSSARY

The concepts below and in the main text are identified in boldface so as to facilitate understanding and reference to this glossary. For related and other concepts, consult *Webster's New International Dictionary* (3d ed.) as a starter and then delve more deeply into such sources as *The Handbook of Sociology*, edited by Neil J. Smelser (1988), the *Encyclopedia of Government and Politics*, edited by Mary Hawkesworth and Maurice Kogan (1992), and *A Dictionary of Marxist Thought*, edited by Tom Bottomore (1983). For example, the concept **Capital** is not included in the glossary but **Capitalism** appears. In Bottomore, capital is defined generally as an asset owned by an individual as wealth, but the specific meanings are complicated and deserving of elaboration, as in Marx's treatment over three volumes.

Accumulation   The process whereby capitalists sell commodities and convert the money from the sale into capital (cf. **Primitive accumulation**).

Analysis   The separation or breaking up of the whole into its fundamental parts and subjecting them to detailed qualitative or quantitative examination; analysis may involve clarification and explication.

Apparatus   Agencies of the state such as repressive apparatus for policy and armed forces, ideological apparatus for the media, and so on. A concept developed by Althusser and Poulantzas (cf. **State**).

Associated dependent capitalist development   Situation in the periphery in which the domestic bourgeoisie ties itself to capitalism, associates with international capital, and stimulates capitalist accumulation. Accumulation and expansion of local capital thus depend on the dynamic of international capitalism (cf. **Dependency**).

Autonomy of the state   (cf. **State**).

Backwardness   A characterization that describes conditions of exploitation and underdevelopment in some countries.

Behavioral approach   A positivist mode of inquiry that focuses empirically on the individual and the small group as the unit of analysis, with attention to motivations, perceptions, and attitudes toward authority.

Bourgeois democratic revolution   The bourgeois revolution usually refers to the transformation of capitalism through the formation and eventual hegemony of a capitalist class (cf. **Bourgeoisie**). The bourgeois democratic revolution usually comes about through parliamentary democracy or social democracy in which proletarian forces support bourgeois rule and reformist action en route to socialism.

Bourgeoisie The capitalist class, the class of owners of the means of production, and the employers of wage labor under capitalism. This class leads the transition to capitalism and may be involved in changes in the direction of socialism (see **bourgeois democratic revolution**).

Bureaucratic authoritarianism A situation where state intervention becomes decisive under authoritarian conditions and serves as an impulse to the developmental process, especially with the exhaustion of the import substitution model of industrialization and where state and national capital are unable to work in isolation from international capital.

Capitalism An economic system characterized by the formation of a bourgeois class that owns and controls the means of production and a class of producers that owns only its labor and must sell its labor power to the owners of the means of production in order to survive.

Circulation of elites A phenomenon arising from competition among the segments of the ruling class and resulting in changes in the composition of the ruling class through the recruitment of members from the lower strata and the incorporation of new social groups.

Class Group or groups characterized by similar socioeconomic criteria, such as income and status. Marx believed that under capitalism society would eventually polarize into two classes, the bourgeoisie and the proletariat. Weber described class in a market situation and emphasized status groups. These writers and others refer to many classes. A ruling class, for example, is an economic class that rules politically; it tends to be a class of varied interests that becomes cohesive. Other classes may include the monopolistic, agrarian, mining, industrial, and commercial bourgeoisie; the petty bourgeoisie; the new middle class, or new petty bourgeoisie; the proletariat; peasants; and the lumpen proletariat.

Colonial dependency The situation in which the land, natural resources, and labor of a colony are tied to the mother country through trade monopolies.

Colonialism The holding of territories under the administration and jurisdiction of dominant countries, such as Great Britain, France, Spain, and Portugal from the fifteenth century; associated with mercantile capitalism.

Communism A type of society characterized by the elimination of a commodity and money economy; the disappearance of inequality, classes, and the state; the overcoming of alienation in work; and the creative use of work and leisure.

Comparative government Traditionally the study of industrial countries or nation-states in Europe, focused on the institutions and functions of those countries, with attention to their executives, legislatures, and judiciaries as well as such supplementary organizations as political parties and pressure groups (cf. **Comparative politics**).

Comparative politics The study of a broad range of political activity, including governments and their institutions as well as other forms of organizations not directly related to national government, for example, tribes, communities, associations, and unions.

Competitive capitalism Capitalism with "free" competition, usually under small-scale enterprise, in contrast to the tendency to concentrate capital through cartels, trusts, and holding companies under monopoly capitalism.

Concept   A theoretical construct of a universal term or idea conceived in the mind and expressed in clear and well-formulated statements; useful in theory building. Conceptualization must occur prior to description and classification, quantification and measurement, and the testing of theory. Concepts may be worked into definitional schema, classificatory arrangements, or systematic orderings that accompany a particular theoretical approach.

Corporatism   Traditionally understood with reference to fascist regimes, especially in Spain, Portugal, and Italy. Political scientists of the 1970s saw the amorphous complex of agencies representing the state and civil society in a corporatist system as somewhat analogous to interest group activity.

Cybernetics   The systematic study of communication and control in all kinds of organizations. The idea was developed by Norbert Wiener based on the assumption that the performance of machines may be corrected and guided by information in a feedback process similar to the functioning of living individuals.

Deduction   The application of the principle that if a universal generalization is true, then a lesser generalization can be true.

Democracy   Derived, according to *Webster's New International Dictionary* (3d ed.), from the Greek roots *demos,* signifying people, and *kratia,* authority, and suggesting government by the people or government in which supreme power is retained by the people and exercised either directly in the form of absolute or pure democracy or indirectly through a system of representation. Representative, indirect, and formal or bourgeois democracy typical of more common practice can be contrasted with participatory, direct, and informal or proletarian democracy.

Dependency   The situation in which accumulation and expansion of capital characterize dominant countries or regions, to the disadvantage of the less developed countries, which become stagnant and unable to expand and be self-sustaining (cf. **Associated dependent capitalism, Colonial dependency, Financial-industrial dependency, New dependency**).

Dependent variables   (cf. **Variables**).

Description   A statement about the parts or relations of something; may involve classification, identification, and specification.

Development   Generally the proposition that all basic needs (health, food, shelter, education, and employment) of all people should be provided for. In a broad sense this might also imply such human needs as survival, belonging, and leisure.

Development of underdevelopment   The thesis (Frank, 1967) that capitalism generates economic growth in the metropolis center through the appropriation of the economic surplus of satellites, thereby contributing to stagnation and underdevelopment in the periphery.

Dialectics   A process of understanding through the juxtaposition of theory and practice or weighing tensions or oppositions between interacting forces; allows for the building of theory upon new facts as well as for the interpreting of facts in relation to new theory. Both Hegel and Marx employed a dialectical method, with the former emphasizing idealism and the latter believing in a materialist, not an idealist, view of history.

Diffusionist development   The view that political and economic democracy, nationalist development, and modernization will result from the diffusion of capital and technology from advanced to backward nations.

Dual power   The traditional Marxist-Leninist thesis that workers and popular forces must mobilize outside the state, agitating through an alternative organization and eventually revolting against the state to bring about its revolutionary transformation.

Economic base   (cf. **Infrastructure**).

Economic surplus   As defined by Baran (1957/1960), the difference between a society's output and its consumption. He suggested different forms, including actual, potential, and planned surplus.

Elitist theory of democracy   The idea that in every society a privileged minority makes the major decisions, an idea that dates to the thought of Plato and Pareto.

Equilibrium   The balance of forces within a social or political system. Mosca conceived equilibrium as a system of interdependent forces moving together. Easton emphasized stability in an interrelated process of inputs (demands and supports) and outputs (decisions and policies).

False consciousness   As envisaged by Marx, the reflection of the superstructure or ideological and political underpinnings of capitalist society in the beliefs and symbols of culture. Thus, under capitalism, culture tends to reflect the interests of the ruling capitalist class.

Feminism   Within liberalism, a defense and promotion of women's rights, opportunities, and equality with men. A separatist form advocates female communities, strengthening of women's relationship to each other, and attacking male brutality. Another current aligns the struggle for women's liberation with socialist and other lines of left politics (cf. **New social movements**).

Finance capital   Bank capital that penetrates and dominates industry; the term originates in Hilferding's *Finance Capital* (1910).

Financial-industrial dependency   A situation in which big bank and industrial capital dominated and expanded outside the hegemonic centers during the period from the end of the nineteenth century to the Second World War.

Forces of production   Productive capacity, including plants and machinery, technology, and labor skills (cf. **Means of production, Mode of production**).

Formal modeling   Simulating situations through a mathematical and statistical model; used in rational choice theory.

Generalization   A general statement of uniformities and regularities. The simplest form of explanation, in which knowledge of subject matter facilitates the capacity to generalize. Meehan (1965) identified three forms of generalization: universal generalizations, which in some cases may be laws, because they have withstood intensive testing; probabilistic generalizations that based on experience likely are valid (frequently referred to as propositions); and tendency generalizations, expressed in tentative and conjectural terms (thus being hypotheses, which may be true but have not yet been tested).

Global or grand theory   A search for universal conceptualizations; also known as macro theory. The efforts to establish such theory for comparative politics have been largely discredited because of generality, vagueness, and abstraction.

Governing class The idea that one elite may take the place of another and that individuals may move from a low to a high stratum in society. Pareto divided this high stratum into a governing class, or elite (those who directly or indirectly govern), and a nongoverning elite.

Group A cluster of individuals or interests that may coincide with class but usually are distinguishable from classes in the analysis of mainstream social scientists.

Hegemony The dominance of some social group or class or bloc of forces in power. Once a crisis in the hegemony of the ruling class occurs, for example, the masses may become disenchanted and rebellious. The concept is important in the thought of Gramsci.

Historicism An outgrowth of German academic debate in the nineteenth century, dealing with history and influencing Hegel, Marx, and other thinkers; sometimes referred to as perspectivism, subjectivism, relativism, or instrumentalism.

Hypothesis A tendency generalization, expressed in tentative and conjectural terms, which may be true but has not yet been tested.

Ideal types Conceptual formulations that describe and classify phenomena that approximate empirical probability. For Weber ideal types served as the basis for his analysis of authority—traditional, charismatic, and legal authority.

Ideology Beliefs, norms, and values incorporated into either a total or particular framework, in the sense suggested by Mannheim in *Ideology and Utopia* (1936). Conceptually understood as false consciousness by Lukács; in Marxism seen as part of the political, religious, and philosophical superstructure, itself a reflection of the capitalist base of society.

Imperialism As defined by Lenin, monopoly capitalism, the highest stage of capitalism, usually associated with the appearance of cartels, trusts, and holding companies and the growth of industrial monopolies along with accumulation within a world market; alternatively, the military and political expansion of aggressive nations beyond their borders (cf. **Monopoly capitalism**).

Import substitution A policy of discouraging the importation of luxury goods through the implementation of tariffs and building of infrastructure to encouraging local industry to meet demands for consumer goods.

Independent variables (cf. **Variables**).

Induction The process of inferring a generalization from a pattern of specific observations. In mainstream comparative politics, induced generalizations and propositions are suspect because they may be viewed as deterministic or deemed to be correct and true when in fact conclusive evidence may be lacking or deviant cases to disprove them may exist.

Infrastructure The economic structures in which the relations of production and material foundations are found and upon which, according to Marx, the legal and political superstructures arise; as used by economists, the roads, power, and other resources that permit industrialization.

Instrumentalism The idea that the state is the instrument of the ruling or dominant class.

Interest group Special interests or issues advocated by groups; associated with notions of pluralism and the idea that groups effectively participate in representative democratic systems.

Internal colonialism   A relationship similar to the colonial relationship between nations but involving dominant and marginal groups within a single society (for example, according to González Casanova, the monopoly of the ruling metropolis in Mexico over the marginal Indian communities).

Internationalization of capital   A theory elaborated by Christian Palloix and others that incorporates an analysis of the movement of capital and class struggle on an international level.

Labor power   Capacity for work, including skills, owned by the class of producers, who under capitalism must sell it to the owners of the means of production in order to survive.

Late capitalism   As defined by Mandel (1975), the capitalism of the post–Second World War period, characterized by the rise of the multinational firm.

Macro theory   Broad-range theory, sometimes referred to as global or grand theory (in the usage of Talcott Parsons); often concerned with general policy questions (as in macroeconomics) oriented to analysis of overall data and trends.

Means of production   The tools, land, buildings, machinery, and raw materials with which workers produce goods for themselves and the society (cf. **Mode of production, Forces of production**).

Merchant capital   An elementary form of capitalism associated with mercantilism, the introduction of money, and the appearance of the merchant in international commerce.

Method   A procedure or process that involves the techniques and tools used in inquiry for examining, testing, and evaluating theory. Methods may be experimental, statistical, or linguistic. The case study method looks at a single (configurative) or a multitude of examples, may be qualitative or quantitative, and offers possibilities for theory building and gathering information.

Methodology   Methods, procedures, working concepts, rules, and the like used for testing theory, guiding inquiry, and searching for solutions to problems of the real world. Methodology is a particular way of viewing, organizing, and giving shape to inquiry.

Micro theory   Has suffered from overemphasis with technique rather than substance; often sensitive issues of politics are obscured by limiting ths scope of inquiry to small problems and easily manageable data.

Middle-range theory   A level of theory between macro and micro emphasizing the study of institutions (structures) and their activities (functions); preferred by most practitioners of social science, especially in comparative politics.

Mode of production   The mix of productive forces and relations of production in a society at a given time in history. Modes may include primitive communism, feudalism, capitalism, and communism (cf. **Forces of production, Means of production**).

Model   A construct that brings disparate parts together and demonstrates relationships. Models tend to simplify representations of the real world. They can facilitate understanding but they do not explain. They help bring order to the mass of information available to students of comparative politics. Models, like typologies and classifications, are limited, however. They are mental constructions, not theories.

Modernization The development of capitalism, especially industrialization, and of the forces of production in a universal drive toward advanced forms of capitalism. In political science the term often implies an advanced form of democracy.

Monopoly capitalism A form of capitalism characterized by the rise of cartels, trusts, and holding companies and the growth of industrial monopolies.

Narrow-gauge theory (cf. **Micro theory**).

National bourgeoisie The domestic class of "progressive" capitalists in a nation whose interests presumably are not tied to international capital but are associated with the development of national resources and industrialization.

Necessary production Production for the subsistence of workers—their food, shelter, and so on (cf. **Surplus production**).

New dependency Dependency characterized by capital investment of multinational corporations in industries oriented to the internal market of underdeveloped counties in the period after the Second World War (cf. **Dependency**).

New social movements Movements organized around particular causes as an alternative (sometimes referred to as identity politics) to traditional participation in politics. The tumultuous events of 1968, driven by some of the early new social movements, were unique in that they were not always working-class led or based. The new social movements tend to be grassroots and popular; involved in protest; and focused on such issues as ethnicity, feminism, ecology, and so on.

Normative approach A traditional tendency, dating to times before philosophy was divorced from politics, that looks to desirable cultural values in society and emphasizes rules, rights, and obligations that are considered desirable; contrasts with perspectives seeking to be empirical, positivist, or purely scientific.

Overdetermination A concept in the thought of Althusser and adapted by Resnick and Wolff (1982) to suggest that "each process has no existence other than as the site of the converging influences exerted by all the other social processes. . . . the class process is a condition of existence of each and every other social process" (2).

Paradigm A scientific community's perspective of the world, its set of beliefs and commitments—conceptual, theoretical, methodological, and instrumental; guides the scientific community's selection of problems, evaluation of data, and advocacy of theory.

Peripheral capitalism As defined by Prebisch and others, an imitative capitalism in backward countries in which capitalism is unable to reproduce itself and capital accumulation is incompatible with the consumer society (cf. **Capitalism**).

Petty bourgeoisie A class of merchants who do not own means of production; also may refer to intellectuals and professionals.

Petty commodity production The production by professional artisans of commodities that they exchange freely for products they need.

Political culture Usually linked with formal representative democracy, but also tied to participatory and pluralistic democracy based on the toleration of individual freedoms, consensus, and order through rational bureaucracy. The mainstream perspective looks to modernization and democracy in the shaping of culture through values such as civic virtue and responsibility, sharing with others, trust and confidence in one's fellow being, and freedom from anxiety.

Political economy The study and analysis of political and economic processes, usually defined as a social science, concerned with economics but related primarily to politics, yet only recently of concern to political science. Marx, Smith, and Ricardo all worked out their theories within a framework of political economy.

Political system As initially conceived by David Easton, illustrated by a black box with inputs of demands and supports and outputs of decisions and policies with feedback to suggest equilibrium. Gabriel Almond applied a structural-functionalism and slightly modified this scheme (cf. **Systems theory**).

Positivism The basis of contemporary social science concerned with knowledge based on objectivity and observations of real experience; evolved from the classical British empiricism associated with Hume and elaborated by Comte.

Postimperialism The notion that global institutions tend to promote the integration of diverse national interests on a new international basis by offering access to capital resources and technologies. For example, dominant class elements and resistant labor movements might coalesce across national boundaries as capital transforms through a globalization process.

Post-Marxism A current of thinking, popular in the 1990s, that suggests Marxism has been transcended by a new politics of identity, new social movements, and postmodernism and that class as agency no longer is relevant in analysis of contemporary society.

Power elite A concept worked out by Mills (1956) in a book with the same title, referring to the upper reaches of power in society, including the military, bureaucrats, and businesspeople.

Primitive accumulation The process whereby the possession of the means of production is taken from the workers or producers in the early stages of capitalism, thus breaking down the precapitalist social formation.

Proletariat A class of workers who only own their labor and must sell this to the owners of the means of production in order to survive.

Proposition A probabilistic generalization that based on experience likely is valid.

Protest A manifestation in the form of complaint, objection, disapproval, or display of resistance or objection to an idea, course of action, or social condition. Protest may be a response to institutional failure to accommodate immediate demands or to suppression, exploitation, or rejection.

Qualitative analysis Inquiry based on research not greatly concerned with formal method and tending toward generality, employing historical chronology and description, and drawing on universal strategies in comparisons.

Qualitative variables (cf. **Variables**).

Quantitative analysis Inquiry emphasizing specificity and exactness; employs variable-oriented comparative research focused on features of social structure identifiable as variables and hypotheses tested usually through multivariate statistical techniques.

Quantitative variables (cf. **Variables**).

Rational choice theory Theory focused on individuals and associated with "micro-foundations," "methodological individualism," and formal theory.

Relations of production   The division of labor that puts productive forces in motion (cf. **Means of production**).

Reproduction of capital   Process by which a capitalist society, to continue producing, reproduces itself by replacing equipment, raw materials, and other essentials used in production. In production, workers consume the means of production or raw materials that go into their product; with their wages, they also consume in order to obtain food and shelter. The capitalist consumes labor power or pays for the labor that is used in the production process.

Resistance   The reaction of a segment of the population to some issue such as social (exploitation) conditions; may evolve into an organizational mobilization aimed at mitigating those conditions.

Ruling class   The dominant social class, usually associated with an aristocracy, oligarchy, or bourgeoisie. Marx referred to the ruling class as an economic class that rules politically. Mosca depicted the ruling class as a political class that represents the interests of important and influential groups, especially in parliamentary democracies.

Socialism   Collective and public rather than individual and private ownership of the means of production and appropriation of the surplus product (cf. **Transition to socialism**).

State   An entity that evolved when the functions of people in primitive communal societies were assumed by separate groups of people, such as armies, judges, and hereditary rulers. Hegel, Marx, and Engels saw the state as emerging from the civil society as a separate entity of apparatuses and activities. An instrumentalist approach emphasizes that the state is only an instrument manipulated by the ruling classes, whereas the structuralist approach stresses that the bourgeois ruling class is unable to dominate the state and the state unifies and organizes the interests of that class through structures or apparatuses such as the army, police, and judiciary.

Status groups   In Weberian thought, related to the location of class in the market and relations of circulation.

Structural approach   Analysis distinguishing between center and periphery in developmental considerations; may focus on the autonomous prospects for the state, institutional concern for separation of governmental powers, and groups and classes (cf. **Structural-functionalism** and **Structuralism**).

Structural-functionalism   Middle-range theory focused on a mix of structures (institutions) and their functions (activities) that are viewed as common to all societies. Popular during the 1960s among mainstream social scientists.

Structuralism   The approach of political economists to analyzing the world in terms of centers and peripheries, metropoles and satellites. Alternatively, in some Marxist writings, the repressive, political, and ideological apparatuses of the capitalist state. Structures are also analyzed in the form of groups and classes and their economic interests so that attention is directed to the struggle between economic classes.

Subimperialism   As defined by Marini, a situation in which the prospects for industrialization in a dependent capitalist economy are not great and therefore the economy attempts to expand by pushing beyond its national borders and dominating the economies of weaker neighbors.

Superstructure The legal, political, religious, philosophical, or ideological forms that according to Marx arise out of the infrastructure or economic base of society (cf. **Infrastructure**).

Surplus production The production of workers beyond their requirements for subsistence (cf. **Necessary production**).

Sustainable development In either capitalist or socialist economies, the enhancement of the quality of life of contemporary peoples without impairing the welfare of future generations. Development must be designed for the human being to provide for basic needs while protecting the environment on a global scale.

Synthesis The combining of the parts into the whole, of diverse ideas and forces into a coherent or cohesive complex.

System (cf. **Political system**).

Systems theory Theory emphasizing equilibrium and structural-functionalism; advocated by Parsons in sociology and Easton in political science.

Theory Set of systematically related generalizations premised on what is happening or might happen in the real world. Theory can lead to changes in the world, and the experiences of the world can shape, revise, and refine theory (cf. **Global or grand theory, Micro theory, Macro theory**).

Transition to socialism Period in which a workers' state replaces the capitalist state, the means of production come under collective rather than private ownership, and proletarian democracy replaces bourgeois democracy, though remnants of capitalism such as a money economy may persist.

Typology A classification or framework that divides and orders information and facts.

Ultra-imperialism A theory worked out by Kautsky proposing that the capitalist nations eventually would rationally and peacefully align with each other and divide up the underdeveloped world.

Underconsumption Traditionally, a condition in which domestic consumption is unable to absorb the products of industrialized nations, thus necessitating imperialism in the search for markets in the exploited colonies and outlying areas; more recently, an explanation for underdevelopment in backward countries in which a bourgeoisie's consumption is limited.

Underdevelopment A theory that suggests the negative consequences of capitalism and the imperialist advance (cf. **Backwardness, Development of underdevelopment, Imperialism**).

Unequal exchange A theory prominent among Third World economists such as Amin who focus on the differences between the impoverished masses and the wealthy minority in the world capitalist system.

Variables Concepts with quantitative or qualitative attributes that are employed in the search for causal explanation. Numerical values, such as age or size, can be utilized with quantitative variables, whereas nonnumerical values are employed with qualitative variables. Variables also may be dependent or independent: Dependent variables depend on at least one other variable, and independent variables are completely autonomous from other variables (cf. **Dependent variables, Independent variables, Qualitative variables, Quantitative variables**).

World systems theory A theory influenced by Fernand Braudel and elaborated by Immanuel Wallerstein that analyzes the origins and evolution of capitalism through center, semiperiphery, and periphery.

REFERENCES

Many classical works appear in the text with the date of the original publication but do not appear in References unless there is a citation to a quote or substantive content in the text. These works generally are identified as examples of scholarship or historical works of significance to the fields of political science and political economy but are not dealt with in depth in the present text. In general, these works were published before 1970 and are easily found in most libraries.

With only a few exceptions, works after 1970 appear in References. Where the original edition was in a foreign language but an English edition exists from which a page reference is given, the date of the original publication will appear first, followed by the date and title of the English edition. Foreign titles appear only where there exists no English edition.

Acuña, Rodolfo. 1972. *Occupied America: The Chicano's Struggle Toward Liberation.* San Francisco: Harper & Row.

Albert, Michael, and Robin Hahnel. 1991a. *Looking Forward: Participatory Economics for the Twenty-First Century.* Boston: South End Press.

_____. 1991b. *The Political Economy of Participatory Economics.* Princeton: Princeton University Press.

Almond, Gabriel A. 1956. "Comparative Political Systems." *Journal of Politics,* 18 (August), 391–409.

_____. 1988. "The Return to the State," *American Political Science Review,* 82 (September), 853–874.

_____. 1990a. *A Discipline Divided: Schools and Sects in Political Science.* Newbury Park, CA: Sage Publications.

_____. 1990b. "Rational-Choice Theory and the Social Sciences," pp. 117–137 in his *A Discipline Divided: Schools and Sects in Political Science.* Newbury Park, CA: Sage Publications.

_____. 1990c. "Separate Tables: Schools and Sects in Political Science," pp. 13–31 in his *A Discipline Divided: Schools and Sects in Political Science.* Newbury Park, CA: Sage Publications. Also in *PS: Political Science and Politics* (Fall 1988), 828–841.

_____. 1991. "Capitalism and Democracy." *PS: Political Science and Politics,* 24 (September), 467–473.

Almond, Gabriel A., and G. Bingham Powell. 1966. *Comparative Politics: A Developmental Approach.* Boston: Little, Brown.

Almond, Gabriel A., and James S. Coleman (eds.). 1960. *The Politics of Developing Areas*. Princeton: Princeton University Press.

Almond, Gabriel A., and Sidney Verba. 1963. *The Civic Culture: Political Attitudes and Democracy in Five Nations*. Princeton: Princeton University Press.

Almond, Gabriel A., and Sidney Verba (eds.). 1980. *The Civic Culture Revisited*. Boston: Little, Brown and Co., 2d ed., Sage Publications, 1989.

Althusser, Louis. 1970. *For Marx*. Translated by Ben Brewster. New York: Vintage Books.

_____. 1971. "Ideology and Ideological State Apparatuses," pp. 121–173 in his *Lenin and Philosophy and Other Essays*. London: New Left Books.

Amin, Samir. 1974. *Accumulation on a World Scale: A Critique of the Theory of Underdevelopment*. New York: Monthly Review Press.

_____. 1976. *Unequal Development: An Essay on the Social Transformations of Peripheral Capitalism*. New York: Monthly Review Press.

_____. 1977a. *Imperialism and Unequal Development*. New York: Monthly Review Press.

_____. 1977b. "Universality and Cultural Spheres." *Monthly Review*, 28 (February), 25–38.

Anderson, Perry. 1974. *Passages from Antiquity to Feudalism*. London: Verso.

_____. 1975. *Lineages of the Absolute State*. London: Verso.

_____. 1980. *Arguments Within English Marxism*. London: New Left Books.

_____. 1990. "A Culture in Contraflow." *New Left Review*, 180 (March-April), 41–78, and 182 (July-August), 85–137.

Aronowitz, Stanley. 1990. "Marxism and Democracy," ch. 8, pp. 256–304, in his *The Crisis of Historical Materialism: Class, Politics and Culture in Marxist Theory*. Minneapolis: University of Minnesota Press.

_____. 1994. "The Situation of the Left in the United States." *Socialist Review*, 23 (3), 5–79.

Arrighi, Giovanni. 1994. *The Long Twentieth Century*. London: Verso.

Baran, Paul. 1960. *The Political Economy of Growth*. 2d ed. New York: Prometheus. Original edition, Monthly Review Press, 1957.

Baran, Paul, and Paul Sweezy. 1966. *Monopoly Capital: An Essay on the American Economic and Social Order*. New York: Monthly Review Press.

Bates, Robert H. 1981. *Markets and States in Tropical Africa: The Political Basis of Agricultural Policies*. Berkeley: University of California Press.

Becker, David G., Jeff Frieden, Sayre P. Schatz, and Richard L. Sklar (eds.). 1987. *Postimperialism, International Capitalism, and Development in the Late Twentieth Century*. Boulder: Lynne Rienner Publishers.

Becker, David G., and Richard L. Sklar. 1987. "Why Imperialism?" pp. 1–18 in David G. Becker, Jeff Frieden, Sayre P. Schatz, and Richard L. Sklar, eds., *Postimperialism, International Capitalism and Development in the Late Twentieth Century*. Boulder: Lynne Rienner Publishers.

Bell, Daniel. 1962. *The End of Ideology: On the Exhaustion of Political Ideas in the Fifties*. 2d ed. New York: Collier Books.

_____. 1988. "The End of Ideology Revisited." *Government and Opposition*, 23 (Spring), 321–331.

Benton, Ted. 1989. "Marxism and Natural Limits: An Ecological Critique and Reconstruction." *New Left Review,* 178 (December), 51–86.

Bettelheim, Charles. 1976. *Class Struggles in the USSR.* New York: Monthly Review Press.

Bill, James A., and Robert L. Hardgrave Jr. 1973. *Comparative Politics: The Quest for Theory.* Columbus, OH: Charles E. Merrill, 2d ed., Washington, DC: University Press of America, 1981.

Binder, Leonard (ed.). 1971. *Crises and Sequences in Political Development.* Princeton: Princeton University Press.

Blaut, James. 1977. "Are Puerto Ricans a National Minority?" *Monthly Review,* 29 (May), 35–55.

Boggs, Carl. 1986. *Social Movements and Political Power: Emerging Forms of Radicalism in the West.* Philadelphia: Temple University Press.

_____. 1995. *The Socialist Tradition: From Crisis to Decline.* New York: Routledge.

Bowles, Samuel, and Herbert Gintis. 1986. *Democracy and Capitalism: Property, Community, and the Contradictions of Modern Social Thought.* New York: Basic Books.

Braverman, Harry. 1974. *Labor and Monopoly Capital: The Degradation of Work in the Twentieth Century.* New York: Monthly Review Press.

Brenner, Robert. 1976. "The Origins of Capitalist Development: A Critique of Neo-Smithean Marxism." *New Left Review,* 104 (July-August), 24–92.

Brewer, Anthony. 1990. *Marxist Theories of Imperialism: A Critical Survey.* London: Routledge and Kegan Paul. Originally published 1980.

Burawoy, Michael. 1985. *The Politics of Production.* London: Verso.

_____. 1989. "Should We Give Up on Socialism?" *Socialist Review,* (1), 59–74. (Critique of Bowles and Gintis, *Democracy and Capitalism* [1989]).

Burris, Val. 1987. "The Neo-Marxist Synthesis of Marx and Weber on Class," pp. 67–90 in Norbert Wiley, ed., *The Marx-Weber Debate.* Newbury Park, CA: Sage Publications.

Caldwell, Malcolm. 1977. *The Wealth of Some Nations.* London: Zed Press.

Cammack, Paul. 1997. *Capitalism and Democracy in the Third World: The Doctrine for Political Development.* London: Leicester University Press.

Canak, William L. 1984. "The Peripheral State Debate: State Capitalist and Bureaucratic Authoritarian Regimes in Latin America." *Latin American Research Review,* 19 (1), 3–36.

Caporaso, James A. (ed.). 1989. *The Elusive State: International and Comparative Perspectives.* Newbury Park, CA: Sage Publications.

Cardoso, Fernando Henrique. 1973. "Imperialism and Dependency in Latin America," pp. 7–33 in Frank Bonilla and Robert Girling, eds., *Structures of Dependence.* Stanford, CA. (See a similar piece, "Associated-Dependent Development: Theoretical and Practical Implications," pp. 142–176 in Alfred Stepan, ed., *Authoritarian Brazil.* New Haven: Yale University Press, 1973.)

Cardoso, Fernando Henrique, and Enzo Falleto. 1979. *Dependency and Development.* Berkeley: University of California Press.

Carnoy, Martin. 1984. *The State and Political Theory.* Princeton: Princeton University Press.

Castells, Manuel. 1973. *Luttes urbaines et pouvoir politique.* Paris: Maspero.

Castoriadis, Cornelius. 1988–1993. *Political and Social Writings.* 3 vols. Translated and edited by David Ames Curtis. Minneapolis: University of Minnesota Press.

Chilcote, Edward B., and Ronald H. Chilcote. 1992. "The Crisis of Marxism: An Appraisal of New Directions." *Rethinking Marxism,* 5 (Summer), 84–106.

Chilcote, Ronald H. 1982. *Theories of Comparative Politics: The Search for a Paradigm.* Boulder: Westview Press.

_____. 1984. *Theories of Development and Underdevelopment.* Boulder: Westview Press.

_____. 1991. "Capitalism and Socialist Perspectives in the Search for a Class Theory of the State and Democracy," pp. 75–97 in Dankwart Rustow and Kenneth Erickson, eds., *Comparative Political Dynamics: Global Research Perspectives.* New York: Harper and Collins.

_____. 1992. "Development." pp. 616–637 in Mary Hawkesworth and Maurice Kogan, eds., *Encyclopedia of Government and Politics,* vol. 1. London: Routledge. (A conceptualization of developmental theory and policy, identification of the major approaches and schools of thought, a bibliography of principal sources.)

_____. 1994. *Theories of Comparative Politics: The Search for a Paradigm Revisited.* 2d ed. Boulder: Westview Press.

_____. Forthcoming. *Theories of Comparative Political Economy.* Boulder: Westview Press.

Chilcote, Ronald H. (ed.). 1972. *Protest and Resistance in Angola and Brazil: Comparative Studies.* Berkeley: University of California Press.

Clawson, Robert W. 1973. "Political Socialization of Children in the USSR." *Political Science Quarterly,* 87 (December), 684–712.

Clegg, Stewart, Paul Boreham, and Geoff Dow. 1985. *Class, Politics and the Economy.* London: Routledge and Kegan Paul.

Cohen, G. A. 1978. *Karl Marx's Theory of History: A Defense.* Princeton: Princeton University Press.

Cohen, Jean L. 1982. *Class and Civil Society: The Limits on Marxian Critical Theory.* Amherst: University of Massachusetts Press.

Cohen, Joshua, and Joel Rogers. 1983. *On Democracy: Toward a Transformation of American Society.* New York: Penguin Books.

Colfax, David, and Jack L. Roach (eds.). 1971. *Radical Sociology.* New York: Basic Books.

Collier, Ruth Berins, and David Collier. 1991. *Shaping the Political Arena: Critical Junctures, the Labor Movement, and Regime Dynamics in Latin America.* Princeton: Princeton University Press.

Conroy, Martin. 1984. *The State and Political Theory.* Princeton: Princeton University Press.

Cunningham, Frank. 1987. *Democratic Theory and Socialism.* New York: Cambridge University Press.

Dahl, Robert A. 1978. "Pluralism Revisited." *Comparative Politics,* 1 (January), 191–203.

Dahrendorf, Ralf. 1959. *Class and Class Conflict in Industrial Society.* Stanford: Stanford University Press.

Domhoff, G. William. 1978a. *The Powers That Be: Process of Ruling Class Domination in America.* New York: Vintage Books.

_____. 1978b. *Who Really Rules? New Haven and Community Power Reexamined.* New Brunswick, NJ: Transaction Books.

Dos Santos, Theotônio. 1970. "The Structure of Dependence." *American Economic Review,* 60, 231–236.

Draper, Hal. 1977. *Karl Marx's Theory of the Revolution. Book 1: State and Bureaucracy.* New York: Monthly Review Press.

Dube, S. C. 1988. *Modernization and Development: The Search for Alternative Paradigms.* London: Zed Books, and Tokyo: United Nations University.

Durkheim, Émile. 1938. *The Rules of Sociological Method.* Translated by Sarah A. Solovay and John H. Mueller and edited by George E. G. Catlin. Chicago: University of Chicago Press.

Duverger, Maurice. 1964. *An Introduction to the Social Sciences with Special Reference to Their Methods.* Translated by Malcolm Anderson. New York: Frederick A. Praeger.

Easton, David. 1953. *The Political System: An Inquiry into the State of Political Science.* New York: Alfred A. Knopf.

_____. 1965. *A Framework for Political Analysis.* Englewood Cliffs, NJ: Prentice Hall.

_____. 1981. "The Political System Besieged by the State." *Political Theory,* 9 (August), 303–325.

_____. 1990. *The Analysis of Political Structure.* New York: Routledge.

Eckstein, Harry. 1982. "The Idea of Political Development: From Dignity to Efficiency." *World Politics,* 34 (July), 451–468.

Elliott, Gregory. 1987. *Althusser: The Detour of Theory.* London: Verso.

Elster, Jon. 1985. *Making Sense of Marx.* Cambridge, UK: Cambridge University Press.

Emmanuel, Arghiri. 1972. *Unequal Exchange: A Study of the Imperialism of Trade.* New York: Monthly Review Press.

Engels, Friedrich. N.d. *Origins of the Family, Private Property, and the State: In the Light of the Researches of Lewis H. Morgan.* New York: International Publishers. Originally published 1884.

Evans, Peter, Dietrich Rueschemeyer, and Theda Skocpol (eds.). 1985. *Bringing the State Back In.* Cambridge, UK: Cambridge University Press.

Evans, Peter, Dietrich Rueschemeyer, and Evelyn Hjuber Stephens (eds.). 1985. *States Versus Markets in the World-System.* Beverly Hills, CA: Sage Publications.

Evans, Peter B., and John D. Stephens. 1988. "Development and the World Economy," pp. 739–773 in Neil J. Smelsor, ed., *Handbook of Sociology.* Newbury Park, CA: Sage Publications.

Fagen, Richard R. 1969. *The Transformation of Political Culture in Cuba.* Stanford: Stanford University Press.

Fagen, Richard R., Carmen Diana Deere, and José Luis Coraggio (eds.). 1986. *Transition and Development: Problems of Third World Socialism.* New York: Monthly Review Press.

Frank, André Gunder. 1967. *Capitalism and Underdevelopment in Latin America: Historical Studies of Chile and Brazil.* New York: Monthly Review Press.

Frankel, Boris. 1987. *The Post-Industrial Utopians.* Madison: University of Wisconsin Press. (A critical appraisal of various "post" forms of society with focus on postindustrialism.)

Fuentes, Marta, and André Gunder Frank. 1989. "Ten Theses on Social Movements." *World Development,* 17 (2), 179–191.

Fukuyama, Francis. 1992. *The End of History and the Last Man.* New York: Free Press.

Furtado, Celso. 1963. *Economic Growth of Brazil: A Survey from Colonial to Modern Times.* Berkeley: University of California Press.

Fusfeld, Daniel R. 1966. *The Age of the Economist: The Development of Modern Economic Thought.* Glenview, IL: Scott, Foresman and Co.

Giele, Janet Z. 1988. "Gender and Sex Roles," pp. 291–323 in Neil J. Smelser, ed., *Handbook of Sociology.* Thousand Oaks, CA: Sage Publications. (A comprehensive overview of issues and directions around gender and sex, the new women's movements, and related topics.)

Gitlin, Todd. 1965. "Local Pluralism as Theory and Ideology." *Studies on the Left,* 5 (Summer), 21–72.

———. 1987. *The Sixties: Years of Hope, Days of Rage.* New York: Bantam Books.

González Casanova, Pablo. 1969. "Internal Colonialism and National Development," pp. 118–139 in Irving Louis Horowitz, ed., *Latin American Radicalism.* New York: Vintage Books. (His thesis on internal colonialism, drawn from his *Sociología de la explotación,* 2d ed., Mexico City: Siglo Veintiuno Editors, 1970.)

———. 1973. "Historical Systems and Social Systems." *Studies in Comparative International Development,* 8 (Fall), 227–246.

———. 1988. "The Theory of the State and Today's World." *Socialism in the World,* 11 (66), 3–25.

Goodman, David, and Michael Redclift. 1982. *From Peasant to Proletarian: Capitalist Development and Agrarian Transitions.* New York: St. Martin's Press.

Goodwin, Jeff. 1990. "The Limits of 'Radical Democracy.'" *Socialist Review,* 90 (4), 131–144.

Gorz, André. 1980. *Farewell to the Working Class.* London: Pluto Press.

Gramsci, Antonio. 1957. *The Modern Prince and Other Writings.* New York: New York University Press.

Grofman, Bernard. 1993. "Lessons of Athenian Democracy." *PS: Political Science and Politics,* 26 (September), 471–494.

Grosfuguel, Ramón. 1996. "From Cepalismo to Neoliberalism: A World Systems Approach to Conceptual Shifts in Latin America." *Review,* 19 (Spring), 131–154.

Guevara, Ernesto Che. 1967. *Man and Socialism in Cuba.* Havana: Book Institute.

Guinier, C. Lani. 1994. *The Tyranny of the Majority: Fundamental Fairness in Representative Democracy.* New York: Free Press.

Gunnell, John G. 1990. "In Search of the State: Political Science as an Emerging Discipline in the U.S.," pp. 123–161 in Wagner B. Whittrock and R. Riley, eds., *Discourses on Society,* vol. 15. Netherlands: Kluwer Academic Publishers.

Gurley, John. 1971. "Capitalist and Maoist Economic Development." *Monthly Review,* 22 (February), 15–35.

Hall, John A. 1985. *Powers and Liberties: The Causes and Consequences of the Rise of the West.* Berkeley: University of California Press.

Halliday, Fred. 1989. "Notes on the New Political Culture." *The Nation* (September 4ff.), 234ff.

Hanson, Russell L. 1989. "Democracy," ch. 4, pp. 68–89, in Terence Ball, James Farr, and Russell L. Hanson, eds., *Political Innovation and Conceptual Change.* New York: Cambridge University Press.

Harrington, Michael. 1976. *The Twilight of Capitalism.* New York: Simon & Schuster.

Harris, Marvin. 1968. *The Rise of Anthropological Theory: A History of Theories of Culture.* New York: Thomas Y. Crowell Co.

Heilbroner, Robert. 1993. *21st Century Capitalism.* New York: W. W. Norton.

Held, David. 1987. *Models of Democracy.* Stanford: Stanford University Press.

Hernández, Rafael, and Haroldo Dilla. 1992. "Political Culture and Popular Participation," pp. 31–46 in Centro de Estudios Sobre América, *The Cuban Revolution into the 1990s.* Boulder: Westview Press.

Hilton, Rodney (ed.). 1976. *The Transition from Feudalism to Capitalism.* London: New Left Books.

Hindess, Barry. 1987. *Politics and Class Analysis.* New York: Basil Blackwell.

_____.1992. "Class and Politics," ch. 34, pp. 555–567, in Mary Hawkesworth and Maurice Kogan, eds., *Encyclopedia of Government and Politics.* London: Routledge.

Hobson, J. A. 1965. *Imperialism: A Study.* Ann Arbor: Ann Arbor Paperbacks, University of Michigan Press.

Holloway, John, and Sol Picciotto (eds.). 1978. *State and Capital: A Marxist Debate.* Austin: University of Texas Press.

Huntington, Samuel P. 1968. *Political Order in Changing Societies.* New Haven: Yale University Press.

_____. 1974. "Paradigms of American Politics: Beyond the One, the Two, and the Many." *Political Science Quarterly,* 89 (March), 1–26.

_____. 1991. *The Third Wave: Democratization in the Late Twentieth Century.* Norman: University of Oklahoma Press.

Jacoby, Russell. 1987. *The Last Intellectuals: American Culture in the Age of Academe.* New York: Basic Books.

Jameson, Fredric. 1991. *Postmodernism or the Cultural Logic of Late Capitalism.* Durham, NC: Duke University Press.

Jessop, Bob. 1982. *The Capitalist State.* Oxford, UK: Martin Robertson.

_____. 1985. *Nicos Poulantzas: Marxist Theory and Political Strategy.* London: Macmillan.

_____. 1990. *State Theory: Putting Capitalist States in Their Place.* University Park: Pennsylvania University Press. (Especially "The Democratic State and the National Interest," ch. 6, pp. 170–189.)

Karl, Terry Lynn. 1990. "Dilemmas of Democratization in Latin America." *Comparative Politics,* 23 (October), 1–22.

Katzenstein, Peter. 1985. *Small States in World Markets: Industrial Policy in Europe.* Ithaca, NY: Cornell University Press.

Kay, Cristóbal.1989. *Latin American Theories of Development and Underdevelopment.* London: Routledge.

Kay, Geoffrey. 1975. *Development and Underdevelopment: A Marxist Analysis.* London: Macmillan.

Kennedy, Paul. 1987. *The Rise and Fall of the Great Powers: Economic Change and Military Conflict from 1500 to 2000.* New York: Random House.

Kesselman, Mark. 1982. "Socialist Pedagogy." *New Political Science* (Summer), 112–136.

Kesselman, Mark, and Joel Krieger (eds.). 1992. *European Politics in Transition.* 2d ed. Lexington, MA: D. C. Heath.

Krasner, Stephen D. 1988. "Sovereignty: An International Perspective." *Comparative Political Studies,* 21 (April), 66–94.

Kuhn, Thomas S. 1970. *The Structure of Scientific Revolutions.* 2d ed. Chicago: University of Chicago Press.

_____. 1977. "Second Thoughts on Paradigms," pp. 293–318 in his *The Essential Tension: Selected Studies in Scientific Tradition and Change.* Chicago: University of Chicago Press.

Laclau, Ernesto, and Chantal Mouffe. 1985. *Hegemony and Socialist Strategy: Towards a Radical Democratic Politics.* London: Verso.

Lenin, V. I. 1918. 1932. *State and Revolution.* New York: International Publishers.

Levine, Daniel H. 1988. "Paradigm Lost: Dependence to Democracy." *World Politics,* 40 (April), 377–393.

Lijphart, Arend. 1984. *Democracies: Patterns of Majoritarian and Consensus Government in Twenty-One Countries.* New Haven: Yale University Press.

Lipset, Seymour Martin. 1960. *Political Man: The Social Bases of Politics.* Garden City, NY: Doubleday.

_____. 1996. *American Exceptionalism: A Double-Edged Sword.* New York: W. W. Norton.

Löwy, Michael. 1991. "Twelve Theses on the Crisis of 'Really Existing Socialism.'" *Monthly Review,* 43 (May), 33–40.

Luke, Timothy W. 1989. "Class Contradictions and Social Cleavages in Informationalizing Post-Industrial Societies: On the Rise of New Social Movements." *New Political Science,* 16–17 (Fall-Winter), 125–153.

Lustig, R. Jeffrey. 1982. *Corporate Liberalism: The Origins of Modern Political Theory, 1890–1920.* Berkeley: University of California Press.

Lutjens, Sheryl L. 1996. *The State, Bureaucracy, and the Cuban Schools: Power and Participation.* Boulder: Westview Press.

MacKinnon, Catharine A. 1989. *Toward a Feminist Theory of the State.* Cambridge, MA: Harvard University Press.

Macridis, Roy C. 1955. *The Study of Comparative Government.* Studies in Political Science, vol. 21. New York: Random House.

Mandel, Ernest 1968. *Marxist Economic Theory.* 2 vols. Translated by Brian Pearce. New York: Monthly Review Press.

_____. 1975. *Late Capitalism.* London: New Left Books.

Mann, Michael. 1986. *The Sources of Social Power: A History of Power from the Beginning to A.D. 1760.* Cambridge, UK: Cambridge University Press.

Mannheim, Karl. 1929. 1936. *Ideology and Utopia: An Introduction to the Sociology of Knowledge.* Translated by Louis Wirth and Edward Shils. New York: Harcourt, Brace, and World.

Marable, Manning. 1983. *How Capitalism Underdeveloped Black America.* Boston: South End Press.

Marini, Ruy Mauro. 1978. "World Capitalist Accumulation and Sub-Imperialism." *Two Thirds,* 1 (Fall), 29–39.

Marx, Karl. 1859. 1904. *A Contribution to the Critique of Political Economy.* Translated from the second German edition by N. I. Stoke. Calcutta: Bharati Library.

_____. 1867, 1893, 1894. 1967. *Capital: A Critique of Political Economy.* 3 vols. New York: International Publishers

_____. 1939. 1973. *Grundrisse: Foundations of the Critique of Political Economy.* Translated with a foreword by Martin Nicolaus. New York: Vintage Books.

_____. 1975a. *Early Writings.* Introduction by Lucio Colletti. New York: Vintage Books.

_____. 1975b. *Critique of Hegel's Doctrine of the State (Philosophy and Right),* in his *Early Writings.* New York: Vintage Books.

Marx, Karl, and Friedrich Engels. 1848. 1958. *Manifesto of the Communist Party,* pp. 33–65 in their *Selected Works in Two Volumes.* Moscow: Foreign Languages Publishing House.

McNall, Scott G., Rhonda F. Levine, and Rick Fantasia (eds.). 1991. *Bringing Class Back In: Contemporary and Historical Perspectives.* Boulder: Westview Press.

Meek, Ronald L. 1956. *The Labour Theory of Value.* London: Lawrence and Wishart.

Meehan, Eugene. 1965. *The Theory and Method of Political Analysis.* Homewood, IL: Dorsey Press.

Mermelstein, David. 1970. *Economics and Mainstream Radical Critiques.* New York: Random House.

Migdal, Joel. 1988. *Strong Societies and Weak States: State-Society Relations and State Capabilities in the Third World.* Princeton: Princeton University Press.

Miliband, Ralph. 1969. *The State in Capitalist Society: An Analysis of the Western System of Power.* New York: Basic Books.

_____. 1990. "Counter-Hegemonic Struggles," pp. 346–365 in Ralph Miliband, Leo Panitch, and John Saville, eds., *Socialist Register 1990.* London: Merlin Press.

Miller, James. 1987. *Democracy in the Streets: From Port Huron to the Siege of Chicago.* New York: Simon and Schuster.

Mitchell, Timothy. 1991. "The Limits of the State: Beyond Statist Approach and Their Critics." *American Political Science Review,* 85 (March), 77–96.

Moore, Barrington, Jr. 1966. *Social Origins of Dictatorship and Democracy: Lord and Peasant in the Making of the Modern World.* Boston: Beacon Press.

Mouffe, Chantal (ed.). 1992. *Dimensions of Radical Democracy: Pluralism, Citizenship, Community.* London: Verso.

North, Douglas. 1981. *Structure of Change in Economic History.* New York: W. W. Norton.

Nove, Alex. 1983. *The Economics of Feasible Socialism.* London: George Allen and Unwin.

O'Connor, James. 1973. *The Fiscal Crisis of the State.* New York: St. Martin's Press.

O'Donnell, Guillermo. 1988. *Bureaucratic Authoritarianism: Argentina, 1966–1973, in Comparative Perspective.* Berkeley: University of California Press.

Ollman, Bertell. 1978. "On Teaching Marxism and Building the Movement." *New Political Science,* 1 (Spring-Summer), 7–12.

Organski, A. F. K. 1965. *The Stages of Political Development*. New York: Alfred A. Knopf.

Packenham, Robert A. 1992. *The Dependency Movement: Scholarship and Politics in Development Studies*. Cambridge, MA: Harvard University Press.

Palloix, Christian. 1977. "The Self-Expansion of Capital on a World Scale." *Review of Radical Political Economy*, 9 (Summer), 1–28. (See also his *L'Internationalisation du capital*. Paris: François Maspero, 1975.)

Palma, Gabriel. 1978. "Dependency: A Formal Theory of Underdevelopment or a Methodology for the Analysis of Concrete Situations of Underdevelopment." *World Development*, 6, 881–894.

Parkin, Frank. 1979. *Marxism and Class Theory: A Bourgeois Critique*. London: Tavistock Publications.

Pateman, Carole. 1991. "A New Democratic Theory? Political Science, the Public, and the Private." Buenos Aires: Paper delivered to the Plenary Session "Democratic Theory Today," International Political Science Association, July 21–25.

Pereira, Luiz Carlos Bresser. 1993. "Economic Reforms and Cycles of State Intervention." *World Development*, 21 (8), 1337–1353.

Petras, James. 1965. "Ideology and United States Political Scientists." *Science and Society*, 19 (Spring), 192–216.

Phillips, Anne. 1991. *Engendering Democracy*. Berkeley: University of California Press.

Poulantzas, Nicos. 1973. *Political Power and Social Classes*. London: New Left Books and Sheed and Ward.

_____. 1976. *The Crisis of the Dictatorships: Portugal, Greece, Spain*. London: New Left Books.

_____. 1977 "The New Petty Bourgeoisie," pp. 113–124 in Alan Hunt, ed., *Class and Class Structure*. London: Lawrence and Wishart.

_____. 1978. *State, Power, and Socialism*. London: New Left Books.

Przeworski, Adam. 1985. *Capitalism and Social Democracy*. New York: Cambridge University Press.

Pye, Lucian W. 1958. "The Non-Western Political Process." *Journal of Politics*, 20 (August), 468–486.

_____. 1963. *Communications and Political Development*. Princeton: Princeton University Press.

Pye, Lucian W., and Sidney Verba (eds.). 1965. *Political Culture and Political Development*. Studies in Political Development, vol. 5. Princeton: Princeton University Press.

Resnick, Stephen, and Richard D. Wolff. 1982. "Classes in Marxian Theory." *Review of Radical Political Economics*, 13 (Winter), 1–18.

Rey, Pierre-Philippe. 1973. *Les alliances de classes*. Paris: Maspero.

Ricci, David. 1984. *The Tragedy of Political Science: Politics, Scholarship, and Democracy*. New Haven: Yale University Press.

Rodney, Walter. 1972. *How Europe Underdeveloped Africa*. London and Dar es Salaam: Bogle-l'Ouverture and Tanzania Publishing House.

Roemer, John. 1988. *Free to Lose*. Cambridge, MA: Harvard University Press.

Rosenau, James N. 1988. "The State in an Era of Cascading Politics: Wavering Concept, Widening Competence, Widening Colossus or Weathering Change?" *Comparative Political Studies*, 21 (April), 13–44.

Rosenau, Pauline M., and Robert Paehlke. 1990. "The Exhaustion of Left and Right: Perspectives on the Political Participation of the Disadvantaged." *International Political Science Review*, 2 (1), entire issue.

Ross, Dorothy 1991. *The Origins of American Social Science*. Cambridge, UK: Cambridge University Press.

Rostow, Walt W. 1960. *The Stages of Economic Growth: A Non-Communist Manifesto*. Cambridge, UK: Cambridge University Press.

Rustow, Dankwart A. 1970. "Transitions to Democracy." *Comparative Politics*, 2 (April), 337–363.

Rustow, Dankwart A., and Kenneth Paul Erickson (eds.). 1991. *Comparative Political Dynamics: Global Research Perspectives*. New York: HarperCollins Publishers.

Said, Edward. 1993. *Culture and Imperialism*. New York: Alfred A. Knopf.

Sanford, Jonathan A. 1971. "Political Development and Economic Change: A Radical Interpretation of Almond and Powell's Developmental Approach." *Journal of International and Comparative Studies*, 4 (Summer), 1–36.

Scase, Richard. 1992. *Class*. Minneapolis: University of Minnesota Press.

Schmitter, Philippe C. 1989. "Corporatism Is Dead! Long Live Corporatism." *Government and Opposition*, 24 (Winter), 54–73.

Schmitter, Philippe C., and Terry Lynn Karl. 1991. "What Democracy Is . . . and Is Not." *Journal of Democracy*, 2 (Summer), 75–88.

Schudson, Michael. 1998. *The Good Citizen: A History of American Civic Life*. New York: Martin Kessler Books.

Scott, James C. 1985. *Weapons of the Weak. Everyday Forms of Peasant Resistance*. New Haven: Yale University Press.

Senghaas, Dieter. 1985. *The European Experience: A Historical Critique of Development Theory*. Dover, NH: Berg Publishers.

Sherman, Howard. 1976. "Dialectics as a Method." *Insurgent Sociologist*, 6 (Summer), 57–66.

_____. 1987. *Foundations of Radical Political Economy*. Armonk, NY: M. E. Sharpe.

Sjolander, Claire Turenne, and Wayne S. Cox (eds.). 1994. *Beyond Positivism: Critical Reflections on International Relations*. Boulder: Lynne Rienner Publishers. (Useful for its synthesis on three great debates in the field of international politics and the search for a postpositivism.)

Sklar, Richard L. 1987. "Developmental Democracy." *Comparative Studies in Society and History*, 29 (October), 686–714.

Skocpol, Theda. 1979. *States and Social Relations: A Comparative Analysis of France, Russia, and China*. Cambridge, UK: Cambridge University Press.

So, Alvin Y. 1990. *Social Change and Development: Modernization, Dependency, and World-System Theories*. Newbury Park, CA: Sage Publications.

So, Alvin Y., and Suwarsono. 1990. "Class Theory or Class Analysis? A Reexamination of Marx's Unfinished Chapter on Class." *Critical Sociology*, 17 (Summer), 35–55.

Stephens, Evelyne Huber. 1989. "Capitalist Development and Democracy in South America." *Politics and Society,* 17 (June), 281–352.

Stephens, John. 1993. "Capitalist Development and Democracy: Empirical Research on the Social Origins of Democracy." pp. 409–447 in D. Chopp, J. Hamton, and J. Roemer, eds., *The Idea of Democracy.* Cambridge, UK: Cambridge University Press.

Stiefel, Matthias, and Marshall Wolfe. 1994. *A Voice for the Excluded. Popular Participation in Development. Utopia or Necessity.* London: Zed Books.

Surkin, Marvin. 1969. "Sense and Nonsense in Politics." *PS: Political Science and Politics,* 2 (Fall), 573–581.

Sweezy, Paul. 1942. *The Theory of Capitalist Development: Principles of Marxian Political Economy.* New York: Monthly Review Press.

Szymanski, Al. 1972. "Malinowski, Marx, and Functionalism." *Insurgent Sociologist,* 2 (Summer), 35–43.

Taylor, John G. 1979. *From Modernization to Modes of Production: A Critique of the Sociologies of Development and Underdevelopment.* New York: Macmillan.

Therborn, Goran. 1978. *What Does the Ruling Class Do When It Rules?* London: New Left Books.

Thompson, E. P. 1963. *The Making of the English Working Class.* New York: Vintage Books.

_____. 1978. *The Poverty of Theory and Other Essays.* London: Merlin.

Tilly, Charles. 1975. *The Formation of National States in Western Europe.* Princeton: Princeton University Press.

Toffler, Alvin. 1981. *The Third Wave.* New York: Bantam Books.

Wallerstein, Immanuel. 1974, 1980, 1989. *The Modern World-System.* Vol. l: *Capitalist Agriculture and the Origins of European World-Economy in the Sixteenth Century.* Vol. 2: *Mercantilism and the Consolidation of the European World-Economy 1600–1750.* Vol. 3: *The Second Era of the Great Expansion of the Capitalist World Economy, 1730–1840s.* New York and San Diego: Academic Press.

Warren, Bill. 1980. *Imperialism: Pioneer of Capitalism.* Edited by John Sender. London: New Left Books.

Weber, Max. 1920. 1958. *The Protestant Ethic and the Spirit of Capitalism.* New York: Scribner's.

_____. 1949. *The Methodology of the Social Sciences.* Translated and edited by Edward A. Shils and Henry A. Finch. New York: Free Press.

_____. 1958. *From Max Weber: Essays in Sociology.* Translated and edited with an introduction by H. H. Gerth and C. Wright Mills. New York: Oxford University Press.

_____. 1962. *Basic Concepts in Sociology.* Translated with an introduction by H. P. Secher. New York: Citadel Press.

Weffort, Francisco C. 1992. "New Democracies. Which Democracies?" Working Paper 198. Washington DC: Latin American Program, Woodrow Wilson Center.

Weiner, Myron, and Samuel P. Huntington (eds.). 1987. *Understanding Political Development.* Boston: Little, Brown.

Wolin, Sheldon S. 1968. "Paradigms and Political Theories," pp. 125–152 in P. King and B. C. Parekh, eds., *Politics and Experience.* Cambridge, UK: Cambridge University Press.

_____. 1993. "Democracy: Electoral and Athenian." *PS: Political Science and Politics*, 26 (September), 475–477.

Wood, Ellen Meiksins. 1982. "The Politics of Theory and the Concept of Class: E. P. Thompson and his Critics." *Studies in Political Economy*, 9 (Fall), 45–71.

_____. 1986. *The Retreat from Class: A New "True" Socialism.* London: Verso.

_____. 1989. "Rational-Choice Marxism: Is the Game Worth the Candle?" *New Left Review*, 177 (September-October), 41–88.

_____. 1995. *Democracy Against Capitalism: Renewing Historical Materialism.* New York and Cambridge: Cambridge University Press.

Wright, Erik Olin. 1978. *Class, Crisis, and the State.* London: New Left Books.

_____. 1985. *Classes.* London: New Left Books.

Zaretsky, Eli. 1976. *Capitalism, the Family, and Personal Life.* New York: Harper & Row. Rev. ed., Perennial Library, 1986.

INDEX

Printed in the United States
44799LVS00002B/430

9 780813 381527